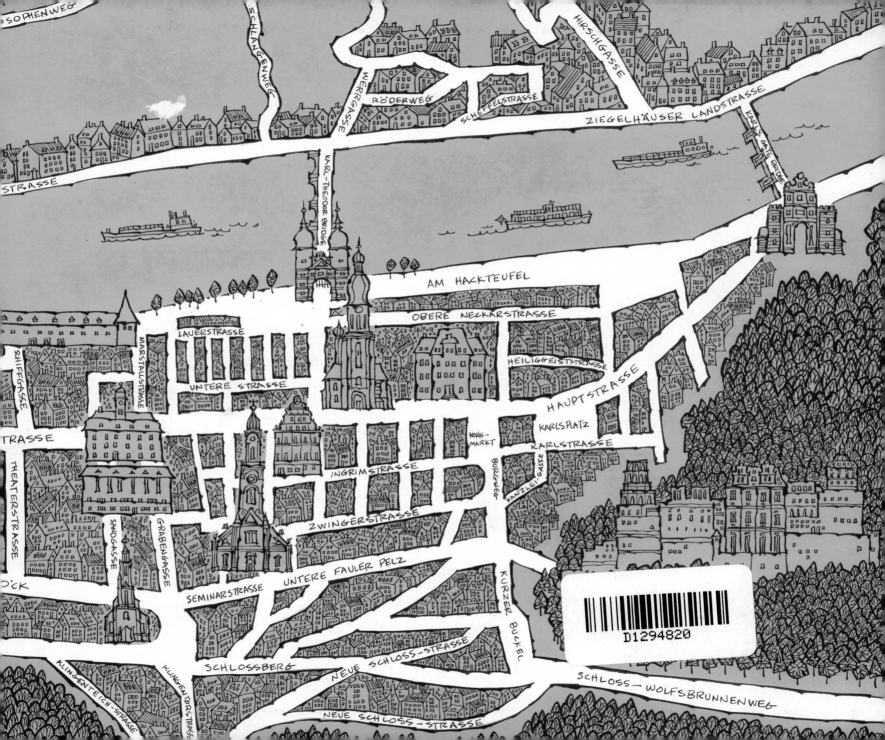

Deutsche Stunden

THE SCRIBNER GERMAN SERIES
General Editor, Harold von Hofe
UNIVERSITY OF SOUTHERN CALIFORNIA

ALLEN I. WEINSTEIN

EDGAR N. MAYER

BARRY J. KARP

ALICE CAROL GAAR

WILLARD TICKNOR DAETSCH

DENNIS J. MAHONEY

DEUTSCHE STUNDEN

CHARLES SCRIBNER'S SONS · NEW YORK

The graphic method of illustrating basic sentences and vocabulary was originated by Mrs. Yvonne Mayer.

Drawings by Mr. Paul Coker, Jr.

Contents

Deutsche Stunden

Introduction

Deutsche Stunden was conceived in an attempt to bring together several recent and most promising developments in foreign language instruction. To be sure, there have been other Elementary German texts designed for an audio-lingual approach in which each lesson centers around a dialog or narrative. This, when thoroughly learned, serves as a storehouse of materials for conversation and as a springboard into succeeding lessons. There have also been texts which apply the principles of modern descriptive linguistics in their presentation of phonology and structure. Other texts have emphasized the patterned structure of the German language, using pattern drills as a primary device for achieving active mastery of the lingual patterns of German. A few texts have used pictures as aids in learning dialogs or sentences, or as stimuli to evoke verbalization in German. **Deutsche Stunden** is intended to combine all of these approaches.

Deutsche Stunden is a basal text designed for the Elementary level. The emphasis is on learning to speak and understand German, with reading and writing treated as skills to be acquired after the two former ones. Thus, while some of the responses to the Pattern Practices have been omitted from the text, all are included in the accompanying tapes, so that written exercises using patterns should not degenerate into mechanical problems which exist only on paper. We wish the student to be constantly reminded that writing is only a symbolization of expressions which must *first* exist in *verbal* form. This is not to say, however, that reading and free or directed composition are to be entirely neglected; one directed composition has been included, as well as a number of suggested topics for free ones. In addition, the exercise material in the later lessons has been purposely kept short, so that the instructor may introduce a reader. This practice, we feel, is highly desirable, both to build vocabulary and to deepen the student's cultural perspective. Experimental use of the text in classes at the State University of New York at Buffalo has shown, at least to our satisfaction, that students introduced to a reader after Lesson XII are able to read aloud with a good deal of success and self-satisfaction, and that the great majority of these students are reading sentences or even paragraphs at a time, rather than proceeding painfully from word to word.

The text was designed for use at the rate of approximately one lesson a week throughout a two-semester course with five class hours per week, and an additional minimum of one hour per week in the language laboratory. More or less time may be spent on a lesson, depending on the needs of the class.

To the Teacher

The Pronunciation section should be thoroughly gone over before beginning Lesson I. Familiarity with this section will make the instructor's task much easier when it comes to learning sentences, since the student will then have far fewer harmful habits to overcome, particularly the one of superimposing the English phonological system on German. In this section it must be constantly emphasized that the student is *not* learning words, but only sounds, or rather, a *sound-system*. Therefore, the student should not be concerned with the *meanings* of any of the German words used—his problem at this point is to re-train his articulatory apparatus, and that is all. By the same token the student should not be held responsible for sounds to which he has not yet been formally introduced. In any given practice in the Pronunciation section, perfect pronunciation of each word is not the goal, but rather only the correct pronunciation of the sounds being drilled, as they occur in different phonological environments, as well as those sounds which have already been encountered and drilled. Thus, while working with the vowels, the student's ability to produce the "*Ich-Laut*" should not matter, but when the latter sound is formally taken up, all of the vowels should be well under control.

Each Lesson consists of a set of "Basic Sentences," a set of "Variations," a "Structure" section, a set of "Pattern Practices" (except for Lesson XXIV) and a Vocabulary list. The Basic Sentences and Variations are meant to supply the student with a stock of sentences which will enable him to speak sensibly, albeit on an elementary level, about one topic of general interest, such as his family, the weather, his studies and so on. The Basic Sentences are not reading selections to be casually perused once or twice; they are to be learned actively and by heart. With the important help of the pictures to make this task easier and more pleasant, the student can soon recite them *verbatim*, so that by the end of the course he has at the tip of his tongue a great number of sentences illustrative of every major structural feature of German. Because they must be learned by heart and must be gone over again and again, the Basic Sentences are kept relatively short and simple. The student is also held responsible for the Variations, but not to the same extent as for the Basic Sentences.

Each set of Basic Sentences and Variations introduces one or more structural items: a new case, a new tense, or new uses of a previously learned item. These structural items are then analyzed in the Structure section and drilled as Pattern Practices.

The structural analyses are purposely kept terse and concise. The intention here is not to be charming but to be clear and brief, and to refrain from giving the student the impression that discussing how the language works is as important as putting the language to use. Actually, the practices take up far more space than do the analyses, which, most language teachers would nowadays agree, is as it should be. Throughout the analyses, we have capitalized on German–English similarities, for we believe that the close linguistic relationship of the two should be turned to our advantage, and should not be overlooked. Similarly, we have written the Structure sections in English, since we have noted that when grammars are written in German students often neglect such material entirely in favor of the ubiquitous English "ponies."

The "slotted" structure of German sentences is constantly stressed, for two reasons. First, this appears to be a good method for teaching word order. Second, it enables the student to produce a vast number of sentences easily and automatically, given only a thoroughly memorized model. While many of these differ from one another by only one lexical item, they are nonetheless individual sentences, expressing different thoughts. When a student realizes that, for example, out of Practice XX, Lesson IV, alone he can independently produce up to *twenty thousand different German sentences*, the positive effect on his morale is considerable. We estimate conservatively that the text contains several million sentence possibilities, and that the average student, learning only between five and ten percent of the material, should at the end of the course be in active control of between half a million and a million sentences. The student's conscious appreciation of his new abilities, we have found, can exert a profound, positive effect on his morale and motivation to learn.

The Pattern Practices are meant *primarily* for the student to study by himself, at home or in the laboratory, and so most of the answers are given. The Practices may be started in the classroom, but probably no attempt should be made to do them all in class—there are far too many of them for this, and class time may be used more effectively. Students must be directed at first, and reminded from time to time later, to cover up the responses and use them only as a check after they have themselves attempted an answer. Some students will probably be lazy, and "cheat." In our experience, however, most students will do the practices in the proper manner. Even if they do "cheat" a little, not much is lost, for at least they have repeated something correctly. *But unquestionably the greatest time-waster and detriment to learning is passive study of the practices.—The student must speak!*

Students will often complain that learning the Basic Sentences and doing the Pattern Practices are boring. Nothing could be more natural, for we are asking the student to go through the same kind of repetitive drill as a piano student practicing his scales, or a basketball player working on his dribbling. But language learning, like the learning of any other kind of skill, necessarily entails a certain amount of repetitive practice before the learner can attain the kind of performance that is needed. We believe the picture technique embodied in this text will go far toward eliminating this complaint.

The picture method of presentation, as used in **Deutsche Stunden**, has three primary objectives: first, to take away a good part of the boredom inherent in repetitive practice; second, to enable the instructor to evoke utterances in German from the student by means of meaningful but non-lingual stimuli, thus making the use of English unnecessary; third, to increase fluency by allowing the instructor to control and graduate the speed of the student's response.

Our procedure is not simply a "direct method" approach, though it has some of the same features. The pictures are not intended to convey completely the meaning of the sentences to which they correspond, but only to act as "cues" for those utterances. The text itself does not necessarily have to be used in the classroom, because the instructor can rely on the pictures for a great part of the work; but many instructors like the students to be able to see in print, at least part of the time, the sentences they are saying; and the book is of course essential for home and laboratory study. A routine that has proven effective and versatile in *our* classes for the week's work on a lesson is as follows:

First day. Present Basic Sentences with pictures. Instructor displays each picture and says the corresponding sentence or phrase. Class repeats in chorus and then individually, with instructor checking and correcting pronunciation. Tempo is rapid from the outset, and speaking speed should be as near normal as possible for each sentence. When students can repeat every sentence after the instructor, they should respond to the pictures without prompting; cumulative drill with the pictures will greatly facilitate this. The goal is choral repetition of all sentences without prompting; if this is not attained, the tempo has probably been too slow and should be quickened in future lessons. Assignment: *Active* oral study of Basic Sentences and Variations, at home or in the laboratory or both; look over Structure.

Second day. Open with *brief* discussion of structure. Divide class into groups of no more than eight students each, and check ability to recite Basic Sentences with each group. (For checking purposes, this is just as effective and far quicker than individual repetition.) Group (responsive) repetition of the Basic Sentences, then individual practice at normal speaking speed. Goal: individual repetition of all sentences with pictures at normal speaking speed. If time permits, begin work on selected Pattern Practices. Assignment: oral and written home study of Basic Sentences and Variations; oral study of selected Pattern Practices.

Third day. Brief, concentrated drill on Basic Sentences. Move on to Pattern Practices, which are conducted at normal speaking speed. As students gain confidence with each pattern, instructor shifts to completely oral work, using the supplementary vocabulary pictures in place of the text. These pictures then become a "bridge" leading to the ultimate goal of the lesson: free conversation on the topic of the week. This is approached by asking the students to expand on the vocabulary pictures, or by placing several of them together and asking the students to respond to the visual situation. Finally, the instructor asks the students questions about the topic of the week's lesson as it applies to their own lives. Assignment: Further study of Variations; write out answers to selected Pattern Practices; finish oral study of all Pattern Practices.

Fourth day. Same as third day, using vocabulary pictures to deal with as many structural situations as is convenient. Directed question-and-answer between students. (The students should speak as much as possible and the instructor as little as possible.) Follow with student question period on structure. Assignment:

Finish studying and review entire lesson; review preceding lessons as directed.

Fifth day. At instructor's option, may include written or oral quiz (with or without pictures), free conversation, short talks by individual students, critique of written assignments, review of preceding lessons; in second semester, may include use of supplementary reader. Assignment: written translation exercise, composition, or other written work. (NOTE: Students are not encouraged to begin studying the next lesson before it has been introduced in class.)

Assuming effective class work at a rapid tempo and hard oral study outside of class (averaging six to eight hours per week), each lesson can be completed in a week. The latter lessons can be completed in less time, so that a reader may also be used to supplement the basal text.

We wish to express our sincere gratitude to Professors René Taube, Albert Martin and Byron Koekkoek of the State University of New York at Buffalo, whose criticisms have been of invaluable assistance; to Miss Ellen Heitmann and Miss Jenny Lechner, whose *Sprachgefühl* for their native German language contributed much to the work; and to Miss Mittie Decker, Mrs. Karen Carbonara and Miss Jo-Ann Vickers for their untiring labor in the preparation of the manuscripts.

Finally, thanks are due the many students at Buffalo whose numerous sincere suggestions were of great help to us. For these students and for students of German everywhere, **Deutsche Stunden** was written, and to them it is dedicated.

THE AUTHORS

To the Student

A great many language teachers today believe what specialists in linguistics and psychology have long maintained: that learning a foreign language is very much like learning a skill such as typing, playing the clarinet, or throwing a forward pass. It involves a certain amount of conscious knowing what to do and how to do it (which is why we study structure); but far more, it involves the ability *automatically* to do the right thing at the right time. This means that, inevitably, a great part of your activities in learning German will have to consist of repeating aloud the same material again and again, and drilling yourself on it until you know you can do it perfectly, automatically, without hesitation. Naturally enough, this will sometimes be boring. But it is *essential*. You must keep going until you no longer have to think consciously about the endings, the word order, and so on. "Once over lightly" is not enough to leave any lasting effect; it simply isn't worth the bother. Never stop work on a given practice until you can do it automatically, by reflex. And work *aloud!* Some part of your homework will be written, but don't assume that you have nothing to do if there is no written assignment; your main task is to learn the Basic Sentences thoroughly and work on the Pattern Practices, all of which means a good deal of oral study. (Our better students tell us that they spend about six to eight hours a week, on the average, on their German outside of class, and that most of this time is spent in oral work.) Don't lose sight of the fact that all this hard work is not an end in itself but only a means to the end that you want: being able to speak, understand, read and write German. If you work conscientiously and regularly—not just before quizzes—you will find yourself approaching that goal by leaps and bounds.

We are not asking you merely to memorize the material without understanding it; the English equivalents in the Basic Sentences and the Variations, as well as the Structure sections, should help you sufficiently. But in an hour of work with the Pattern Practices you will learn far more about what is going on than in an hour spent poring over the Structure.

Nor should you let yourself translate continually. The trick in learning a language is to get directly from an idea or a visual image to an utterance without any English coming between them. As you study, try to connect images and ideas to German utterances, and German utterances to ideas and images. That is, *Baum* should literally make you see a picture of a tree—not just the English word "tree," and vice versa. Very early in the course you will find that German phrases and sentences will come into your mind in response to something going on around you. When that starts to happen, you will know that you are really "thinking in German."

Above all, don't get discouraged. The hardest part may well be behind you before you realize it. Although we have done our best to make things easy, our students tell us that they begin to be worried around Lesson IV, think they will never get through the course at about Lesson XI, and sink to new depths of despair by Lesson XVII. However, after Lesson XVIII things look brighter again and much of the material that seemed so difficult before then comes much more easily.

A word about vocabulary: Many students find that the structure is hard only at the beginning, and that vocabulary (including noun genders and verb forms) soon becomes their major problem. We strongly recommend that you prepare for this right from the start. One of the best devices for this purpose is word-cards.

You can buy ready-made word-cards, but it is probably better to make your own, since the very act of making the card will help you remember the item you are writing. Cut some ordinary index cards into halves or quarters. On one side of the card write the German word or other item—*in a whole phrase or sentence that occurs in the textbook*. On the other side of the card place something to "cue" the German—draw a sketch, use another German word that you already know as an equivalent, but only as a last, desperate resort should you use an English translation, because where an English word may translate a German word in one situation, it may not work at all in another. Carry the cards around with you, and go through them at odd moments. If you work through the cards once or twice a day, you will find yourself learning rapidly. When you know a given item without hesitation, remove its card from the active pack and put it aside, ready for review when needed.

Pronunciation and Spelling

I. GENERALITIES

A. Introduction

The pronunciation of German, you will find, is relatively easy if you remember two basic facts:

1. Both English and German have two kinds of vowel sounds, called "lax" (=relaxed) and "tense." In English the lax ones are short, but the tense ones are **long and diphthongized**—that is, they start with one sound and end with another. For example, the **ee** in s**ee**m is just as long and as diphthongized as the **ai** in m**ai**n. In German, on the other hand, the lax vowels are very much like English lax ones, but THE TENSE ONES ARE "PURE"— that is, **not** diphthongized; the sound does not change detectably from beginning to end. **This is essential to good German pronunciation.**

2. **Many letters and combinations of letters do not represent the same sounds in German as in English.** To give just one example, in German the letter **j** represents a y-sound, and not a **j**-sound at all. **It is essential to learn these differences.**

Now go rapidly through Section B below for a brief over-all view of the German sounds. Imitate your instructor or the tape carefully. Details about specific sounds and spellings will be treated in Sections II and III.

B. Brief Survey of the Sounds of German

The following table shows all of the sounds of German with examples. It is meant to be brief, and is therefore necessarily oversimplified. Details will be found in the rest of this pronunciation section.

a. Vowels and Diphthongs

Sound		Spellings	Examples	Nearest English sound (if any)	Differences from English sound
Tense	I (IH)	ie, ih, i	wie, Ihnen, wir	we, see, eat	Not diphthongized
Lax	I	i	ich, bitte, bin	bin, hit, risk	Shorter
Tense	U (UH)	uh, u	gut, du, Uhr	do, loot, soup (no y-sound as in pure, use)	Not diphthongized; tenser
Lax	U	u	und, Schulze, Kurt	put, cook, could	Shorter
Tense	Ü (ÜH)	üh, ü, y	drüben, Bücher, früh, Lyrik	—(French du)	
Lax	Ü	ü, y	Müller, hübsch, München, Symphonie	—(French buffet)	

Sound		Spellings	Examples	Nearest English sound (if any)	Differences from English sound
Tense	E (EH)	eh, ee, e, ä, äh	geht, verstehe, täglich	ape, take, gait	Not diphthongized; tenser
Lax	E	e, ä	es, jetzt, Länder	bet, yet, very	Shorter
Unstressed	E	e	danke, guten, Abend	about, open	
Tense	O (OH)	oh, o	Johann, also, wiederholen	joke, most, boat	Not diphthongized
Lax	O	o	Morgen, Post, dort	Boston or British top, hot, lock	
Tense	Ö (ÖH)	öh, ö, oe	schön, Bahnhöfe, Söhne, Goethe	Boston or British bird, firm	
Lax	Ö	ö	bewölkt, öfter, Töchter	—(French heure)	
Tense	A (AH)	ah, aa, a	wahr, Abend, Bahnhof, Saal	pa, Shah, father	Not diphthongized
Lax	A	a	danke, Johann, also	top, hot, lock (not as in all)	Made with tongue farther back in the mouth
	EI	ei, ai	heiße, Fräulein, nein, Kaiser	nine, ice, line	Shorter
	OY	eu, äu	Fräulein, Häuser, Freund	boy, hoist, toy	Shorter
	AU	au	auch, Frau, Hause	now, house, out	Farther back and shorter

b. Consonants

Sound	Spellings	Examples	Nearest English sound (if any)	Differences from English sound
P	p, pp, final b	Peter, Lautsprecher, halb	Peter, speak, help	
B	b non-final	bitte, bin, Abend	bitter, bin, ribbon	
T	t, tt, final d; rarely, th	Tag, gut, und, Roth, bitte	too, till (not as in better, wrote)	Not softened medially or finally
D	d non-final	danke, wiederholen, Trudi	dank, do, Judy	
K	k, ck, final g	danke, Tag, Karl	Carl, knock, locker	
G	g non-final	gut, Morgen, geht	give, go, get (not as in gem, gym)	
F	f, ff, initial v	verstehe, Frau, auf	off, fine, if (not like v in vine)	

Sound	Spellings	Examples	Nearest English sound (if any)	Differences from English sound
V	Initial w; non-initial v	wie, wiederholen, wahr; Universität	vine, ever, vest (not like w in wine, west)	
SS	ss, ß, medial and final s	es, heißen, best, Hans	miss, rice, lesson (not as in is)	
Z	s initial in syllable	also, sehr, Hause	zoo, risen (not as in see, miss)	
SH	1. sch	Schmidt, schön, Geschäft	show, ship, push	
	2. initial s before t, p	Straße, Stunden, Strauß	show, ship, schmoo (not like so, sip, smear)	
GE	g before ei or i, in French or English words	Garage, Ingenieur	measure, pleasure (not like jello, gem)	
CH	1. ch after a, o, u, au	1. nach, auch, Nacht	—(Spanish jamás)	Not like church or kick
	2. ch elsewhere	2. ich, nicht, Brecht, Kirche		
H	h (non-final)	heißen, hier, Eckhardt	home, hear, hot	
R	1. r, rr	1. Frau, Maria, Roth	—(like French r in rue, rouge)	Not made with the lips but with the back of the tongue
	2. r final or before consonant	2. Karl, mir, sehr	New York, Boston, or British fear, hard	
M	m, mm	Morgen, mir, Müller	me, men, more	
N	n, nn	Ihnen, und, nicht	now, nice, not	
NG	ng	Lang, Engel, singen	sing, ring, thing (no g-sound as in finger)	
	n before k	danke, links	thanks, think, sink	
L	l, ll	Müller, also, Lang	Miller, long, all	Very liquid-sounding
Y	j	Johann, jetzt, ja	you, yes, yen (not like j in jump)	
PF	pf	Pfeife, Apfel, Kopf	stop fooling, top flight	
TS	z, tz	Schulze, jetzt, zu	puts, Schultz (not like zoo, jazz)	
TCH	tsch	Deutsch	much, church	

C. Basic Principles of German Spelling

1. Tense and Lax Vowels

The distinction between **lax** and **tense** vowel sounds is fundamental. The spelling **usually** shows whether the vowel sound in a given syllable is lax or tense **by means of the vowel letter or letters plus the following consonant letter or letters:**

A **lax** vowel sound is spelled with one vowel letter plus a **double** consonant letter, or with one vowel letter plus **two different** consonant letters.

A **tense** vowel sound is spelled with one vowel letter plus **one consonant** letter, or with one vowel letter plus **h**, or with two vowel letters. (Note that a double consonant letter does not represent **two** consonant sounds but **one**.) Examples:

Lax	Tense			Lax	Tense		
(VCC)	(VC)	(VH)	(VV)	(VCC)	(VC)	(VH)	(VV)
krumme	Krume			Hütte	Hüte		
Hölle		Höhle		Gotte	Gote		
Schiff			schief	fällt		fehlt	
füllen		fühlen		dünne	Düne		
Kamm	kam			kann		Kahn	
Fell		Fehl		Bett			Beet
Stadt			Staat	Lamm		lahm	
Bock	bog			offen	Ofen		
Bulle		Buhle		wenn	wen		

Unfortunately, these principles are not carried out completely; there are many exceptions which will have to be learned as you go along.

2. Unvoicing of Final Voiced Consonant Sounds

If you put your hand on your Adam's apple and say "sss..." and then "zzz...," you will notice that "zzz" has a vibration that "sss" does not. This vibration is called **voicing**; a consonant that has it is called **voiced,** and one that does not is called **voiceless**. Some of the German consonant sounds come in pairs of which one is voiced and the other is similar except that it is voiceless:

Voiced	B	D	G	Z	V
Voiceless	P	T	K	SS	F

Now: **German does not let these voiced consonant sounds end a word or precede a voiceless consonant.** If a voiced consonant happens to become final or to come before a voiceless consonant, **it changes to the corresponding voiceless sound. The spelling, however, does not show the change.**

For example:

in these words b represents a P sound: gab, liebt, gehabt, blieb, halb

,,　,,　　,,　d　　,,　　,, T　,,　: Freund, Mädchen, Kind, Stadt, und, Abend

,,　,,　　,,　g　　,,　　,, K　,,　: Tag, stieg, sagt, liegt

,,　,,　　,,　s　　,,　　,, SS　,,　: es, Haus, das, dies, was

Notice that as a result of this, in the various forms of many words a voiced consonant will actually alternate with a voiceless one. For instance:

Voiceless	Voiced	Meanings	
gab :	gaben	(he) gave	: (we) gave
Tag :	Tage	day	: days
Kind:	Kinder	child	: children
Haus:	zu Hause	house	: at home

The G-sound has another voiceless correspondent besides K. It unvoices to CH (instead of K) in the pronunciation of many speakers in certain kinds of situations, the most important of which is the ending **-ig**. For example, these words end in a CH-sound for some speakers but a K-sound for others:

billig, eckig, schmutzig.

D. Stress

German stress is similar to that of English, and not at all like French or Spanish. The basic principle of German word stress is that the main stress in a word falls on the root syllable of the word, i.e. the first syllable of that portion of the word which remains when all prefixes and suffixes have been removed.

With Prefix	ver**sag**en	be**arb**eiten	emp**fin**den	wieder**hol**en	Ge**birg**e
Without Prefix	**sag**en	**arb**eiten	**fin**den	**hol**en	**Berg**

However, word compounds, consisting of several words written as one, usually have the main stress on their first syllable:

Vorsicht **Fern**sehen **aus**gehen **ein**laden **Bahn**hof **An**fang **Kin**dergarten **auf**machen **ab**steigen **Haupt**stadt

A set of exceptions to the pattern are loan words which in their original languages have stress on a syllable other than the root syllable. Notice the occurrence of the main stress in the following examples:

Foreign Borrowings

French	Universit**ä**t nati**o**nal **Na**tion Tro**ttoir** Restau**rant**
Others	Fa**mi**lie (Latin) Mu**se**um (Latin) Li**no**leum (Latin) at**lan**tisch (Greek) Ana**ly**ze (Greek)

E. The German Alphabet

The German alphabet consists of 30 characters, including the 26 of the English, plus three "umlaut" letters and **ß**. The symbol for "umlaut" (¨) is the remnant of what was once an **e** written above (or sometimes next to) another vowel. This older device survives today in such proper names as Go**e**the and Mu**e**ller. **ß**, as its name implies, resulted from German printers' creation of a single character from **s**+**z**. Today Germans also think of **au, ei, eu, äu, ch, ck, st,** and **tz** as "letters of the alphabet," but have no special names for them. The names of the present individual German characters are:

a	ah	**d**	deh	**g**	geh	**j**	jot	**m**	em	**p**	peh	**s**	ess	**v**	fau	**y**	ypsilon	**ö**	oh-umlaut
b	beh	**e**	eh	**h**	hah	**k**	kah	**n**	en	**q**	kuh	**t**	teh	**w**	weh	**z**	tset	**ü**	uh-umlaut
c	tseh	**f**	eff	**i**	ieh	**l**	ell	**o**	oh	**r**	er	**u**	uh	**x**	iks	**ä**	ah-umlaut	**ß**	ess-tset

II. DETAILS: VOWELS

Tense I (IH)

Spellings: ie; ih

The English sound in kn**ee**, m**ee**t, is very diphthongized. For the German sound keep tongue very high, spread lips energetically.

No diphthongization!

Listen to the difference between this German sound and the nearest English one:

English	meet	knee	fee	sheaf	brief	deep	least	sheen	beer	leap	feel	keel
German	miet'	nie	Vieh	schief	Brief	Dieb	liest	schien	Bier	lieb	viel	Kiel

Lax I

Spelling: i before two consonants (except in some one-syllable words)

Practically the same as the English vowel in s**i**t, but shorter. Compare:

English	fish	in	Dick	film	kin	mitt	links	built	bin
German	Fisch	in	dick	Film	Kinn	mit	links	Bild	bin

IH versus I

Compare:

Tense	Lax	Tense	Lax	Tense	Lax
ihn	in	wieder	Widder	ihm	im
schief	Schiff	mieten	mitten	Bienen	binnen
biete	bitte	siech	sich	Stiel	still
spiel	Spill	Kien	Kinn	hießen	hissen

Practice:

Tense	Lax	Tense	Lax	Tense	Lax
wie	Wind	nie	in	ihm	sich
Bier	bis	die	nicht	Brief	Film
schief	Himmel	Kino	ich	vier	ging
Musik	Milch	Klima	immer	lieben	irgend
viel	richtig	hier	Schiff	nieder	beginnt
Lieder	Zimmer	wir	will	ziemlich	hinter
wieder	gewiß	sieben	Himmel	fliegen	Zimmer

Tense U (UH)

Spelling: uh; u before one consonant or final

English d**o** and n**oo**n are diphthongized. The German sound is made with lips far forward, tongue quite high and back; **no diphthongization!** Do not let the spelling trick you into pronouncing it like **u** in **up, hub, nun.**

Compare:

English	moot	coo	hoot	rue	moose	do	toot	root	shoe	noon	tune	room
German	Mut	Kuh	Hut	Ruh'	Mus	du	tut	Ruth	Schuh	nun	tun	Ruhm

Lax U

Spelling: u before two consonants (except in a few monosyllables)

Very much like English **put, book,** but shorter. **Not** like **up, hub, nun.**

English	bush	pulls	puts	bull	looks	rook
German	Busch	Puls	Putz	Bulle	Luchs	Ruck

UH versus U

Tense	Lax		Tense	Lax		Tense	Lax
Ruhm	Rum		Krume	krumme		Kuren	kurren
Mus	muß		spuken	spucken		Buhle	Bulle

Practice:

Tense	Lax		Tense	Lax		Tense	Lax
gut	dumm		nun	muß		zu	und
Fuß	um		Buch	Hund		Zug	kurz
nur	Durst		Musik	Kursus		tun	durch
Bruder	Hunger		Student	Mutter		Schuh	Kunst
Uhr	jung		versuchen	Stunde		genug	dunkel
Schule	zum		rufen	unter		Bruder	gesungen

Tense Ü (ÜH)

Spellings: üh; ü before one consonant; rarely (in a few Greek derivatives) **y**

This sound is made with the tongue position for IH but with the lips far forward as for tense U. It is not like any English sound. It is like French **u** in **rue.**

Listen to these English and German sets:

Eng.	Ger.	Eng.		Eng.	Ger.	Eng.		Eng.	Ger.	Eng.
keen	kühn	coon		breeder	Brüder	brooder		ream	rühm	room
tear	Tür	tour		free	früh			keel	kühl	cool
me	Müh'	moo		fear	für			green	grün	

Lax Ü

Spellings: ü before two consonants; in a few Greek derivatives, **y**

The same comments apply here as for tense Ü. Compare:

English	din	rick	mist	miller	dinner	physic
German	dünn	rück	müßt	Müller	dünner	Physik

ÜH versus Ü

Compare:

Tense	Lax		Tense	Lax		Tense	Lax
Hüte	Hütte		Brühle	brülle		Düne	dünne
			fühlen	füllen			

Practice:

Tense	Lax	Tense	Lax	Tense	Lax
Tür	hübsch	grün	fünf	für	Glück
Züge	würde	früh	müssen	müde	bürsten
üben	Hündchen	Prüfung	dürfen	kühl	wüßte
Hüte	Kürze	über	Künste	Füße	Hütte
Frühling	Lüste	drüben	Mütter	Bücher	Mütze
Brüder	Brüste	Büro	Rücken	Gemüse	entzücken

IH vs. ÜH vs. UH

Compare:

sieht	Süd	Sud	vier	für	fuhr			Güte	gute
Kien	kühn	Kuhn	mied	müht	muht	Biene	Bühne	Buhne
mied	müd	Mut	Kiel	kühl		Tier	Tür	Tour
spielen	spülen	Spulen		Brüder	Bruder	liege	Lüge	Luge

I vs. Ü vs. U

Compare:

Mist	müßt	mußt		Mütter	Mutter	nützen	nutzen
	münden	Munden		Kürze	kurze	Mücke	Mucke
	Glück	Gluck		wüßte	wußte	Würden	wurden
			Schippe	Schüppe	Schuppe		

Tense A (AH)

Spellings: aa; ah; a before one consonant or final

Very much like the **a**-sound in c**a**lm, Sh**a**h, p**a**, f**a**ther. Do not let the spelling trick you into other sounds as in h**a**t or b**a**ll. Compare:

English	German	English	German	English (various)	German
calm	kam	farm	Farm	moll	mal
Shah	Schah	bar	bar	tot	Tat
Khan	Kahn	par	paar	far	fahr'

Lax A

Spelling: a before two consonants (except in some monosyllables)

Much like the vowel in **hot, con,** but shorter; *not* like hat, lass, fast. Compare:

Eng.	Ger.	Eng.		Eng.	Ger.	Eng.		Eng.	Ger.	Eng.
don	dann			sot	satt	sat		con	kann	can
	Bank	bank			lang	Lang		Bock	back	back
	fast	fast			sang	sang			laß	lass

AH vs. A

Compare:

Tense	Lax		Tense	Lax		Tense	Lax
Saat	satt		Wahn	wann		Schlaf	schlaff
Staat	Stadt		kam	Kamm		lahm	Lamm
Kahn	kann		Hahns	Hans		rate	Ratte
las	laß					Bahn	Bann

Practice:

Tense	Lax		Tense	Lax		Tense	Lax
sah	man		kam	fallen		las	Ball
Abend	wann		Saat	dann		fahren	alt
las	nach		Tage	Laden		wahr	falsch
bade	alle		Bahn	Fang		schlafen	halb
Name	Hand		Staat	Bank		frage	mache
aber	bald		bat	als		war	Arzt
Haar	fast		Vater	ander		Magen	Antwort
sage	lassen		waren	lang		Paar	Mann

Tense E (EH)

Spellings: ee; eh; äh; sometimes **e** or **ä** before one consonant

The English sound in **gate** is diphthongized. The German sound must be tense; tongue high, lips well spread, **no diphthongization.**

Compare:

English	gate	vain	fail	bait	Dane	laden	gay	lame	hair
German	geht	wen	Fehl	Beet	den	Läden	geh'	Lehm	her

Lax E

Spellings: e or ä before two consonants

Practically the same as **e** in **bet, deck, Ben,** but shorter.   Compare:

English	bet	deck	Ben	mess	fell	den	best	elf	next
German	Bett	Deck	Benn	mess	Fell	denn	best	elf	nächst

EH vs. E

Tense	Lax		Tense	Lax		Tense	Lax
wen	wenn		Weg	weg		Väter	Vetter
Beet	Bett		schräg	Schreck		den	denn
her	Herr		fehlt	fällt		Fehl	Fell
Kehle	Kelle		Sehne	Senne		stehlen	stellen

Practice:

er	denn		schläfrig	sechs		wen	wenn
zehn	essen		Zähne	beste		Fee	erst
Feder	gern		nämlich	Ecke		jeder	Herr
gegen✓	elf		lesen	Bett		legen	Eltern
her	gestern		sehr	Hotel		Lehrer	fertig
stehe	bedeckt		See	Englisch		Theater	nächst✓
Väter	lerne		während	letzt		gehen	Mensch

Unstressed E

Spelling: e (in unstressed syllables)*

Note that this **e** is not a "silent letter" (as it often is in English). Practically the same as the English weak vowel in **about, open.**

Compare:

English	often	comma	Keller	Rosa	oxen	common	began	before	houses
German	offen	komme	Keller	Rose	Ochsen	kommen	begann	bevor	Hauses

---

* In some words the spelling **ie** represents I (with the sound of English **y**) plus unstressed E, instead of the usual tense I: Famil**ie**, Italien.

Unstressed E vs. other weak-stressed vowels

E is the only vowel sound that changes its pronunciation when it becomes unstressed. All others remain essentially as they would be if stressed. Compare:

Unstressed E	Other	E	Other	E	Other
komme	Komma	Rose	rosa	Studenten	Studentin
Gote	Gotha	Prime	prima	Museen	Museum
jene	Jena	Note	Nota	bete	Beta

Practice:

Verzeihung	Kaffee	Theater	etwas	spazieren	Klavier
Amerika	Klima	Philosophie	Grammatik	Museum	Heimat
Professor	Apparat	modern	dahin	zunächst	herein
Kursus	erklären	natürlich	Familie	Monat	Hotel
Zigarette	Fabrik	Literatur	Europa	niemand	Ingenieur
langsam	Konzert	Minute	danach	rasieren	erzählen
zusammen	Geometrie	prima	Geographie	Laboratorium	jemand

Tense O (OH)

Spellings: oo; oh; o before one consonant, or final

The English sound in **tone, boat** is diphthongized. For the German one, keep tongue back, lips far forward; **no diphthongization!** Compare:

English	tote	hope	shone	coal	boat	dome	tone	owner	note	photo	wrote	odor
German	tot	hob	schon	Kohl	Boot	Dom	Ton	ohne	Not	Photo	rot	oder

Lax O

Spelling: o before two consonants (except for a few monosyllables)

This sound is quite like the British or Boston **o**-sound in **shock, got, hot**. It is **not** like the sound in those same words as pronounced by most Americans. Compare:

English	shock	clots	mops	locked	hop	locker	common	got	trots
German	Schock	Klotz	Mops	lockt	hopp	locker	kommen	Gott	trotz

OH vs. O vs. A

Compare:

OH	O	A		OH	O	A		OH	O	A
bog	Bock	back'			komm'	Kamm			noch	nach
Floß	floß				Ost	Ast		Ofen	offen	Affen
	Bonn	Bann			ob	ab		Schoß	schoß	
	kosten	Kasten		Gote	Gotte	Gatte			doch	Dach
	voll	Fall			gewonnen	gewannen			Wochen	wachen
	wollen	wallen			begonnen	begannen				

Practice:

OH	O	A		OH	O	A
bloß	ob	alt		hoch	kommt	bald
schon	kommen	fast		Boden	gesprochen	fallen
Radio	Osten	nach		groß	dort	daß
Monat	Konzert	falsch		oben	oft	Platz
Sohn	Sonne	Mann		Oper	Tochter	macht
Note	trotz	Nacht		Brot	Post	lassen
oder	sonst	wach		komisch	von	wachen

Tense Ö

Spellings: öh; ö before one consonant or final; **eu** in French words; rarely, **oe.**

This sound does not exist in English. Make it with your tongue in the same position as for tense E but lips forward as for U. There is no **r**-like element as in **burr.** Compare:

English	burden	learner	earl	hurt	fern	bursar	Hearst	turner	flirter
German	Böden	löhne	Öl	hört	Föhn	böser	hörst	Töne	Flöte

Lax Ö

Spelling: ö before two consonants; rarely **oe**; in words of foreign origin, **eu.**

Same remarks as for tense Ö.

English	murder	Burl	Kerner	firster	hurt
German	Mörder	Böll	Körner	Förster	hört

ÖH vs. Ö

Tense	Lax	Tense	Lax	Tense	Lax
Höhle	Hölle	Schöße	schösse	Goethe	Götter

Practice:

Tense	Lax	Tense	Lax	Tense	Lax
hören	bewölkt	Bahnhöfe	zwölf	mögen	Köpfe
Ingenieur	Wörter	Vögel	Dörfer	Söhne	Röcke
Öfen	möchte	Böden	öffentlich	französisch	könnte
böse	könnten	gehören	plötzlich	möglich	öfter
Köchin	kahlköpfig	höflich	öftest	schöner	möchten
töten	eröffnen	größer	können	öde	erschöpft

EH vs. ÖH vs. OH

Compare:

EH	ÖH	OH	EH	ÖH	OH	EH	ÖH	OH
lehne	löhne	lohne	lesen	lösen	losen		öde	Ode
	Föhr	vor		Goethe	Gote	Sehne	Söhne	Sohne
	schön	schon		Böden	Boden		Vögel	Vogel
	Öfen	Ofen		Größe	große		Bögen	Bogen
kehre	Chöre	Chore				täten	töten	toten

E vs. Ö vs. O

Compare:

E	Ö	O	E	Ö	O	E	Ö	O
Lenz	Löns		kennen	können			Töchter	Tochter
Beck	Böck	Bock	helle	Hölle	Holle	Mächte	möchte	mochte
			könnten	konnten				

AI

Spelling: ai, ei

Much like nine, mice; starts with a vowel sound which is like the **o** in hot but made with the tongue rather far back. Keep this diphthong shorter than in English, and tenser. Compare:

English	nine	mine	high	buy	mice	fine	vice	shine	ice	dine	my	vine	fry
German	nein	mein	Hai	bei	Mais	fein	weiß	Schein	Eis	dein	Mai	Wein	frei

Practice:

ein	Mai	Eis	bei	klein	weit
kein	sein	leicht	Wein	weil	dein
nein	schneit	frei	steigt	Zeit	einst
dreizehn	mein	Arbeit	zeigen	Zeitung	Schein
Bleistift	scheinen	Verzeihung	Fräulein	schreiben	beiden

Spelling: ei versus ie

Remember that the spelling **ei** represents the diphthong AI, whereas **ie** represents the tense I sound (IH).

Practice:

heißen	hießen	schreiben	schrieben	stiegen	steigen
bleiben	blieben	leider	Lieder	fleißig	fliegen
heiß	viele	nein	frieren	scheinen	niedrig
weiter	schienen	rief	Tier	nieder	schneien
Verzeihung	wieder	weil	Viertel	wieviel	Weine
beiden	Arbeit	vielleicht	dreizehn	bereit	Briefe

EU

Spelling: eu, äu

More like O plus Ü than O plus I. Shorter than in English **boy**. Compare:

English	loiter	boiler	foist
German	Leute	Beule	Faüste

Practice:

neu	läuft	freut	deutsch	läuft	Freund
Leute	Fräulein	neuer	Bäume	teuer	heute
Gebäude	Europa	Deutschland	Freundin	bedeuten	Flugzeug
Deutscher	neulich	freuen	Verkäufer	freundlich	überzeugt

AU

Spelling: au

Much like h**ou**se, **ou**t, but the same remarks apply here as were made for AI. Compare:

English	house	brown	mouse	bow	dower	foul
German	Haus	braun	Maus	bau	Dauer	faul

Practice:

auch	blau	aus	Haus	Baum	auf
braun	Frau	kaum	laufen	grau	heraus
schauen	Auge	rauchen	außer	plaudern	Schauspiel
Brause	Hauptfach	dauert	draußen	Auto	glauben
brauchen	darauf	verkaufen	traurig	Aufsatz	Bauwesen

III. DETAILS: CONSONANTS

R

Spelling: r, rr

There are several varieties of **r**-sound. Which is used depends on

1. the position in the word;
2. the part of the German-speaking area the speaker comes from;
3. the individual speaker.

We will describe the three commonest varieties. You should imitate your instructor's usage.

Variety #1 (back or velar R)

This variety has absolutely nothing in common with American **r**. In American **r**, the lips are more or less rounded and do a good deal of the work; the tongue tip points upward toward the front part of the roof of the mouth. In German **r**, the lips are neutral, and **the work is done by the back of the tongue.* The back of the tongue is raised toward the back of the roof of the mouth ("velum")** —about where we make a **g**-sound as in **get**. The tongue does not **touch** the velum; it just comes close to it, and the air rushing past makes a frictional noise. The sound is voiced, but may become voiceless next to a voiceless consonant.

---

* If you have had French, it will help you to know that this variety of German R is almost exactly the same as the **r**-sound in standard Parisian French.

Variety #2 (front or trilled R)

This variety too has nothing in common with the usual American **r**. It is made with the lips neutral. **The tip of the tongue taps or flaps against the gums behind the top front teeth.*** It is voiced.

Some Americans (particularly telephone operators) use this kind of an **r**-sound in words like three, thrust, through. Most Americans use a sound very much like it as a variety of **t**-sound in words like better, butter. Most American children use it when they imitate the sound of a motorboat or airplane. Finally, the British use it as a variety of **r**-sound in words like **very** ("veddy") or **berry**.

Compare: (The German words may have either variety of r-sound.)

English	Rhine	dry	roofed	ring	heron	wrote	fry	reckon	rock	era	gross	room	roar	Rosa	foreign
German	Rhein	drei	ruft	Ring	Herren	rot	frei	recken	Rock	ihre	groß	Ruhm	Rohr	Rose	fahren

Practice:

ruft	bereit	Recht	brachte	Frau	Freund	reiste	groß	Lehrer	richtig
krank	Radio	rechts	Rat	gerade	Rose	regnet	draußen	reist	schreibe
Brief	Brot	Rathaus	trinkt	Haare	rufen	Ring	warum	raucht	Frage

Variety #3 (offglide or "vocalic")

This variety is used by many speakers, but **only in certain positions in the word**—namely, **before a consonant, or at the very end of the word.** (In any **other** position in the word, the same speakers will use one of the other two varieties of **r**.) It sounds somewhat like the vowel-like "offglide" that British and many Eastern Americans (from the South, New England, or New York City) use in the same positions: **lore** (pronounced like **law**), **lord** (pronounced like **laud**). However, this English offglide is towards the **middle** of the mouth, and is like the weak vowel sound in **about**, **open**, or like German unstressed E; whereas German offglide R is made with the tongue moving towards the **back** of the mouth. Compare first the offglide R with American **r**:

English	fear	beer	four	poor	par	fort	heart	dare	here	hair	party	mare
German	vier	Bier	vor	pur	paar	fort	hart	der	hier	her	Party	mehr

and now with unstressed E:

-R vs. unstressed E

R	E	R	E	R	E
Ruhr	Ruhe	sehr	sehe	Kür	Kühe
Wehr	wehe	hör'	Höhe	Zier	ziehe

---

* This variety is almost the same as the Spanish **r**-sounds in **pero** or **perro**.

Practice (alternating **r**)

R-	-R	R-	-R	R-	-R
ruft	paar	groß	Haar	Lehrer	der
Brot	Bier	trifft	hört	rechts	darf
Haare	sehr	Brief	erst	früh	her
Freund	dort	regnet	Durst	streng	Uhr
Frau	für	brachte	Herbst	warum	Tier
rauchen	Jahr	spricht	durch	berühmt	Herr
Bruder	schwer	fahren	hier	Büro	kurz
draußen	Stern	darum	gar	drüben	gern
hören	fern	richtig	lernt	Fräulein	Tür
Rathaus	wahr	freuen	Park	geboren	Arzt
während	nur	Brause	lehrt	lehren	Klavier
darauf	wer	Lehrer	warm	niedrig	dürfen
Frage	Wort	Fabrik	Kirche	schreiben	modern
Straße	daher	Krankenhaus	natürlich	Lehrerin	nirgends
Prüfung	studiert	Radio	Party	reisen	morgen
rasieren	fertig	gerade	Arbeit	ausruhen	vorbei
spazieren	Kursus	Ausdruck	Vorlesung	Sprache	Karte
Arithmetik	Viertel	studieren	werden	bereit	warte

Unstressed -ER vs. Unstressed E

In unstressed -ER the effect of the R is again to move the sound to the back of the mouth, whereas unstressed -E is central. Keep these sharply apart. Compare:

-E	-ER	-E	-ER	-E	-ER
Sonde	sonder	übe	über	Sonden	sondern
bitte	bitter	schneide	Schneider	Höhe	höher
diese	dieser	Liebe	lieber	Güte	Güter
fehle	Fehler	Lehre	Lehrer	alten	altern
Gästen	gestern	Deutsche	Deutscher	Ode	oder

Practice:

diese	Eltern	danke	aber	Briefe	selber
abends	aber	alle	dauern	Minute	Kinder
dunkel	Bruder	eine	aller	Ende	bitter
fließend	ander	bitte	außer	Dame	Bilder
Auge	Feder	Familie	oder	ohne	Fenster
Gebäude	plaudern	bekannt	Schwester	Himmel	Bücher
Boden	sondern	bedeckt	unter	außen	verstehen

Spelling: ir, er, ur, war, wor

In German, **the vowel letter in combinations like ir, er, war represents the same sound as anywhere else.** For example, **ir** represents an I-sound (lax) followed by an R-sound; it does **not** represent the sound in English **first, shirt.** Similarly, **wor** represents a V-sound (weiß) plus an O-sound plus an R-sound—**not** as in **word, work** and so on.

Practice:

wird	erst	nur	lernt	fern	ernst
durch	Stern	war	gern	schwer	warm
kurz	Berg	Durst	ernste	Wort	ferner
Kirche	lernen	warten	wurden	erben	Antwort
nirgends	Kursus	werden	durfte	lernte	geworden
wirklich	modern	Geschirr	Geburtstag	bemerken	Erfolg
gestorben	fertig	gedurft	sterben	furchtbar	erfrischt

Back CH

Spelling: ch after a, o, u, au

This sound is quite different from K and from SH (or English sh). It has nothing to do with the English sound we spell **ch** in **much.** It has two varieties, depending on the position in the word. Both are voiceless frictional sounds. The first variety is made by bringing the back of the tongue close to (**but not close enough to touch**) the back of the roof of the mouth—about where we make a **k**-sound, or even farther back. English has nothing like it.

English k	German CH	German K	German CH	German K	German CH
knock	nach	Lacke	lache	sackt	sacht
mocked	macht	Pocken	pochen	Dock	doch
bock	Bach	nackt	Nacht	Akt	acht
dock	Dach	Flug	Fluch	Bug	Buch
book	Buch				
knocked	Nacht				

Practice:

ach!	Bach	hoch	Buch	Nacht	Frucht	auch	hoch
Fach	doch	suche	acht	noch	wach	Koch	mache
nachts	dachte	brachte	besuchen	rauchen	Sprache	mochte	wachen
Tochter	danach	besuchen	gemocht	brachten	versucht	gesprochen	machten
mochten	schwach	Woche	brauche	versuchen	lachen	abgemacht	gebraucht

Front CH

Spelling: ch everywhere else other than after **a, o, u, au**

The second variety is made in the front of the mouth. Put your tongue and lips into the same position as for **ee** in see, and push the air through.* **Don't round your lips, but spread them.** (If you round them, you get a **sh**-sound.) Compare:

English sh	German CH	German SCH	German CH	German SCH	German CH
dish	dich	Gischt	Gicht	Bresche	breche
fished	ficht	fischt	ficht	Kirsche	Kirche
		misch'	mich	herrschen	Herrchen
		welsch	welch	wischen	wichen

Practice:

ich	echt	rechts	sich	Reich	nicht	durch	mich
Kirche	Milch	Früchte	leicht	Recht	nächst	dich	schlecht
richtig	Mädchen	nichts	Nächte	höchst	möchte	bißchen	**richtig**
endlich	Bücher	manchmal	sprechen	ziemlich	Geschichte	Chemie	gewöhnlich
Köchin	natürlich	Töchter	Unterricht	plötzlich	welche	Fächer	wirklich

Alternating back and front CH:

Back	Front	Back	Front	Back	Front
ach!	ich	Buch	Bücher	hoch	sich
acht	echt	doch	mich	Bach	Milch
Frucht	Recht	Nacht	nicht	auch	leicht
suchen	spricht	Fach	dich	Woche	Kirche
Tochter	Töchter	wachen	bißchen	Sprache	sprechen
gemocht	Geschichte	besuchten	richtig	gebraucht	wirklich

---

* Some English speakers make a sound like this, instead of a regular **h**-sound, in words like **hue, human, huge.**

NG

Spelling: -ng-; -n-

The spelling **ng** in English represents either one sound, as in **singer**, or two sounds (-ng- plus -g-) as in **finger**. In German, NG in the stressed syllable always represents the **ng**-sound as in **singer** and never ends with a G-sound.* Compare:

English (ng+g)	German NG	English	German	English	German
finger	Finger	angle	Angel	English	Englisch
hunger	Hunger	mangle	Mangel	anger	Anger

The same NG-sound before a K-sound, as in **Bank**, **links**, presents no problem to an English speaker: we will not mention it further.

Practice:

Engel	Lunge	singen	Finger	enge	lange	sangen
hungrig	strenger	bringen	Englisch	Menge	Hunger	fangen
springen	Zeitungen	gelingen	gesungen	Dinge	Einladungen	Ringel
Zunge	länger	Junge	hangen			

L

Spelling: l, ll

German L is strikingly different from English l. English l is made with the tongue in a hollow curve, much as for a **u**-sound as in **put**; German L is made with the tongue bunched forward, much as for an I-sound. Only the tip of the tongue touches the gums in English; in German, the whole front of the tongue is in contact with the top of the mouth. To an English speaker's ear, German L is "liquid." Compare:

English	lout	links	lease	loan	leaked	fowl	hell	feel	elf	light	built	felt	vile	film	hotel
German	laut	links	ließ	Lohn	liegt	faul	hell	viel	elf	leid	Bild	Feld	weil	Film	Hotel

Practice:

soll	alles	will	als	Onkel	Vogel	klein	niemals	Klima
Spiel	wieviel	Schule	hell	lassen	Eltern	lang	mild	sollen
leicht	vielmals	einmal	Land	Politik	selten	schlecht	fiel	Lehrer
all	Schallplatte	welcher	Platz	Ball	legen	letzt	Geld	nämlich
schnell	links	lernen	stellt	lacht	fliegen	bleiben	Film	Ratskeller
half	Lied	langsam	Ballett	läuft	Viertel	dunkel	bald	
Laden	wohl	spielen	schlafen	alt	liegen	fallen	kühl	
wollen	Milch	Leute	Fehler	kalt	liebt	lustig	selber	
lesen	falsch	viel	möglich	halb	Bild	gefallen	helfen	

---

* An obvious exception is in words like **angestellt, ungemein**, where the **-n-** belongs to a prefix (**an-, un-,** etc.); here, the pronunciation is -N plus G-, just as in English **ungrateful, ingoing**.

UNVOICING OF B, D, G, Z†

Review the discussion of unvoicing on page 10.

In each of these pairs of forms, both items are from the same stem; for example, **blieben**="(we) stayed," **blieb**="(he) stayed." In each pair, the last consonant of the stem becomes voiceless when final or when before a voiceless consonant, but stays voiced anywhere else. Compare:

B	P	D	T	G	K	Z	SS
blieben :	blieb	Freunde :	Freund	sagen :	sagt	Hause :	Haus
lieben :	liebt	Hunde :	Hund	liege :	liegt	lasen :	las
haben :	gehabt	Kinder :	Kind	Tage :	Tag	reise :	reiste
gaben :	gab	Lieder :	Lied	stiegen :	stieg	dieser :	dies

NOTE 1: Remember that these four consonants become voiceless at the end of a word even when that word is within a "compound." (By "compound" we mean a combination like **Hauptstraße**, from **Haupt** and **Straße**, which is parallel to English **Main Street.** The main difference is that in English we more often than not continue to write the two elements as separate words, whereas in German they are joined in the spelling as one word.) Thus in **Mittagessen** the **g** is pronounced as K, just as it is in **Mittag.** This also occurs before certain suffixes: **-lich, -sam.**

NOTE 2: The suffix **-ig** is pronounced -IK by some Germans but -ICH by others. Imitate your instructor's pronunciation.

Practice:

blieb	Mond	Haus	schrieb	Land	mag
ob	Bild	Tag	las	stand	lag
gab	und	stieg	halb	Hund	zog
hübsch	Kind	liegt	Herbst	Hand	fragt
gibt	Lied	fragt	schreibt	mild	legt
bleibt	bald	tags	selbst	Freund	sagt
liest	Geld	Krieg	lieb	Stadt	Zug
obwohl	Abend	glaubte	absteigt	endlich	möglich
während	fleißig	Flugzeug	reise	Mädchen	Mittag
niemals	Deutschland	fertig	abends	Hündchen	niemand
gehabt	fließend	nirgends	Verwandte	wenig	übrigens
schweigsam	Handschuh	diesseits	rundlich	abholen	Landstraße
Fremdsprache	abgemacht	Mittagessen	überzeugt	Gesundheit	genug
Schwierigkeit	Abendbrot	vereinigten	obgleich	Untergrundbahn	langweilig

T, D, N, SS, Z

Spelling:

T: **t, tt**; final **d**; **dt**; in some words, **th**.

D: **d** non-final.

N: **n, nn**.

SS: **ss, ß***; **s** final or next to a voiceless consonant (except initial **sp-**; **st-**).

Z†: **s** initial before vowel, between vowels, or after a voiced consonant.

All these sounds are made in approximately the same way as in English, and should cause no trouble. However: T is always released (that is, the tongue leaves the teeth at the end of the sound)‡ and is never made with the flapping that English **t** has in words like **letter, bitter.** Compare:

English	toot	tear	bet	mitt	do	odor	dome	dear	nine	in	knee	owner	
German	tut	Tier	Bett	mit	du	oder	Dom	dir	nein	in	nie	ohne	
English	press	house	fasten	ice	rosin	zeal	zone	reason	fetter	bitter	rotten	beater
German	preß	Haus	fassen	Eis	Rasen	Siel	Sohn	Riesen	fetter	bitte	Rotten	biete

Practice:

an	tun	wann	so	was	tat
die	Mann	nun	Eis	denn	gut
noch	Fuß	doch	sagt	neu	sein
dann	Tag	sieht	Tisch	ein	tun
saß	neun	seit	daß	nur	naß
Sohn	Hand	dies	müde	nett	heiß
bitte	etwas	Sonne	später	nieder	Damen
Kind	müssen	finden	arbeite	Theater	wissen
wieder	Minute	Butter	Kino	Mutter	Ende
sieben	Name	Nase	danke	sollen	gewesen
Monat	Gewitter	besser	Süden	Mittel	essen

---

* ß usually occurs after a tense vowel, or finally.

† By Z we mean the **z**-sound as in **zoo**.

‡ *Exception*: before unstressed **-en**: warten, Noten, arbeiten.

EASY SOUNDS

The following consonants normally present no difficulties to English speakers, either in spelling or in sound.

Sound	Spelling	Examples			
P	p, pp; b	Post	ob	halb	gab
		hübsch	lieb	Lampe	Politik
B	b, except final	Baum	Brot	Bank	best
		bei	Abend	über	aber
K	k, ck; g; in some Greek words, ch	Kind	lag	Ecke	genug
		Musik	kommen	danke	Chaos
G	g, except final	Auge	gehe	genug	ganz
		gegen	mögen	regnet	sagen
SH (made with tongue farther back and lips rounder than in English)	sch; in some French words, ch	schön	hübsch	Schiff	Tisch
		Chef	komisch	scheinen	waschen
GE (about the same as in measure, pleasure, lesion)	g before e or i, in French words	Corsage	Courage	Garage	Ingenieur
TCH (about the same as in church, much, pitch)	tsch	Deutsch	Putsch	klatschen	Deutscher
M	m, mm	Mann	um	mit	im
		kommen	Lampe	immer	komisch
H	h (except after vowel in the same syllable)	hat	hier	hoch	hin
		heute	dahin	Hunger	daher

EASY SOUNDS WITH MISLEADING SPELLINGS

F

Spelling: f, ff; initial **v;** in some Greek words, **ph. Notice that initial v does NOT represent v as in vine but an F-sound as in "fine."**
Practice:

von	auf	fast	vor	Frau	viel
früh	Vater	Freund	Schiff	Brief	rufen
helfen	viele	Feder	Prüfung	Vogel	offen
Viertel	Physik	wieviele	vereinigten	Verkäufer	Kaffee

V

Spelling: w; non-initial **v**

This sound can be approximately the same as the **v**-sound in **vine**. In some speakers the friction is not made by the lower lip and upper teeth but by the two lips—as for **b** but with friction instead of complete closing of the lips. **Notice particularly that this is NOT the same as the w-sound in wine.**

Practice:

wird	wann	weil	wahr	was	warm
Winter	Wasser	Westen	warten	Wetter	warum
wenig	schwer	während	Schwester	schwimmen	waschen
wohne	wirklich	auswendig	Universität	Wörter	Revolution

Y

Spelling: j; rarely, **y**

Essentially the same as in English **yes, you**, but tenser and with more friction. **Notice particularly that j does NOT represent a j-sound as in just, jam, judge.**
Practice:

ja	je	jung	jetzt	Junge
Major	jeder	Jacke	jenseits	Jahr
Johannes	jedermann	Sportjacke	jawohl	jemand

TS

Spelling: z, tz. Like the **ts** in **puts; never just a z-sound as in zoo.**
Practice:

stolz	kurz	Schweiz	Herz	holz	ganz
fünfzehn	dazu	neunzehn	vierzehn	erzogen	dreizehn
vierzig	erzählen	bezahlen	spazieren	erziehen	bezogen

Combined practice:

war	vor	Wort	jawohl	jetzt	viel
jung	Vogel	vierzig	schwer	Anzug	warum
dazu	wegen	schwarz	vorbei	wieviel	spazieren
Verzeihung	Wanderjahr	geworden	verkaufen	Winter	erzogen

CONSONANTS IN DIFFICULT CLUSTERS AND DIFFICULT POSITIONS

Initial TS

Spelling: z

This combination (like **ts** in English pu**ts**) is not difficult in itself. But it *is* difficult for us when it occurs at the beginning of a word in German, since it never occurs in that position in English. It is *not* just an **s**-sound or a **z**-sound. Compare:

English z	German TS	English s		English z	German TS	English s
zinc	Zink	sink		zoo	zu	sue
Czar	Zar	Saar			Zeit	sight
	zehn	sane			Zimmer	simmer
zoom	zum			zeal	Ziel	seal

German Z	German TS	Z	TS	Z	TS
seit	Zeit	sauber	Zauber	Siegel	Ziegel
Sahne	Zahne	Siel	Ziel	sieht	zieht
See	Zeh	sein	ziehen	Saum	Zaum
Sünder	Zünder	sangen	Zangen	so	Zoo
		Sie	Zieh!		

Practice:

zu	zwei	zeigt	zum	zweite	zog	Zahn	Zeit
zur	zunächst	zwar	Zähne	Zimmer	zwischen	Zug	zehn
ziemlich	Zigarre	zwanzig	zogen	zeigen	zurück	Zeitung	Zehen
zuhören	zuschauen	zusehen	zusammen	Zigarette	zumachen	Zentrum	erzählen
ausziehen	Flugzeug	Zeiten	zerrissen				

Initial and Final PF

The same kind of remarks apply here as for initial TS: English never has initial or final **pf**, though it has that combination in phrases. PF is *not* just an **f**-sound. Compare:

English f	German PF	German F	German PF	German F	German PF
font	Pfand	fade	Pfade	Falz	Pfalz
false	Pfalz	fahl	Pfahl	fand	Pfand
file	Pfeil	flicht	Pflicht	Flug	Pflug
fool	Pfuhl	Fund	Pfund		
toff	Topf				

Practice:

Pflug	Pfahl	Pferd	Pfeil	Kopf	Pfalz	Pfeife
Pfand	Pfund	Pfropf	Topf	Pflicht	Pflug	Pfarre
hüpfen	Pflanze	Pfuhl	Pfeffer	Pflege	pfänden	Pfennig

Initial SH plus consonant

Spelling: initial **s-** plus **p** or plus **t**; **sch** plus other consonant

The remarks for initial TS and PF apply here as well. These combinations do *not* begin with an **s**-sound but with a **sh**-sound. Compare:

English sp-, etc.	German SHP-, etc.	English	German	English	German
spiel	Spiel	slier	Schleier	steel	Stiel
slim	schlimm	style	steil	swear	schwer
still	still	spear	Spier	stool	Stuhl

Notice, however, that **medial** and **final** **sp** and **st** represent SSP and SST—*not* SHP, SHT! **Examples:** best, Fenster, Gast, gestern, fliehst, Kunst, liest, Osten, Post, tust, erst, reiste, selbst, sonst, Westen, ist, gehst.

Practice:

stand	Staat	spät	schlief	streng	Spiel	Stuhl	Sprache
schwer	schnell	Stamm	schlecht	schwamm	Stern	Schnee	Stadt
schreiben	stellen	Straße	schlafen	spielen	schwatzen	bestand	Schwester
Stunde	schneien	angestellt	Frühstück	schläfrig	absteigen	steil	Stimme
Schauspiel	sprechen	schwierig	Bierstube	spazieren	Gaststätte	steigen	studieren
gestanden	Fremdsprache	Studentin	einschlafen	stehen	Bleistift	stolz	verstehen

GLOTTAL STOP

By "glottal stop" we mean the little catch or click, made with the vocal cords, that we often use in English just before an initial vowel sound—particularly in phrases like **an iceman** (just before the **i**). If you whisper "Not a *nice* man but an *ice*man," you will probably hear the glottal stop clearly.

In English the glottal stop is always optional. In German it is required before any word (even within a "compound") that **begins with a vowel that is stressed.** You will often hear people say that German is "staccato" or "choppy," or that "in German it is easy to tell where one word ends and the next begins." The glottal stop is one very important reason behind that impression.

Practice:

geradeaus	Verabredung	vereinigt	Postämter	außerordentlich	geantwortet	Beachtung	Fernsehapparat
das ‿ Eis	die ‿ andere	die ‿ Oper		ich ‿ esse		um zu ‿ üben
als ‿ ob	nur ‿ einmal	zum ‿ Osten		auf ‿ Englisch		hat ‿ unrecht
die ‿ Ecke	meine ‿ Eltern	ohne ‿ Antwort		nach ‿ Europa		und ‿ übrigens
sehr ‿ angenehm	nicht ‿ einmal	sehr ‿ interessant		gestern ‿ Abend		zu ‿ übersetzen
drei ‿ Uhr	zog sich ‿ um	ist ‿ unbekannt		auf der ‿ Universität		zum ‿ Abendessen
das ‿ USA	ganz ‿ unrichtig	von ‿ Anfang ‿ an		ihr ‿ Akzent		im ‿ allgemeinen
in ‿ Amerika	das ‿ Ende	nicht ‿ amerikanisch		und ‿ endlich		mein ‿ Onkel

Lesson I

BASIC SENTENCES

Müller—Good morning.	(1) **Müller—Guten Morgen.**
How are you?	(2) **Wie geht es Ihnen?**
Strauss—I'm fine, thank you.	(3) **Strauß—Es geht mir gut, danke.**
And you?	(4) **Und Ihnen?**
M. —I'm fine, too.	(4a) **M. —Es geht mir auch gut.**

(2)

(1)

(3)

(4)

(4-a)

S.	—What's your name?	(5)	S.	—Wie heißen Sie?
M.	—My name is Müller.	(6)	M.	—Ich heiße Müller.
S.	—I don't understand.	(7)	S.	—Ich verstehe nicht.
	Please say it again /repeat/.*	(8)		Wiederholen Sie bitte!

_____

* English words or phrases enclosed in slashes indicate literal equivalents of the German.

(5)

(6)

(7)

(8)

M.	—I am Johann Müller.	(9)	M.	—Ich bin Johann Müller.
	Do you understand now?	(10)		Verstehen Sie jetzt?
S.	—Yes, thank you, I understand.	(11)	S.	—Ja, danke sehr, ich verstehe.
	Well, I'm going home now.	(12)		Also, jetzt gehe ich nach Hause.
M.	—Good-bye.	(13)	M.	—Auf Wiedersehen.
S.	—So long.	(14)	S.	—Auf Wiedersehen.

(9)

(10)

(11)

(12)

(13)

(14)

VARIATIONS

Who am I?	**Wer bin ich?**
Who is he?	**Wer ist er?**
Who is she?	**Wer ist sie?**
Who is that?	**Wer ist das?**
Who are they?	**Wer sind sie?**
Is that Mr. Müller?	**Ist das Herr Müller?**
Is that Mrs. Schmidt?	**Ist das Frau Schmidt?**
Is that Miss Eber?	**Ist das Fräulein Eber?**
Are you Mr. Schulze?	**Sind Sie Herr Schulze?**
Are you Johann?	**Bist du Johann?**
Are you Irmgard?	**Bist du Irmgard?**
Are you Irmgard and Johann?	**Seid ihr Irmgard und Johann?**
No, we're Trudi and Karl.	**Nein, wir sind Trudi und Karl.**
Are you Mr. and Mrs. Braun?	**Sind Sie Herr und Frau Braun?**
Yes, we're Mr. and Mrs. Braun.	**Ja, wir sind Herr und Frau Braun.**
Are you Peter Strauss?	**Sind Sie Peter Strauß?**
No, I'm not Peter Strauss;	**Nein, ich bin nicht Peter Strauß;**
I'm Johann Müller.	**ich bin Johann Müller.**
Is that Miss Stein?	**Ist das Fräulein Stein?**
No, that isn't Miss Stein;	**Nein, das ist nicht Fräulein Stein;**
that's Mrs. Müller.	**das ist Frau Müller.**
And who is that?	**Und wer ist das?**
That's Mrs. Berg.	**Das ist Frau Berg.**
What's my name?	**Wie heiße ich?**
What's your name?	**Wie heißen Sie?**
What's her name?	**Wie heißt sie?**
What's his name?	**Wie heißt er?**
What are their names?	**Wie heißen sie?**
Is your name Schmidt?	**Heißen Sie Schmidt?**
Yes, my name is Schmidt.	**Ja, ich heiße Schmidt.**

Is your name Anna?	**Heißt du Anna?**
No, my name is Trudi.	**Nein, ich heiße Trudi.**
Are your names Karl and Peter?	**Heißt ihr Karl und Peter?**
Yes, our names are Karl and Peter.	**Ja, wir heißen Karl und Peter.**
Who is that?	**Wer ist das?**
That's Mr. Müller, isn't it?	**Das ist Herr Müller, nicht wahr?**
That's Mrs. Müller, isn't it?	**Das ist Frau Müller, nicht wahr?**
You're Hans, aren't you?	**Du bist Hans, nicht wahr?**
You're Miss Schulze, aren't you?	**Sie sind Fräulein Schulze, nicht wahr?**
You're Peter and Fritz, aren't you?	**Ihr seid Peter und Fritz, nicht wahr?**
You're Mr. and Mrs. Engel, aren't you?	**Sie sind Herr und Frau Engel, nicht wahr?**
Is Johannes here?	**Ist Johannes hier?**
Yes, he's here.	**Ja, er ist hier.**
No, he's not here.	**Nein, er ist nicht hier.**
Is Irmgard here?	**Ist Irmgard hier?**
Yes, she's here.	**Ja, sie ist hier.**
No, she's not here.	**Nein, sie ist nicht hier.**
Are Mr. and Mrs. Schmidt here?	**Sind Herr und Frau Schmidt hier?**
Yes, they're here.	**Ja, sie sind hier.**
No, they're not here.	**Nein, sie sind nicht hier.**
Are you children here?	**Seid ihr Kinder hier?**
Yes, we're here.	**Ja, wir sind hier.**
Good morning!	**Guten Morgen!**
Morning!	**Morgen!**
Hello! Good day!	**Guten Tag!**
(NOTE: *Not* in the sense of "Good-bye!")	
Hi!	**Tag!**
(NOTE: Unlike German, English has no shorter form of "Good day!")	
Good evening!	**Guten Abend!**
Evening!	**Abend!**

Good night!	Gute Nacht!
	(NOTE: *Not* "Guten!")
Good-bye!	Auf Wiedersehen!
'Bye! Be seeing you!	Wiedersehen!
Thanks a lot.	Danke sehr.
You're welcome.	Bitte sehr.

STRUCTURE

A. Personal Pronouns

TABLE I A

	Singular	Plural
First Person	**ich** *I*	**wir** *we*
Second Person	**du** *you*	**ihr** *you*
	Sie *you*	
Third Person	**er** *he* **sie** *she*	**sie** *they*

NOTES:

1. The pronouns **du** and **ihr** are used only when addressing immediate relatives, small children, persons with whom one has a close relationship (e.g. fiancés) or animals.

2. **Sie** is the commonest equivalent of English *you*. It is used in all circumstances not mentioned in Note 1. As in English, and in contrast with **du-ihr, Sie** is always a grammatical plural, irrespective of the number of persons being addressed. Thus we say:

Du bist Hans.	**Ihr seid Hans und Ida.**		**Sie sind Herr Schmidt.**	**Sie sind Herr und Frau Schmidt.**
You are Hans.	*You are Hans and Ida.*	but	*You are Mr. Schmidt.*	*You are Mr. and Mrs. Schmidt.*

3. As in English, the first word of every German sentence is capitalized. Note that in initial position, **Sie** (=*you*) is in writing indistinguishable from **sie** (=*they*), and in speech the two are always identical; they have to be distinguished through the context.

4. The pronoun **Sie** (=*you*) is always capitalized in writing. The others are not ordinarily capitalized, except at the beginning of a sentence.

5. The German equivalents of English *it* will be discussed later.

B. The verb *be*—**Present tense**

TABLE I B

ich bin	**wir sind**
I am	*we are*
du bist	**ihr seid**
you are	*you are*
	Sie sind
	you are
er, sie ist	**sie sind**
he, she is	*they are*

NOTE:

The pronoun **sie** (=*she*) is distinguished from **sie** (=*they*) and **Sie** (=*you*) by the singular verb form that goes with it when it is the subject.

PATTERN PRACTICES

I. *Answer in the affirmative:*

Das ist Herr Engel,	nicht wahr?	Ja, das ist Herr Engel.
Fräulein Hirsch,		Fräulein Hirsch.
Johannes,		Johannes.
sind Herr und Frau Schmidt,		sind Herr und Frau Schmidt.
Peter und Karl,		Peter und Karl.
Frieda und Ilse,		Frieda und Ilse.
ist Ursula,		ist Ursula.

II. *Answer in the affirmative:*

Ist das Fräulein Engel?	Ja, das ist Fräulein Engel.
Herr Schulz?	Herr Schulz.
Heinrich?	Heinrich.
Kurt?	Kurt.
Sind das Peter und Dieter?	Ja, das sind Peter und Dieter.
Herr und Frau Braun?	Herr und Frau Braun.
Maria und Gertrud?	Maria und Gertrud.
Herr Hirsch und Fräulein Eckhardt?	Herr Hirsch und Fräulein Eckhardt.

III. *Answer with* **"Sie"** *when you hear* **"ich"** *and vice versa, substituting your own name for the brackets:*

Sind Sie ( )?	Ja, ich bin ( ).
Bin ich Herr Lautsprecher?	Sie sind Herr Lautsprecher.
Bist du ( )?	ich bin ( ).
Sie sind ( ), nicht wahr?	ich bin ( ).
Du bist ( ),	ich bin ( ).
Ich bin Herr Lautsprecher,	Sie sind Herr Lautsprecher.

IV. *Answer in the negative:*

Ist das Karl?	Nein, das ist nicht Karl.
Fräulein Schulz?	das ist nicht Fräulein Schulz.
Bist du Johannes?	ich bin nicht Johannes.
Seid ihr Heinrich und Hans?	wir sind nicht Heinrich und Hans.
Sind Sie Herr Brecht?	ich bin nicht Herr Brecht.
Bist du Ursula?	Ursula.
Sind Sie Frau Roth?	Frau Roth.
Sind Sie Herr und Frau Braun?	wir sind nicht Herr und Frau Braun.

V. *Answer in the negative if the question is affirmative, and vice versa, using the appropriate pronoun:*

Ist	Karl	hier?	Nein, er ist nicht hier.
Sind	Herr und Frau Weiß hier?		Nein, sie sind nicht hier.
Sind	Johannes und Peter nicht hier?		Ja, sie sind ___ hier.
Ist	Trudi nicht hier?		Ja, sie ist ___ hier.

Kinder, seid ihr nicht hier?   Ja,   wir sind ____ hier.

Sind   Heinz und Fritz hier?   Nein, sie sind nicht hier.

Sind Sie Herr Braun?   Nein, ich bin nicht Herr Braun.

Ist das nicht Karl?   Ja,   das ist ____ Karl.

Bist du   Hans?   Nein, ich bin nicht Hans.

VI. *Give appropriate answers:*

Sind Sie Herr Schmidt?   Ich heiße Schulz, nicht wahr?

Sind Sie Fräulein Engel?   Heißt er Peter?

Bin ich Herr Lautsprecher?   Wer ist das?

Ich bin Herr Lautsprecher, nicht wahr?   Wer ist sie?

Sie sind Fräulein Schulz, nicht wahr?   Ist das Frau Braun?

Ich bin Herr Lang, nicht wahr?   Wer sind sie?

Sie heißen Müller, nicht wahr?   Heißen Sie Schmidt?

VII. *Copy carefully each of the basic German sentences.*

VIII. *Write out, in German, answers to the last pattern practice, then translate the entire exercise into English. Then, from your translation, reproduce the original German.*

VOCABULARY

Abend! Evening!
also well...
Amerika America
auch also, too
Auf Wiedersehen! Good-bye! So long!
bitte please
danke thank you
das that
du you (familiar singular)
er he, it
es it
die Frau,* -en the woman
   Frau __ Mrs. __

das Fräulein, __ young woman
   Fräulein __ Miss __
gehen go
   Es geht mir gut. I'm fine.
gut good, well
Guten Abend! Good evening!
Gute Nacht! Good night!
Guten Morgen! Good morning!
Guten Tag! Hello! Good day!
Haus:
   nach Hause gehen go home
heißen be called
   Ich heiße Müller. My name is Müller.

---

* Nouns are entered in the singular and plural.

der **Herr, -en**   gentleman
   Herr __   Mr. __
hier   here
ich   I
ihr   you (familiar plural)
ja   yes
jetzt   now
das Kind, -er   child
Morgen!   Morning!
die Nacht, ⁼e   night
nein   no
nicht   not
nicht wahr?   isn't it?   aren't you?   doesn't it? etc.
sehr:
   danke sehr   thank you very much, thanks a lot
   bitte sehr   you're welcome

sein (ist)   be
Sie   you
sie   she, they, it
Tag!   Hi!
und   and
verstehen   understand
wer   who
wie   how
   Wie geht es Ihnen?   How are you?
wiederholen   repeat
Wiedersehen!   Bye! Be seeing you!
wir   we

Lesson II

BASIC SENTENCES

Peter	—Excuse me/Pardon/.		(1)	Peter	—Verzeihung.
	Is that the railroad station?				**Ist das der Bahnhof?**
Johannes	—No, it isn't		(2)	Johannes	—Nein, das ist nicht
	/No, that isn't the railroad station/.				**der Bahnhof.**
	That's the city hall.		(3)		**Das ist das Rathaus.**
P.	—Well, where is the station?		(4)	P.	—Wo ist denn der Bahnhof?

(1)

(2)

(3)

(4)

J.	—It's straight ahead.	(5)
	It's not far.	(6)
	I'm going there too.	(7)
P.	—What's that over there?	(8)
J.	—That's a hotel.	(9)
	And here is a church.	(10)
P.	—It's very pretty, isn't it?	(11)
J.	—And, finally, here's the station.	(12)
P.	—Thank you very much.	(13)

J.	—Er ist geradeaus.
	Er ist nicht weit.
	Ich gehe auch dahin.
P.	—Was ist das dort drüben?
J.	—Das ist ein Hotel.
	Und hier ist eine Kirche.
P.	—Sie ist sehr schön, nicht wahr?
J.	—Und hier ist endlich der Bahnhof.
P.	—Danke vielmals.

(5)

(6)

(7)

(8)

(9)

(10)

(11)

(12)

(13)

VARIATIONS

Who	is that?	Mr. Schmidt?	Wer ist das? Herr Schmidt?

Who   is that?   Mr. Schmidt?
Where is that?   Straight ahead?
What's   that?   The station?
Is   that   the railroad station?
Is   that   the church?
Is   that   the city hall?

Wer ist das?   Herr Schmidt?
Wo ist das?   Geradeaus?
Was ist das?   Der Bahnhof?
Ist das   der Bahnhof?
Ist das   die Kirche?
Ist das   das Rathaus?

That's the station, isn't it?
This is the park, isn't it?
　　　　the square (plaza), isn't it?
　　　　the library, isn't it?
　　　　(the) Main Street, isn't it?
　　　　the post office, isn't it?
　　　　the university, isn't it?
　　　　the movie theater, isn't it?
　　　　the hospital, isn't it?

Das ist der Bahnhof, nicht wahr?
Dies ist der Park, nicht wahr?
　　　　der Platz, nicht wahr?
　　　　die Bibliothek, nicht wahr?
　　　　die Hauptstraße, nicht wahr?
　　　　die Post, nicht wahr?
　　　　die Universität, nicht wahr?
　　　　das Kino, nicht wahr?
　　　　das Krankenhaus, nicht wahr?

The stations　　　　are downtown.
The parks
The plazas
The libraries
The restaurants
The post offices
The universities
The movie theaters
The hospitals
The park   is pretty, isn't it?
　　　tree
　　　plaza
　　　street
　　　church
　　　house

Die Bahnhöfe   sind in der Stadt.
Die Parks
Die Plätze
Die Bibliotheken
Die Gaststätten
Die Postämter
Die Universitäten
Die Kinos
Die Krankenhäuser
Der Park   ist schön, nicht wahr?
Der Baum
Der Platz
Die Straße
Die Kirche
Das Haus

The parks are pretty, aren't they?	**Die Parks** **sind schön, nicht wahr?**
trees	**Die Bäume**
plazas	**Die Plätze**
streets	**Die Straßen**
churches	**Die Kirchen**
houses	**Die Häuser**
What's that?	**Was ist das?**
That's a store.	**Das ist ein Laden.**
a tree.	**ein Baum.**
a church.	**eine Kirche.**
a school.	**eine Schule.**
a bank.	**eine Bank.**
That's not a factory.	**Das ist keine Fabrik.**
a restaurant.	**keine Gaststätte.**
a hotel.	**kein Hotel.**
a shop.	**kein Geschäft.**
a department store.	**kein Warenhaus.**
What are these?	**Was ist dies?**
These are shops.	**Dies sind Läden.**
trees.	**Bäume.**
churches.	**Kirchen.**
schools.	**Schulen.**
banks.	**Banken.**
factories.	**Fabriken.**
restaurants.	**Gaststätten.**
hotels.	**Hotels.**
stores.	**Geschäfte.**
department stores.	**Warenhäuser.**

Is that a bank or a shop?	Ist das eine Bank oder ein Laden?
3. That's not a (that's no) bank; it's a shop.	Das ist keine Bank, das ist ein Laden.
? That's not a shop; it's a bank.	Das ist nicht ein Laden, sondern eine Bank.
Where is the station?	Wo ist der Bahnhof?
It is straight ahead.	Er ist geradeaus.
Where is the shop?	Wo ist der Laden?
It is to the left.	Er ist links.
Where is the park?	Wo ist der Park?
It is to the right.	Er ist rechts.
Where is the church?	Wo ist die Kirche?
It is around the corner.	Sie ist um die Ecke.
Where is the school?	Wo ist die Schule?
It is over there, to the left.	Sie ist dort drüben links.
Where is the factory?	Wo ist die Fabrik?
It is around the corner.	Sie ist um die Ecke.
Where is the hotel?	Wo ist das Hotel?
It is over there, to the right.	Es ist dort drüben rechts.
Where is the department store?	Wo ist das Warenhaus?
It is around the corner, to the right.	Es ist rechts um die Ecke.
Where is the hospital?	Wo ist das Krankenhaus?
It is around the corner, to the left.	Es ist links um die Ecke.
Where are the hotels?	Wo sind die Hotels?
They are downtown.	Sie sind in der Stadt.
Where are the department stores?	Wo sind die Warenhäuser?
They are downtown.	Sie sind in der Stadt.
Where are the restaurants?	Wo sind die Gaststätten?
They are downtown.	Sie sind in der Stadt.
Where is the station?	Wo ist der Bahnhof?
It's here.	Er ist hier.
Here it is.	Hier ist er.

STRUCTURE

A. Gender of Nouns

In English we think of three types of nouns, those describing male beings, female beings, and inanimate or "sexless" things, such as plants, to which we refer by the pronouns "*he*," "*she*," and "*it*" respectively. However, we sometimes quite arbitrarily assign gender to inanimate things, as for example when we speak of a country as "*she*."

German makes a similar distinction, but the German genders are not based on biological considerations; they seem almost arbitrary. The three grammatical genders of German are called **masculine, feminine,** and **neuter.** The gender of a German noun is seldom apparent from the form of the noun itself, but is shown— at least a good deal of the time—by the form of its accompanying modifiers (adjectives, articles). The gender of each German noun must be learned along with the noun.

B. The Nominative Case

By "case" we mean the function which a noun has within a sentence, as shown by variations in the noun itself or in its modifiers. The "name form" of a noun (i.e. the one you will find listed in a dictionary), which is also that form which the noun has when it is a subject or equivalent to a subject, is called the **nominative case.** All the German nouns and pronouns which we have used up to now* have been in the nominative case, and all of the following remarks apply to the nominative case only.

C. The Definite Article—*the*

German has three nominative forms of the definite article, which are used as shown in Table IIA.

TABLE II A

der	masculine singular **der Bahnhof; der Park; der Laden**
die	feminine singular and *all* plurals **die Gaststätte; die Bank; die Bahnhöfe**
das	neuter singular **das Haus; das Kino; das Geschäft**

The best way to learn the gender of any German noun is to learn it *as a phrase with its definite article*—**der Park, die Bank, das Haus** (not just *Park, Bank, Haus*). At the same time, learn its plural: **der Park, die Parks,** and so on.

---

* Except for two nouns in fixed expressions.

D. The Indefinite Article—*a, an*

The indefinite article has only two forms in the nominative:

TABLE II B

ein	masculine and neuter singular **ein Park; ein Hotel; ein Laden; ein Geschäft**
eine	feminine singular **eine Gaststätte; eine Kirche; eine Bank**

E. The Negative Article—*not a, not any*

TABLE II C

kein	masculine and neuter singular **kein Park; kein Geschäft; kein Bahnhof**
keine	feminine singular and *all* plurals **keine Schule; keine Bank; keine Geschäfte**

F. Agreement of Pronouns—*it*

TABLE II D

Referring to	Pronoun	English Equivalent
Masculine singular	**er**	*it; he*
Feminine singular and *all* plurals	**sie**	*it; she; they*
Neuter singular	**es**	*it*

PATTERN PRACTICES

I. *Answer in the affirmative:*

Ist das der Platz?	Ja, das ist der Platz.
die Ecke?	die Ecke.
die Bibliothek?	die Bibliothek.
das Krankenhaus?	das Krankenhaus.
die Hauptstraße?	die Hauptstraße.
die Kirche?	die Kirche.
der Park?	der Park.
das Hotel?	
die Schule?	
das Geschäft?	
das Rathaus?	
die Universität?	

II. *Answer in the negative:*

Ist das die Fabrik?	Nein, das ist nicht die Fabrik.
das Haus?	das Haus.
der Laden?	der Laden.
die Post?	die Post.
das Warenhaus?	das Warenhaus.
der Park?	der Park.
die Universität?	die Universität.
die Straße?	
der Bahnhof?	
die Gaststätte?	
die Bank?	
der Baum?	

III. *Answer in the affirmative:*

Ist das ein Kind?	Ja, das ist ein Kind.
eine Bibliothek?	eine Bibliothek.
ein Platz?	ein Platz.
ein Krankenhaus?	ein Krankenhaus.
ein Herr?	ein Herr.
eine Frau?	eine Frau.
ein Rathaus?	ein Rathaus.
eine Gaststätte?	
eine Schule?	
ein Laden?	
ein Fräulein?	
ein Baum?	

IV. *Answer in the negative, changing* **ein** *to* **kein:**

Das ist eine Universität, nicht wahr?	Nein, das ist keine Universität.
ein Bahnhof,	kein Bahnhof.
eine Kirche,	keine Kirche.
ein Haus,	kein Haus.
eine Fabrik,	keine Fabrik.
ein Park,	kein Park.
eine Post,	keine Post.
ein Kino,	
eine Ecke,	
ein Geschäft,	
eine Straße,	
ein Baum,	

V. *Answer in the negative, with* **nicht:**

KEINE?

Sind das die Banken?	Nein, das sind nicht die Banken.
Hotels?	Hotels.
Plätze?	Plätze.
Gaststätten?	Gaststätten.
Kinder?	Kinder.
Häuser?	Häuser.
Herren?	
Bäume?	
Schulen?	
Straßen?	
Geschäfte?	

VI. *Change the noun to the plural:*

a.

Die Bibliothek ist in der Stadt.	Die Bibliotheken sind in der Stadt.
Der Platz	Die Plätze
Das Kino	Die Kinos
Der Herr	Die Herren
Die Kirche	Die Kirchen
Das Warenhaus	Die Warenhäuser
Das Krankenhaus	Die Krankenhäuser
Die Bank	Die Banken
Der Bahnhof	Die Bahnhöfe
Die Fabrik	Die Fabriken
Das Geschäft	
Die Gaststätte	
Der Laden	
Das Hotel	

b.   Das ist ein Laden.   Das sind Läden.

                                    ein Haus.   Häuser.

                                    eine Universität.   Universitäten.

                                    eine Kirche.   Kirchen.

                                    ein Platz.   Plätze.

                                    eine Frau.   Frauen.

                                    ein Hotel.   Hotels.

                                    ein Park.   Parks.

                                    ein Geschäft.   Geschäfte.

                                    eine Bibliothek.

                                    ein Kind.

                                    eine Straße.

                                    ein Baum.

                                    eine Schule.

VII. *Now reverse query and answer in Practice VI.*

VIII. *Answer with the noun in parentheses:*

            Ist das der Bahnhof?   (Hotel)   Nein, das ist das Hotel.

                    die Schule?   (Krankenhaus)   das Krankenhaus.

                    der Park?   (Platz)   der Platz.

                    das Warenhaus?   (Fabrik)

                    die Schule?   (Rathaus)

                    die Universität?   (Warenhaus)

                    die Post?   (Bahnhof)

                    das Krankenhaus?   (Bank)

IX. *Repeat VIII, using* **"ein"** *and substituting answer for query and vice versa.*

                    Example: Ist das ein Hotel?   Nein, das ist ein Bahnhof.

X. *Answer in the negative with* **kein:**

Ist das ein Hotel?	Nein, das ist kein Hotel.	Ist das ein Park?
Sind das Gaststätten?	sind keine Gaststätten.	ein Haus?
Sind das Bäume?	sind keine Bäume.	eine Bibliothek?
Ist das eine Kirche?	ist keine Kirche.	ein Bahnhof?
Ist das eine Straße?	ist keine Straße.	ein Platz?
Sind das Kinos?	sind keine Kinos.	
Sind das Geschäfte?	Geschäfte.	

XI. *Answer in the negative, followed by* **"sondern"** *and the suggested noun:*

Ist das der Bahnhof? (Krankenhaus)   Nein, das ist nicht der Bahnhof, sondern das Krankenhaus.

Ist das eine Bibliothek? (Rathaus)   Nein, das ist nicht eine Bibliothek, sondern ein Rathaus.

Ist das die Schule? (Post)   Nein, das ist nicht die Schule, sondern die Post.

Sind das die Hotels? (Gaststätten)

Sind das die Gaststätten? (Warenhäuser)

Ist dies ein Krankenhaus? (Universität)

Ist dies eine Schule? (Bibliothek)

Ist dies eine Fabrik? (Bahnhof)

XII. *Answer with the phrase,* "_____ **ist in der Stadt,**" *using the proper personal pronoun:*

Wo ist die Post?	Sie ist in der Stadt.	Wo ist der Baum?
ist der Bahnhof?	Er ist	sind die Kinder?
ist das Hotel?	Es ist	ist der Park?
ist die Gaststätte?	Sie ist	ist das Kind?
sind die Kinos?	Sie sind	sind die Frauen?
ist der Platz?	Er ist	
ist die Hauptstraße?	Sie ist	
sind die Hotels?	Sie sind	
ist das Fräulein?	Sie ist	
sind die Herren?	Sie sind	

XIII. *Answer, placing the suggested noun into the phrase used in the question:*

    Example: Was ist das dort drüben? (Post)   Das ist die Post dort drüben.

Was ist das dort	drüben?	(Post)		Was ist das hier?	(Bibliothek)
	geradeaus?	(Haus)		um die Ecke?	(Kirche)
	rechts?	(Hotel)		rechts?	(Gaststätte)
	links?	(Fabrik)		links?	(Banken)
	hier?	(Bank)		hier?	(Bahnhof)
	links?	(Krankenhaus)		dort drüben?	(Läden)
	rechts?	(Bahnhof)		links?	(Warenhaus)
	dort drüben links?	(Kirche)		geradeaus?	(Warenhäuser)
	geradeaus?	(Schule)		dort drüben?	(Häuser)
	dort drüben rechts?	(Geschäfte)		rechts?	(Kind)
	geradeaus?	(Hotels)		dort drüben?	(Kinos)

XIV. *Copy the Basic Sentences.*

XV. *Write out the answers to practice XIII.*

XVI. *Repeat XV, substituting the proper pronouns.*

VOCABULARY

der Bahnhof, ⸚e railroad station
die Bank, -en bank
der Baum, ⸚e tree
die Bibliothek, -en library
dahin (to) there, to that place
denn well (then)
der, die, das the (definite article)
dies this
dort drüben over there
die Ecke, -n corner
  um die Ecke around the corner
ein, eine a, an (indefinite article)
endlich final(ly)
die Fabrik, -en factory
die Gaststätte, -n restaurant
geradeaus straight ahead
das Geschäft, -e shop

Haupt- main, chief
  die Hauptstraße, -n (the) Main Street
das Haus, ⸚er house
das Hotel, -s hotel
in in
kein, keine not any, no, not a (negative article)
das Kino, -s movie theater
die Kirche, -n church
das Krankenhaus, ⸚er hospital
der Laden, ⸚ store
links to the left
oder or
der Park, -s park
der Platz, ⸚e square, plaza
die Post, Postämter post office
das Rathaus, ⸚er city hall
rechts to the right

schön pretty
die Schule, -n school
sehr very
sondern rather, but
die Stadt, ⸚e city
  in der Stadt in the city, downtown
die Straße, -n street
die Universität, -en university
Verzeihung! Excuse me!
vielmals many times
  Danke vielmals. Thank you very much.
das Warenhaus, ⸚er department store
was what
weit far
wo where

Lesson III

(1)

BASIC SENTENCES

This is Johannes Dietrich Müller.

He's called Hans.

He's a German.

He lives in Heidelberg

and goes to the University/studies at the University/.

(1) **Dies ist Johannes Dietrich Müller.**

(2) **Er heißt Hans.**

(3) **Er ist Deutscher.**

(4) **Er wohnt in Heidelberg**

(5) **und studiert auf der Universität.**

(2)

(3)

(4)

(5)

And this is Peter Strauss.	(6)	**Und dies ist Peter Strauß.**
He's called Peter.	(7)	**Er heißt Peter.**
He's an American,	(8)	**Er ist Amerikaner,**
but he's in Germany now.	(9)	**aber er ist jetzt in Deutschland.**
He's been there for three weeks/is since three weeks there/.	(10)	**Er ist seit drei Wochen da.**
Peter speaks, understands, reads, and writes a little German.	(11)	**Peter spricht, versteht, liest und schreibt ein bißchen Deutsch.**
He wants to speak it well.	(12)	**Er will es gut sprechen.**
Hans and Peter are friends.	(13)	**Hans und Peter sind Freunde.**
Hans has pictures of Heidelberg,	(14)	**Hans hat Bilder von Heidelberg,**
and Peter wants to see them.	(15)	**und Peter will sie sehen.**

VARIATIONS

This man is a German.	**Dieser Mann ist Deutscher.**
This gentleman is an American.	**Dieser Herr ist Amerikaner.**
This boy is a student.	**Dieser Junge ist Student.**
Is this boy a student?	**Ist dieser Junge Student?**
Yes, he's a student.	**Ja, er ist Student.**
This lady is a German.	**Diese Dame ist Deutsche.**
This woman is an American.	**Diese Frau ist Amerikanerin.**
Is she a co-ed?	**Ist sie Studentin?**
Yes, she's a co-ed.	**Ja, sie ist Studentin.**
No, she's not a co-ed.	**Nein, sie ist keine Studentin.**
This girl is an American.	**Dieses Mädchen ist Amerikanerin.**
This girl is a German.	√ **Dieses Mädchen ist Deutsche.**
Does she study?	**Studiert sie?**
Yes, she studies at the University.	**Ja, sie studiert auf der Universität.**
These men are Germans.	**Diese Männer sind Deutsche.**
These people are Americans.	**Diese Leute sind Amerikaner.**
Are these girls co-eds?	√ **Sind diese Mädchen Studentinnen?**
Yes, and they're Americans.	**Ja, und sie sind Amerikanerinnen.**
Are these boys Germans?	**Sind diese Jungen Deutsche?**
Yes, they're friends.	**Ja, sie sind Freunde.**
No, they're not friends.	**Nein, sie sind keine Freunde.**
That man is an American.	**Der Mann ist Amerikaner.***
Is that boy a student?	**Ist der Junge Student?**
Is that woman a German?	**Ist die Frau Deutsche?**
No, that woman is an American.	**Nein, die Frau ist Amerikanerin.**
Is that girl a co-ed?	**Ist das Mädchen Studentin?**
No, she's no co-ed.	**Nein, sie ist keine Studentin.**
Are those boys students?	**Sind die Jungen Studenten?**
Yes, those boys are students.	**Ja, die Jungen sind Studenten.**

---

* Notice the strong stress on **der, die, das, die** in this and the following sentences.

Yes, those boys are friends.	Ja, die Jungen sind Freunde.
Those people are Americans.	Die Leute sind Amerikaner.
Hans is my friend.	Hans ist mein Freund.
Peter, is Hans your friend?	Peter, ist Hans dein Freund?
Where is his friend?	Wo ist sein Freund?
Where is her friend?	Wo ist ihr Freund?
Karl is our friend.	Karl ist unser Freund.
Children, is Karl your friend?	Kinder, ist Karl euer Freund?
Yes, Karl is their friend.	Ja, Karl ist ihr Freund.
Where is your friend, Mr. Schmidt?	Wo ist Ihr Freund, Herr Schmidt?
That co-ed is my girl friend.	Die Studentin ist meine Freundin.
Peter, is this girl your friend?	Peter, ist dieses Mädchen deine Freundin?
That's his girl friend.	Das ist seine Freundin.
That's her girl friend.	Das ist ihre Freundin.
Where are our (girl) friends?	Wo sind unsere Freundinnen?
Ida and Ilse, your girl friend is here!	Ida und Ilse, eure Freundin ist hier!
This is my book.	Dies ist mein Buch.
Hans, that's your book.	Hans, das ist dein Buch.
That's his book.	Das ist sein Buch.
That's her child.	Das ist ihr Kind.
Where is our book?	Wo ist unser Buch?
Is this your book, children?	Ist dies euer Buch, Kinder?
No, this isn't their book.	Nein, dies ist nicht ihr Buch.
Is this your child, Mrs. Eber?	Ist dies Ihr Kind, Frau Eber?
Those are my books, aren't they?	Das sind meine Bücher, nicht wahr?
Peter, are these children your friends?	Peter, sind diese Kinder deine Freunde?
Those girls are his students.	Die Mädchen sind seine Studentinnen.
Who is that?	Wer ist das?
That's Mr. Müller.	Das ist Herr Müller.
What's/How is/his first name?	Wie ist sein Vorname?
His first name is Otto.	Sein Vorname ist Otto.
What's your name?	Wie ist Ihr Name?

My first name is Heinrich,	**Mein Vorname ist Heinrich,**
and my family name is Schmidt.	**und mein Familienname ist Schmidt.**
I'm writing. (I write.)	**Ich schreibe.**
Hans, are you writing? (Do you write?)	**Hans, schreibst du?**
Peter is writing. (Peter writes.)	**Peter schreibt.**
We're writing. (We write.)	**Wir schreiben.**
Children, are you writing? (Do you write?)	**Kinder, schreibt ihr?**
Are they writing? (Do they write?)	**Schreiben sie?**
Are you writing? (Do you write?)	**Schreiben Sie?**
Do you understand German, Mr. Eck?	**Verstehen Sie Deutsch, Herr Eck?**
No, but I understand English.	**Nein, aber ich verstehe Englisch.**
Hans, do you understand English?	**Hans, verstehst du Englisch?**
Children, do you understand German?	**Kinder, versteht ihr Deutsch?**
Children, you understand English, don't you?	**Kinder, ihr versteht Englisch, nicht wahr?**
No, we don't understand English.	**Nein, wir verstehen kein Englisch.**
Ilse doesn't understand German.	**Ilse versteht kein Deutsch.**
What are you doing?	**Was machen Sie?**
I'm reading now.	**Ich lese jetzt.**
Karl, you're reading now, aren't you?	**Karl, du liest jetzt, nicht wahr?**
Mrs. Schmidt is reading now.	**Frau Schmidt liest jetzt.**
We're reading, too.	**Wir lesen auch.**
Are you reading, children?	**Lest ihr, Kinder?**
Do you speak German?	**Sprechen Sie Deutsch?**
Yes, I speak German.	**Ja, ich spreche Deutsch.**
Hans, you speak English, don't you?	**Hans, du sprichst Englisch, nicht wahr?**
Yes, and Ilse speaks it, too.	**Ja, und Ilse spricht es auch.**
Children, do you speak German?	**Kinder, sprecht ihr Deutsch?**
No, we don't./We speak no German./	**Nein, wir sprechen kein Deutsch.**
But our friends speak German.	**Aber unsere Freunde sprechen Deutsch.**
My girl friend speaks German, too.	**Meine Freundin spricht auch Deutsch.**
Does she read English?	**Liest sie Englisch?**
Yes, she reads a little English.	**Ja, sie liest ein bißchen Englisch.**

Where do you/does one/speak German?	**Wo spricht man Deutsch?**
They speak* German in Germany.	**Man spricht Deutsch in Deutschland.**
You speak*	
One speaks*	
And where do you speak English?	**Und wo spricht man Englisch?**
You speak English in England and America.	**Man spricht Englisch in England und Amerika.**
What do you speak here?	**Was spricht man hier?**
Does anybody (someone) here speak German?	**Spricht hier jemand Deutsch?**
Yes, everyone speaks German.	**Ja, alle sprechen Deutsch.**
But no one speaks English.	**Aber niemand spricht Englisch.**
What are you doing now?	**Was machen Sie jetzt?**
I'm working.	**Ich arbeite.**
Otto, you're working, aren't you?	**Otto, du arbeitest, nicht wahr?**
Yes, and Richard's working, too.	**Ja, und Richard arbeitet auch.**
Where are you working?	**Wo arbeiten Sie?**
We're working in America,	**Wir arbeiten in Amerika,**
but our friends are working in Germany.	**aber unsere Freunde arbeiten in Deutschland.**
Children, where do your friends work?	**Kinder, wo arbeiten eure Freunde?**
What are you doing?	**Was machen Sie?**
I'm reading something.	**Ich lese etwas.**
writing	**schreibe**
studying	**lerne**
And Hans? What's he doing now?	**Und Hans? Was macht er jetzt?**
Oh, he's reading.	**Oh, er liest.**
writing.	**schreibt.**
working.	**arbeitet.**
Do you understand everything?	**Verstehen Sie alles?**
No, I don't understand anything./No, I understand nothing./	**Nein, ich verstehe nichts.**
Hans, are you doing something?	**Hans, machst du etwas?**

---

* In the meaning of "People in general speak..."

I'm not studying anything.	Ich lerne nichts.
reading	lese
writing	schreibe
Is Seppl writing?	Schreibt Seppl?
No, he's not writing.	Nein, er schreibt nicht.
reading.	liest
studying.	lernt
working.	arbeitet
I want to understand German well.	Ich will Deutsch gut verstehen.
read	lesen.
write	schreiben.
speak	sprechen.
Hans, do you want to study something?	Hans, willst du etwas studieren?
read	lesen?
write	schreiben?
This student wants to work in America.	Dieser Student will in Amerika arbeiten.
study in America.	studieren.
learn English in America.	Englisch lernen.
speak German in America.	Deutsch sprechen.
live in America.	wohnen.
We want to (Let's) read something.	Wir wollen etwas lesen.
write	schreiben.
study	studieren.
Children, do you want to speak English?	Kinder, wollt ihr Englisch sprechen?
learn	lernen?
read	lesen?
write	schreiben?
They want to study here, don't they?	Sie wollen hier studieren, nicht wahr?
work	arbeiten,
read	lesen,
speak	sprechen,

Do you speak German?	**Sprechen Sie Deutsch?**
Yes, certainly.	**Ja, gewiß.**
I speak German well.	**Ich spreche gut Deutsch.**
poorly.	**schlecht**
already.	**schon**
only.	**nur**
little.	**wenig**
Peter doesn't speak German yet.	**Peter spricht noch nicht Deutsch.**
any more.	**nicht mehr**
either.	**auch nicht**
at all.	**gar kein**
We always speak English.	**Wir sprechen immer Englisch.**
usually	**gewöhnlich**
often	**oft**
sometimes	**manchmal**
seldom	**selten**
never	**nie**
How do you say that in German?	**Wie sagt man das auf Deutsch?**
How long have you been studying?	**Seit wann studieren Sie?**
I've been studying for three weeks.	**Ich studiere seit drei Wochen.**
four months.	**vier Monaten.**
two years.	**zwei Jahren.**

STRUCTURE

A. Nationalities and Occupations

Unmodified names of nationalities or occupations are often not accompanied by the indefinite article **ein**, in sentences like the following:

Hans ist   Deutscher.
Ich bin   Amerikaner.
Ilse ist   Studentin.

However, we sometimes say:

Hans ist ein Deutscher.
Ich bin ein   Amerikaner.
Ilse ist eine Studentin.

B. Dieser—*this*

"**Dieser**" is actually composed of a stem (**dies**—), to which endings are added. In the nominative case this word is structured as follows:

TABLE III A

dieser	masculine singular
this	**dieser Bahnhof**
diese	feminine singular and *all* plurals
this; these	**diese Studentin; diese Studentinnen**
dieses	neuter singular
this	**dieses Haus**

NOTE: Compare the endings of **dieser** with the definite article in Table II A.

C. Der, etc., Ein, etc., With Strong Stress—*that, those; one.*

Der, die, das, die, spoken with strong stress, are used as demonstrative adjectives meaning "*that*," "*those*." In their use as definite articles, equivalent to English "*the*," they are spoken with *weak* stress.

In the same way, **ein, eine,** spoken with strong stress, are used as the numeral "*one*."

D. The Present Tense

Most German verb forms consist of a stem with some kind of ending. For most verbs the pattern is as follows:

TABLE III B

Pronoun(s)	Ending	Examples
ich	**-e**	ich studiere; ich verstehe
du	**-st**	du studierst; du verstehst
er, sie, es, ihr	**-t**	er studiert; sie versteht; ihr versteht
wir, Sie, sie	**-en**	wir studieren; Sie verstehen; sie verstehen

A verb whose stem ends in **"d"** or **"t,"** as for example **arbeit-,** follows a slightly different pattern.

TABLE III C

Pronoun(s)	Ending	Examples
ich	-e	ich arbeite
du	-est	du arbeitest
er, sie, es, ihr	-et	er arbeitet
wir, Sie, sie	-en	wir arbeiten

In certain verbs, the stems in the forms for **du**, **er**, **sie** and **es** have vowels other than those found in the remaining forms. You will have to familiarize yourself with these variations in the stem vowel as you learn each verb, although later on a pattern will develop which will enable you to predict this change. Two such verbs which we have already met are **ich lese** and **ich spreche**. Study the forms of these verbs found in Table III D.

TABLE III D

ich	spreche	ich	lese
du	sprichst	du	liest
er, sie, es	spricht	er, sie, es	liest
wir, Sie, sie	sprechen	wir, Sie, sie	lesen
ihr	sprecht	ihr	lest

E. The Infinitive

All German verbs possess a "name form" (i.e., a form which is used, for example, for listing purposes) called the infinitive. For all German verbs with the exception of "be," the infinitive is identical in form with the present tense form that goes with **wir** and **Sie.**

F. The Verb Wollen—*want*

This is a special kind of verb, with present tense forms differing from those of the other verbs we have met:

TABLE III E

Ich **will** ein Buch lesen.	Wir **wollen** nach Hause gehen.
I want to read a book.	*We want to go home.*
Willst du Deutsch lernen?	Ihr **wollt** arbeiten, nicht wahr?
Do you want to learn German?	*You want to work, don't you?*

Wollen Sie etwas schreiben?

Do you want to write something?

Hans **will** sprechen.	Hans und Irma **wollen** hier sein.
Hans wants to speak.	*Hans and Irma want to be here.*

Note that **"wollen"** occurs with an infinitive of another verb, which is found at the end of the sentence or clause.

G. Word Order

In German, the main finite verb (i.e., the verb with a personal ending) is always the second element of a simple sentence, except in the case of a question which may be answered with **"ja"** or **"nein,"** or a command, where the verb occurs first.

TABLE III F

Statement			Question			
Hans	**spricht**	Deutsch.	**Spricht**	Hans	Deutsch?	
Ich	**schreibe**	Deutsch.	**Schreibe**	ich	Deutsch?	
Sie	**wollen**	Deutsch lernen.	**Wollen**	sie	Deutsch lernen?	

H. Possessive Adjectives

TABLE III G

Personal pronoun	Possessive adjective	Personal pronoun	Possessive adjective
ich	**mein**	wir	**unser**
du	**dein**	ihr	**euer***
er, es	**sein**	Sie	**Ihr**
sie (="she" *or* "they")	**ihr**		

The German possessive adjectives always have the same endings as **ein** and **kein**.

* NOTE: The second **e** of **euer** is often dropped when any ending is added. Thus we say: **Eu*e*r Freund ist hier**; but **Eu*re* Freunde sind hier.**

PATTERN PRACTICES

I. *Answer in the affirmative:*

Ist Hans	Deutscher?	Ja, Hans	ist Deutscher.
dieser Student		dieser Student	
der Mann		der Mann	
Ihr Freund		mein Freund	
die Frau	Deutsche?	die Frau	Deutsche.
Ilse		Ilse	
meine Freundin		Ihre Freundin	
Fräulein Schmidt		Fräulein Schmidt	

II. *Answer in the affirmative:*

Ist Herr Jones	Amerikaner?	Ja, Herr Jones	ist Amerikaner.
Ihr Freund		mein Freund	
der Student		der Student	
diese Studentin	Amerikanerin?	diese Studentin	Amerikanerin.
Fräulein Green		Fräulein Green	
Baxter		Baxter	
meine Freundin		Ihre Freundin	
Sind Ihre Freundinnen	Amerikanerinnen?	meine Freundinnen sind	Amerikanerinnen.
die Frauen		die Frauen	
diese Studentinnen		diese Studentinnen	
Ihre Freunde	Amerikaner?	meine Freunde	Amerikaner.
diese Studenten		diese Studenten	

III. *Answer in the affirmative, substituting the proper pronoun:*

Ist Herr Jones	Amerikaner?	Ja, er ist	Amerikaner.
Frau Green	Amerikanerin?	sie	Amerikanerin.
Fräulein Bixby			
Frau Hahn	Deutsche?		Deutsche.
Herr Wolff	Deutscher?	er ist	Deutscher.
Sind Herr und Frau Gunther	Deutsche?	sie sind Deutsche.	
die Studenten		sie sind Deutsche.	
meine Freunde	Amerikaner?		Amerikaner.

IV. *Answer in the negative, substituting the proper pronoun:*

Ist Herr Schulz	Amerikaner?	Nein, er ist	kein	Amerikaner.
Frau Jones	Amerikanerin?	sie ist	keine	Amerikanerin.
Sind Ihre Freundinnen	Amerikanerinnen?	sie sind	keine	Amerikanerinnen.
Freunde	Amerikaner?		keine	Amerikaner.
Ida und Max	Deutsche?		keine	Deutsche.
Ist Irma		ist	keine	Deutsche.
Peter	Deutscher?	er ist	kein	Deutscher.
Herr Brummel	Amerikaner?	er ist	kein	Amerikaner.

V. *Answer by changing the nationality in the question from German to American, and vice versa:*

Ist Herr Jones	Deutscher?	Nein, er ist	Amerikaner.
Sind die Leute	Amerikaner?	sie sind	Deutsche.
diese Studentinnen	Deutsche?		Amerikanerinnen.
Sie _____	Deutsche(r)?	ich bin	Amerikaner(in).
Bin ich _____	Amerikaner?	Sie sind	Deutscher.
Sind Herr und Frau Eck	Deutsche?	sie	Amerikaner.
Ist Herr Jones	Deutscher?	er ist	

VI. *Answer with the phrase,* **"Dies- _____ ist schön, nicht wahr?":**

Hier ist	eine Kirche.	Diese Kirche	ist	schön, nicht wahr?
	der Bahnhof.	Dieser Bahnhof		
Dort	eine Studentin.	Diese Studentin		
	sind die Hotels.	Hotels	sind	
Hier ist	eine Gaststätte.	Diese Gaststätte ist		
Dort sind die Läden.				
Hier ist	das Warenhaus.			
	sind die Häuser.			
Dort ist	eine Bibliothek.			
	der Platz.			

VII. *Answer in the affirmative, using the suggested possessive adjective:*

Ist	das	das	Hotel?	(sein)	Ja, das ist	sein	Hotel.
	sein	die	Gaststätte?	(mein)		meine	Gaststätte.
		eine	Schule?	(ihr)		ihre	Schule.
Sind		die	Häuser?	(ihr)		sind ihre	Häuser.
		die	Fabriken?	(unser)		unsere	Fabriken.
Ist		die	Post?	(unser)		ist unsere	Post.
		das	Buch?	(sein)		sein	Buch.
Sind		die	Bücher?	(unser)		sind unsere	Bücher.

VIII. *Say the whole sentence, using the suggested subject in the model sentence and making the appropriate change in the verb.*

Model:	Ich verstehe noch nicht gut.	*Model:*	Ich spreche schon Deutsch.
(er)	Er versteht noch nicht gut.	(wir)	Wir sprechen schon Deutsch.
(wir)	Wir verstehen	(er)	Er spricht
(Sie)	Sie verstehen	(ihr)	Ihr sprecht
(du)	Du verstehst	(die Frau)	Die Frau spricht
(ich)	Ich verstehe	(ich)	Ich spreche
(ihr)	Ihr versteht	(du)	Du sprichst
(das Fräulein)	Das Fräulein versteht	(Sie)	Sie sprechen

Model:	Ich arbeite seit zwei Wochen.	*Model:*	Ich lese gewöhnlich Englisch.
(wir)	Wir arbeiten seit zwei Wochen.	(die Studenten)	Die Studenten lesen gewöhnlich Englisch.
(Herr Schmidt)	Herr Schmidt arbeitet	(wir)	Wir lesen
(Sie)	Sie arbeiten	(er)	Er liest
(du)	Du arbeitest	(Sie)	Sie lesen
(ihr)	Ihr arbeitet	(ihr)	Ihr lest
(ich)	Ich arbeite	(du)	Du liest
(meine Freunde)	Meine Freunde arbeiten	(das Fräulein)	Das Fräulein liest

Model:	Ich will Deutsch gut sprechen.		
(wir)	Wir wollen	Deutsch gut sprechen.	
(er)	Er will		
(Sie)	Sie wollen		
(du)	Du willst		
(ich)	Ich will		
(die Studenten)	Die Studenten wollen		

IX. *Complete the statement in the affirmative, using the suggested pronoun:*

Peter	schreibt,	(ich)	und ich schreibe auch.
Herr Schmidt	spricht,	(ich)	spreche
Die Studenten	lesen,	(ich)	lese
Er _____	arbeitet,	(du)	du arbeitest
	schreibt,	(du)	schreibst
	spricht,	(du)	sprichst
Mein Freund	liest,	(sie)	sie liest
Ich _____	verstehe,	(er)	er versteht
	lese etwas,	(er)	liest auch etwas.
	mache etwas,	(Sie)	Sie machen
	verstehe Englisch,	(ihr)	ihr versteht auch Englisch.
Sie	spricht Deutsch,	(wir)	wir sprechen Deutsch.
	ist hier,	(wir)	wir sind hier.

X. *Complete the statement in the negative, using the suggested pronoun:*

Er versteht Deutsch,	(ich)	aber ich verstehe kein Deutsch.
	(wir)	wir verstehen
Ich spreche Englisch,	(er)	er spricht Englisch.
	(du)	
lese Englisch,	(ihr)	
arbeite.	(sie)	
Sie sind hier,	(er)	
verstehen Englisch,	(wir)	

XI. *Complete the statement, using the suggested pronoun and* **"wollen"** :

Peter	liest,	(ich)		und ich will	auch lesen.
	schreibt,	(du)		du willst	schreiben.
Ich	verstehe,	(er)		er will	verstehen.
Wir	sprechen,	(du)		du willst	sprechen.
	arbeiten,	(ihr)			
Ihr	arbeitet,	(ich)			
Sie	liest,	(wir)			
Der Student	versteht,	(sie)			
Mein Freund	spricht,	(ich)			

XII. *Complete the statement, using the suggested adverb:*

Peter	spricht	selten	Deutsch,	(immer)		aber er will	es immer sprechen.
	liest	manchmal	Deutsch,	(oft)			oft lesen.
Baxter	spricht	noch nicht	Deutsch,	(gut)			es gut sprechen.
Ich	verstehe	wenig	Deutsch,	(gut)		ich will	verstehen.
Wir	verstehen			(gut)		wir wollen	

XIII. *Give a suitable answer, but not in the negative:*

Wollen Sie Deutsch sprechen?

Will Hans in Amerika arbeiten?

Will sie ein Buch lesen?

Wollen Sie nach Hause gehen?

Ist der Student Ihr Freund?

Wo ist der Bahnhof?

Ist die Kirche rechts um die Ecke?

Wo wollen Sie studieren?

Seit wann lernen Sie Deutsch?

Seit wann studiert Johannes?

XIV. *Give negative answers for each of the above.*

XV. COMPOSITION: *Write a German composition, by giving suitable German equivalents for each of the following sentences:*

1. Peter Kruger is in Germany.
2. He wants to study there.
3. He wants to study at the University in Heidelberg.
4. But he doesn't speak, understand, read, or write German.
5. He's an American.
6. He speaks and understands English.
7. He reads and writes it, too.

8. But now he wants to study German.
9. He wants to speak it well.
10. His girl friend doesn't speak English.
11. She's a German.
12. Yes, Peter wants to speak German very well.
13. You understand, don't you?

VOCABULARY*

aber but
alle everyone
alles everything
der Amerikaner, - American (man)
die Amerikanerin, -nen American (woman)
an at
arbeiten work; study (be at work over one's books)
auch nicht not...either
das Bild, -er picture
ein bißchen a little
das Buch, ¨er book
die Dame, -n lady
dein, deine your
das Deutsch German (language)
auf Deutsch in German
der Deutsche, -en German (man)
die Deutsche, -n German (woman)
Deutschland Germany
dieser, diese, dieses this (adj.)
drei three
England England
das Englisch English (language)
etwas something
euer, eure your
der Familienname, -n family name
die Frau, -en woman, wife
der Freund, -e friend
die Freundin, -nen girl friend
gar kein no...at all, not...any at all
gewiß certainly
gewöhnlich usually
haben (hat) have
ihr, ihre her, their
Ihr, Ihre your
immer always
das Jahr, -e year
jemand anybody, someone
der Junge, -n boy
lernen study; learn
lesen (ie) read

die Leute (pl.) people
machen do
das Mädchen, - girl
man you, one
manchmal sometimes
der Mann, ¨er man
mehr:
   nicht mehr not any more
mein, meine my
der Monat, -e month
der Name, -n name
nichts nothing
nie never
niemand no one, nobody
noch nicht not yet
nur only
oft often
schlecht poor(ly)
schon already
schreiben write
sehen (sieht) see
sein, seine his, her, its
seit:
   Er ist seit drei Wochen da. He's been there for three weeks.
   seit wann...? for how long...?, since when...?
selten seldom
sprechen (i) speak
der Student, -en student (at a university)
die Studentin, -nen co-ed
studieren study (be taking courses)
unser, unsere our
vier four
von of, about
der Vorname, -n first name
wenig little (adv.)
die Woche, -n week
wohnen live
wollen (will) want
zwei two

---

* Verbs are entered in the infinitive only, except that we enter the stem vowel for the 2nd and 3rd person singular forms of verbs like **sprechen (sprichst, spricht).**

Lesson IV

BASIC SENTENCES

Johannes	—Here is Heidelberg.	(1)	**Johannes**	**—Hier ist Heidelberg.**
	It's a German city.	(2)		**Es ist eine deutsche Stadt.**
Peter	—What kind of a city is it?	(3)	**Peter**	**—Was für eine Stadt ist es?**

(1)   (2)   (3)

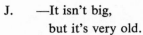

J.　—It isn't big, (4)
　　　but it's very old. (5)

J.　—Es ist nicht groß,
　　　aber es ist sehr alt.

(4)

(5)

(7)

(6)

A hundred thousand people live in Heidelberg. (6)　　Heidelberg hat einhunderttausend Leute.

P.　—What can you see here?/What is here to see/? (7)　　P.　—Was ist hier zu sehen?

(8)

(9)

(10)

J.	—There's a famous university here.	(8)	**J.** —Es gibt hier eine berühmte Universität.
	The streets are very pretty.	(9)	**Die Straßen sind sehr schön.**
P.	—What else can you/one/see in Heidelberg?	(10)	**P.** —Was kann man in Heidelberg noch sehen?

J.	—Here we have a beautiful park,	(11)		J.	—Hier haben wir einen schönen Park,
	and here the city hall.	(12)			und hier das Rathaus.
	Naturally, there are churches.	(13)			Natürlich gibt es Kirchen.

(11)

(12)

(13)

	There are also hotels, movie theaters and stores.	(14, 14a, 14b)	**Es gibt auch Hotels, Kinos und Geschäfte.**
P.	—What's the name of the main street?	(15)	**P. —Wie heißt die Hauptstraße?**
J.	—What else? "Main Street"!	(16)	**J. —Was sonst? „Hauptstraße"!**
P.	—And what's the name of the university?	(17)	**P. —Und wie heißt die Universität?**

(14)

(14-a)

(14-b)

(15)

(16)

(17)

(18)

(19)

(20)

(21)

(18)	J.	—It's called the Ruprecht-Karl University.
		—**Sie heißt die Ruprecht-Karl-Universität.**
(19)	P.	—Tell (some) more about Heidelberg.
		—**Erzählen Sie mehr von Heidelberg.**
(20)	J.	—Wait a minute/Wait a bit/.
		—**Warten Sie ein bißchen.**
(21)		One thing at a time./Always one thing after the other/.
		Immer eins nach dem anderen.

VARIATIONS

One, two, three, four, five.	Eins, zwei, drei, vier, fünf.
Six, seven, eight, nine, ten.	Sechs, sieben, acht, neun, zehn.
Eleven, twelve, thirteen, fourteen, fifteen.	Elf, zwölf, dreizehn, vierzehn fünfzehn.
Sixteen, seventeen, eighteen, nineteen, twenty.	Sechzehn, siebzehn, achtzehn, neunzehn, zwanzig.
Twenty-one, twenty-two, twenty-three, twenty-four, twenty-five.	Einundzwanzig, zweiundzwanzig, dreiundzwanzig, vierundzwanzig, fünfundzwanzig.
Twenty-six, twenty-seven, twenty-eight, twenty-nine.	Sechsundzwanzig, siebenundzwanzig, achtundzwanzig, neunundzwanzig.
Ten, twenty, thirty, forty, fifty.	Zehn, zwanzig, dreißig, vierzig, fünfzig.
Sixty, seventy, eighty, ninety, one hundred.	Sechzig, siebzig, achtzig, neunzig, hundert.
One hundred one, one hundred two.	Hunderteins, hundertzwei.
One hundred thirteen, one hundred twenty-seven.	Hundertdreizehn, hundertsiebenundzwanzig.
Two hundred, three hundred, four hundred, five hundred.	Zweihundert, dreihundert, vierhundert, fünfhundert.
Six hundred, seven hundred, eight hundred, nine hundred, one thousand.	Sechshundert, siebenhundert, achthundert, neunhundert, tausend.
Six hundred seventy-eight.	Sechshundertachtundsiebzig.
Three thousand four hundred eighty-two.	Dreitausendvierhundertzweiundachtzig.
Nineteen thirty-eight. (1938)	Neunzehnhundertachtunddreißig.
Nineteen sixty-one. (1961)	Neunzehnhunderteinundsechzig.
Six and eight is fourteen.	Sechs und acht ist vierzehn.
Twenty-three and thirty-two is fifty-five.	Dreiundzwanzig und zweiunddreißig ist fünfundfünfzig.

What kind of a city   is that?

Was für eine Stadt   ist das?

park	ein Park
building	ein Gebäude
church	eine Kirche

What is there here?	Was gibt es hier?
There is a park here.	Es gibt hier einen Park.

station	Bahnhof.
church	eine Kirche.
restaurant	Gaststätte.
hotel	ein Hotel.
building	Gebäude.

What do you have here?	**Was haben Sie hier?**
We have a park.	**Wir haben einen Park.**
university.	**eine Universität.**
city hall.	**ein Rathaus.**
We also have hotels.	**Wir haben auch Hotels.**
factories.	**Fabriken.**
department stores.	**Warenhäuser.**
restaurants.	**Gaststätten.**
libraries.	**Bibliotheken.**
schools.	**Schulen.**
What do you have there, Franz?	**Was hast du da, Franz?**
I have a book.	**Ich habe ein Buch.**
What does Mr. Müller have?	**Was hat Herr Müller?**
Mr. Müller has a store.	**Herr Müller hat ein Geschäft.**
What do you have, children?	**Was habt ihr, Kinder?**
We have two books here.	**Wir haben zwei Bücher hier.**
We're reading them.	**Wir lesen sie.**
What do you see?	**Was sehen Sie?**
I see the station.	**Ich sehe den Bahnhof.**
man.	**Mann.**
library.	**die Bibliothek.**
bank.	**Bank.**
hotel.	**das Hotel.**
building.	**Gebäude.**
department stores.	**die Warenhäuser.**
restaurants.	**Gaststätten.**
What do you see, Fritz?	**Was siehst du, Fritz?**
Fritz sees the park.	**Fritzt sieht den Park.**
restaurant.	**die Gaststätte.**
movie theater.	**das Kino.**
trees.	**die Bäume.**
What do you see, children?	**Was seht ihr, Kinder?**

We see that store	over there.		Wir sehen den Laden	dort.	
street			die Straße		
building			das Gebäude		
those streets			die Straßen		
girls			Mädchen		
boys			Jungen		
children			Kinder		
men			Männer		
women			Frauen		
ladies			Damen		

What can you see?

Was können Sie sehen?

I can see that store.		Ich kann den Laden sehen.
these streets.		diese Straßen
the school.		die Schule
those hospitals.		die Krankenhäuser

What can you see, Hans?

Was kannst du sehen, Hans?

Hans can see his friend.		Hans kann seinen Freund sehen.
girl friend.		seine Freundin
hotel.		sein Hotel
books.		seine Bücher

I can see my shop.		Ich kann meinen Laden sehen.
girl friend.		meine Freundin
hotel.		mein Hotel

Children, can you read this book?		Kinder, könnt ihr dieses Buch lesen?
that		das
your		euer
my		mein
their		ihr

Do you see	the	boy?	I see him.
	the	station?	I see it.
	the	shop?	
	my	girl friend?	I see her.
	his	restaurant?	I see it.
	her	hotel?	
	your	house?	
	those	students?	I see them.
	these	co-eds?	
	the	Americans?	

What can you see?
I can see something.
Fritz, can you see something?
I can't see anything.
I can't see anything at all.
Mr. Müller, can you see me?
Yes, I can see you.
Franz, can you see me?
Yes, I can see you.
Who can see us?
You children can see us.
And we can see you, too.
That street is famous. It's a famous street.
Your hotel is beautiful. It's a beautiful hotel.
His building is modern. It's a very modern building.
My house is new. It's a very new house.
That girl is young. She's a very young girl.
These churches are old. They're old churches.
Those hotels are poor. They're very poor hotels.
These hotels are good. They're good hotels.
Our streets are side. They're very wide streets.
Your streets are narrow. They're narrow streets.

Sehen Sie	den	Jungen?	Ich sehe ihn.
	den	Bahnhof?	Ich sehe ihn.
	den	Laden?	
	meine	Freundin?	sie.
	seine	Gaststätte?	
	ihr	Hotel?	es.
	Ihr	Haus?	
	die	Studenten dort?	sie.
	diese	Studentinnen?	
	die	Amerikaner?	

Was können Sie sehen?
Ich kann etwas sehen.
Fritz, kannst du etwas sehen?
Ich kann nichts sehen.
Ich kann gar nichts sehen.
Herr Müller, können Sie mich sehen?
Ja, ich kann Sie sehen.
Franz, kannst du mich sehen?
Ja, ich kann dich sehen.
Wer kann uns sehen?
Ihr Kinder könnt uns sehen.
Und wir können euch auch sehen.
Die Straße dort ist berühmt. Sie ist eine berühmte Straße.
Ihr Hotel ist schön. Es ist ein schönes Hotel.
Sein Gebäude ist modern. Es ist ein sehr modernes Gebäude.
Mein Haus ist neu. Es ist ein sehr neues Haus.
Das Mädchen dort ist jung. Es ist ein sehr junges Mädchen.
Diese Kirchen sind alt. Sie sind alte Kirchen.
Die Hotels dort sind schlecht. Sie sind sehr schlechte Hotels.
Diese Hotels sind gut. Sie sind gute Hotels.
Unsere Straßen sind breit. Sie sind sehr breite Straßen.
Ihre Straßen sind eng. Sie sind enge Straßen.

Do you want to see the new station?	Wollen Sie den neuen Bahnhof sehen?
this old shop?	diesen alten Laden sehen?
that beautiful park?	den schönen Park dort sehen?
Mr. Müller wants to see the old school.	Herr Müller will die alte Schule sehen.
that modern bank.	die moderne Bank dort sehen.
this ugly factory.	diese häßliche Fabrik sehen.
Hans wants to see the old book.	Hans will das alte Buch sehen.
that new hotel.	das neue Hotel dort sehen.
this famous building.	dieses berühmte Gebäude sehen.
We can see the narrow streets.	Wir können die engen Straßen sehen.
We can see these big factories.	Wir können diese großen Fabriken sehen.
We can see those beautiful girls.	Wir können die schönen Mädchen dort sehen.
Here is a big station.	Hier ist ein großer Bahnhof.
your old friend.	Ihr alter Freund.
their new school.	ihre neue Schule.
a modern library.	eine moderne Bibliothek.
our small hospital.	unser kleines Krankenhaus.
his new house.	sein neues Haus.
Here are my old books.	Hier sind meine alten Bücher.
your new pictures.	Ihre neuen Bilder.
his German friends.	seine deutschen Freunde.
I can see a small shop.	Ich kann einen kleinen Laden sehen.
a tall student.	einen großen Studenten
their modern bank.	ihre moderne Bank
his ugly factory.	seine häßliche Fabrik
my old store.	mein altes Geschäft
your big hospital.	Ihr großes Krankenhaus
He can't see any old buildings.	Er kann keine alten Gebäude sehen.
young students.	jungen Studenten
tall Americans.	großen Amerikaner
new factories.	neuen Fabriken
beautiful girls.	schönen Mädchen
wide streets.	breiten Straßen

We can't see my German friends.	**Wir können meine deutschen Freunde nicht sehen.**
We can't see his new pictures.	**Wir können seine neuen Bilder nicht sehen.**
There are many American students in Heidelberg.	**Es gibt viele amerikanische Studenten in Heidelberg.**
a lot of beautiful streets	**viele schöne Straßen**
old buildings	**alte Gebäude**

STRUCTURE

A. The Accusative Case

Peter is the student	=	*The student is Peter*

Note that in the English sentence above, the two nouns can be reversed without altering the basic meaning of the sentence. This is *not* true of the sentence below.

Peter sees the student	≠	*The student sees Peter*

In this sentence the noun which occurs *before* the verb is called the *subject*, and the noun occurring *after* the verb is called the *object*.

In German, the relationship of subject and object, whether nouns or pronouns, is indicated by position in the sentence, and partly also by case endings attached to the subject and object and/or their modifying words (articles and adjectives). The German object is usually in the accusative case.

Peter sieht den Studenten	=	**Den Studenten sieht Peter**
Peter sieht ihn		**Ihn sieht Peter**

Most German verbs take accusative objects. We say these verbs "govern" the accusative case. The verb "*be*" (Infinitive: **sein**), is usually followed by the nominative case. There are other types of German verbs which will be taken up later.

B. The Accusative Case of Nouns

Most German nouns are the same in the accusative as they are in the nominative. A few masculine nouns, however, have accusative forms which differ from their nominative ones. We have already seen two of this kind: **Herr**, whose accusative form is **Herrn**, and **Student**, whose accusative form is **Studenten**.

C. The Accusative Case of Personal Pronouns

TABLE IV A

Nominative			Accusative		
ich *I*			mich *me*		
du *you*			dich *you*		
er *he, it*	sie *she, it*	es *it*	ihn *him, it*	sie *her, it*	es *it*
wir *we*			uns *us*		
ihr *you*			euch *you*		
sie *they*	Sie *you*		sie *them*	Sie *you*	

D. The Ein- Words

This group of words consists of **ein, kein,** and the possessive adjectives **mein, dein, sein, ihr, unser, euer, Ihr.** Once you have learned the proper ending for **ein** in a given situation, you also know the proper ending for all the other **ein-** words in the same situation, because they all have the same set of endings.

E. The Accusative Endings of the Definite Article, Dieser, and the Ein- Words

The endings for the accusative case are identical with the corresponding nominative endings, except for the masculine singular, which is always **-en.** (See Tables IV B and IV C.)

F. Predicate Adjectives

Predicate adjectives are not followed by nouns. They never have endings. *Examples:* **Das Haus ist groß. Ich bin jung.**

G. Attributive Adjectives

An adjective which precedes the noun it modifies is called an attributive adjective or an adjective in attributive position. Such adjectives *always* have endings. *Example:* **Heidelberg ist eine schöne Stadt.**

H. Attributive Adjective Endings after the Definite Article and Dieser

TABLE IV B

Gender	Nominative ending	Accusative ending
Masculine	**-e** dieser schöne Park der junge Mann	**-en** diesen schönen Park* den jungen Mann*
Feminine	**-e** diese alte Stadt die berühmte Fabrik	**-e** diese alte Stadt die berühmte Fabrik
Neuter	**-e** dieses gute Hotel das junge Mädchen	**-e** dieses gute Hotel das junge Mädchen
Plural	**-en** diese breiten Straßen die neuen Kinos	**-en** diese breiten Straßen die neuen Kinos

* NOTE: The masculine singular accusative ending for **dieser** and the definite article is **-en**.

I. Attributive Adjective Endings After Ein- Words

TABLE IV C

Gender	Nominative ending	Accusative ending
Masculine	**-er** unser großer Bahnhof	**-en** unseren großen Bahnhof*
Feminine	**-e** eine enge Straße	**-e** eine enge Straße

* NOTE: The masculine accusative ending for the **Ein-** words is **-en**.

Gender	Nominative ending	Accusative ending
Neuter	**-es** kein gutes Warenhaus	**-es** kein gutes Warenhaus
Plural	**-en** Ihre guten Banken	**-en** Ihre guten Banken

J. The Verb "können"—*can*

"**Können**" usually occurs with an infinitive, as does "**wollen.**" Note the present tense forms of "**können**" in Table IV D.

TABLE IV D

Ich kann ein Buch lesen.
I can read a book.

Wir können jetzt nach Hause gehen.
We can go home now.

Kannst du Englisch lesen?
Can you read English?

Ihr könnt schreiben nicht wahr?
You can write, can't you?

Können Sie etwas sagen?
Can you say something?

Trudi kann arbeiten.
Trudi can work.

Karl und Ilse können nicht hier sein.
Karl and Ilse can't be here.

after definite article & dieser

m	e	en
F	e	e
N	e	e
P	en	en

after ein words

	er	en
	e	e
	es	es
	en	en

PATTERN PRACTICES

I. *Do the following additions in German:*

Eins	und zwei	ist	drei
Sechs	und vier		zehn.
Fünfzehn	und fünf		zwanzig.
Achtzehn	und neun		siebenundzwanzig.
Zweiundzwanzig	und dreiundzwanzig		fünfundvierzig.
Zweihundertneun	und achtundvierzig		zweihundertsiebenundfünfzig.

II. *Complete the statement, using a form of* **ein** *and the suggested noun:*

Es gibt   in Heidelberg. (Park)   Es gibt einen Park   in Heidelberg.

(Bank)	eine Bank
(Bahnhof)	einen Bahnhof
(Schule)	eine Schule
(Bibliothek)	eine Bibliothek
(Laden)	einen Laden
(Geschäft)	ein Geschäft
(Kino)	ein Kino

III. *Complete the question, using the plural of the suggested noun:*

Gibt es auch   in Heidelberg? (Student)   Gibt es auch Studenten in   Heidelberg?

(Haus)	Häuser
(Baum)	Bäume
(Geschäft)	Geschäfte
(Kino)	Kinos
(Hotel)	Hotels
(Amerikanerin)	Amerikanerinnen

IV. *Answer in the affirmative each of the questions you have just formed.*

V. *Form new sentences by interchanging the subject and object in the sentences given:*

Fritz sieht den Mann.	Der Mann sieht Fritz.
Der Student sieht diese Studentin.	Diese Studentin sieht den Studenten.
Ich sehe Herrn Müller.	Herr Müller sieht mich.
Ich will Frau Müller sehen.	Frau Müller will mich sehen.
Siehst du sie? *= she*	Sieht sie dich?
Seht ihr ihn? *more then one = him*	Sieht er euch? *(MORE THAN ONE)*
Wir sehen Sie. *3 Person*	Sie sehen uns.
Ich sehe Sie. *3 Person*	Sie sehen mich.
Sie sehen Franz, nicht wahr?	*FRANZ SIEHT SIE*
Ich sehe euch.	*Ihr sieht mich*
Er sieht dich.	*Du siehst ihn.*
Wir sehen ihn.	*Er sieht uns.*
Wir wollen euch sehen.	*Ihr wollt uns sehen.*

VI. *Respond to the following with the sentence:* „**Ich kann ____ sehen.**"

Dort ist der	Park.		Ich kann den	Park	sehen.
	die	Bibliothek.		die	Bibliothek
	sein	Warenhaus.		sein	Warenhaus
	unser	Platz.		unseren	Platz
	der	Student.		den	Studenten
	die	Studentin.		die	Studentin
sind die	Läden.				
	die	Straßen.			
	unsere	Studenten.			
ist der	Mann.				

VII. *Answer in the affirmative, using the appropriate pronoun:*

why not SEIT IHR

Sehen Sie die	Studenten dort?	Ja, ich sehe sie.	
den	Studenten		ihn.
die	Studentin		sie.
diesen	Laden		ihn.
das	Mädchen		es.

Sehen Sie das Gebäude	dort?	Ja, ich sehe es.	
den Bahnhof			ihn.
das Warenhaus			es.
die Bäume			sie.

VIII. *Answer in the affirmative, using the appropriate pronoun:*

Kann Herr Müller den	Park	sehen?	Ja, er kann ihn sehen.
die	Bibliothek		sie
die	Gaststätten		sie
den	Bahnhof		ihn
mein	Geschäft		es
Ihre	Freunde		sie
diesen	Studenten		ihn
diese	Studenten		
diesen	Jungen		
diese	Jungen		
die	Universität		
mein	Buch		

IX. *Answer in the negative:*

Haben Sie eine	Universität?	Nein, wir haben keine	Universität.
einen	Bahnhof?	keinen	Bahnhof.
einen	Laden?	keinen	Laden.
ein	Geschäft?	kein	Geschäft.
ein	Haus?	kein	Haus.
eine	Gaststätte?	keine	Gaststätte.

X. *Answer with* **kein,** *using the plural form of the noun:*

Hat Nirgendsberg eine	Universität?	Nein, es hat gar keine	Universitäten.
einen	Bahnhof?		Bahnhöfe.
ein	Warenhaus?		Warenhäuser.
einen	Park?		Parks.
eine	Bank?		Banken.
eine	Post?		Postämter.
einen	Laden?		Läden
ein	Gebäude?		Gebäude.
etwas?			gar nichts.

XI. *Enlarge the given statements by adding the suggested adjective:*

Das ist ein	Park.	(schön)	Das ist ein	schöner	Park.
		(berühmt)		berühmter	
		(alt)		alter	
		(klein)		kleiner	
	eine Straße.	(breit)		eine breite	Straße.
		(eng)		enge	
		(schön)		schöne	
		(häßlich)		häßliche	
	ein Kino.	(groß)		ein großes	Kino.
		(klein)		kleines	
		(neu)			
		(schlecht)			
sind Ihre Freunde.		(alt)			
		(gut)			
		(deutsch)			

XII. *As above, but now using the given possessive adjectives:*

Hier ist unsere	Universität.	(alt)	Hier ist unsere	alte	Universität.
Ihre	Schule.	(schön)	Ihre	schöne	Schule.
unser	Bahnhof.	(neu)	unser	neuer	Bahnhof.
mein	Haus.	(klein)	mein	kleines	Haus.
sind unsere	Straßen.	(berühmt)			
deine	Freunde.	(deutsch)			
eure	Bücher.	(neu)			
ist unser	Park.	(klein)			
sind meine	Bilder.	(neu)			

XIII. *Use the suggested adjectives in your responses to the following questions:*

Wo ist	dieser	Park?	(schön)		Dieser	schöne	Park	ist in Heidelberg.
	die	Universität?	(berühmt)		Die	berühmte	Universität	
	die	Bibliothek?	(groß)		Die	große	Bibliothek	
	der	Bahnhof?	(klein)		Der	kleine	Bahnhof	
	das	Geschäft?	(neu)		Das	neue	Geschäft	
	dieses	Rathaus?	(groß)		Dieses	große	Rathaus	

XIV. *As above:*

Wo sind	diese	Gaststätten?	(klein)		Diese	kleinen	Gaststätten sind in Heidelberg.
	die	Schulen?	(alt)		Die	alten	Schulen
	die	Straßen?	(eng)		Die	engen	Straßen
	die	Fabriken?	(groß)				
	diese	Kirchen?	(berühmt)				
	die	Straßen?	(breit)				
	die	Studentinnen?	(amerikanisch)				
	diese	Deutschen?	(jung)				

XV. *Form questions from the given statements, adding the suggested adjective:*

Hier ist	der	Park.	(berühmt)		Ist das	der	berühmte	Park?
	eine	Bibliothek.	(neu)			eine neue		Bibliothek?
	das	Hotel.	(groß)			das große		Hotel?
sind die	Straßen.		(eng)					
	Mädchen.		(schön)					
ist	eine	Frau.	(alt)					
	ein	Student.	(gut)					
	eine	Stadt.	(amerikanisch)					

XVI. *Answer in the affirmative, placing the adjective before the noun:*

Ist	dieser	Student	jung?		Ja, er ist	ein	junger	Student.
	die	Kirche	berühmt?		sie	eine berühmte		Kirche.
	das	Hotel	groß?		es	ein	großes	Hotel.
	die	Post	neu?		sie	eine neue		Post.

Sind Ihre	Straßen	eng?		sie sind	enge	Straßen.
die	Gebäude	klein?			kleine	Gebäude.
diese	Kirchen	berühmt?				
Ist der	Mann	alt?				
dieses	Mädchen	schön?				
die	Dame	jung?				
der	Junge	groß?				

XVII. *Complete the following statements, using the suggested subject and substituting a pronoun for the noun given:*

Ich kann den	schönen	Park sehen,	(Sie)		und Sie	können ihn auch sehen.
	eine	alte	Schule,	(er)		er	kann	sie
	das	neue	Haus,	(du)		du	kannst	es
	mein	altes	Geschäft,	(ihr)		ihr	könnt	es
	Ihren	schönen	Laden,	(Hans)		Hans kann	ihn
	Ihre	schönen	Läden,	(Irma)			
Er	die	engen	Straßen,	(wir)			
	den	alten	Herrn,	(Sie)			
	die	schöne	Frau,	(ich)			
	ein	großes	Warenhaus,	(du)			

XVIII. *Answer in the affirmative, adding the suggested adjective:*

Gibt es einen	Bahnhof	in Berlin?	(groß)		Ja, es gibt einen	großen	Bahnhof	in Berlin.
eine	Universität		(berühmt)		eine	berühmte	Universität
ein	Hotel		(alt)		ein	altes	Hotel
ein	Warenhaus		(neu)		ein	neues	Warenhaus
einen	Park		(groß)		einen	großen	Park
eine	Bank		(schön)		eine	schöne	Bank
—	Krankenhäuser		(viel)		—	viele	Krankenhäuser
—	Kirchen		(viel)		—	viele	Kirchen

XIX. *Answer, beginning with the phrase* „**Man sieht. . .**":

Wo ist dieser große	Bahnhof?		Man sieht diesen großen	Bahnhof	in Heidelberg.
der schöne	Park?		den schönen	Park	
diese berühmte	Fabrik?		diese berühmte	Fabrik	
die alte	Bank?		die alte	Bank	
das neue	Gebäude?		das neue	Gebäude	
das große	Krankenhaus?		das große	Krankenhaus	
sind diese breiten	Straßen?		diese breiten	Straßen	
die jungen	Amerikaner?		diese jungen	Amerikaner	

XX. *Use the subjects given as objects in the sentence,* „**Fritz will _____ sehen**":

Das kleine Rathaus	ist	in Berlin.		Fritz will das kleine Rathaus sehen.
Diese engen Straßen	sind			diese engen Straßen
Der große Bahnhof	ist			den großen Bahnhof
Die jungen Amerikaner	sind			
Das alte Gebäude	ist			
Der große Herr	ist			
Das junge Mädchen	ist			
Die schönen Studentinnen	sind			

XXI. *Give the appropriate answers to the following questions:*

Wieviel ist sechs und acht?

　　　　vierzehn und sechzehn?

　　　　zweiundzwanzig und hunderteins?

Wie heißt die Hauptstraße in Heidelberg?

Ist Macy's ein kleines Warenhaus?

Ist Heidelberg eine schöne Stadt?

Was kann man in Heidelberg sehen?

XXII. *In 100 German words, give a brief description of the town or city in which you live.*

XXIII. *Translate the last pattern drill into English, then try to reproduce the original German from your translation.*

VOCABULARY

alt old
amerikanisch American (*adj.*)
berühmt famous
breit wide
deutsch German (*adj.*)
dort there
eins one
eng narrow
erzählen tell
gar nichts nothing at all
das Gebäude, __ building
es gibt (*acc.*) there is, there are
groß big
häßlich ugly
Immer eins nach dem anderen. One thing at a time.

For numbers, see Variations.

jung young
klein small
können (kann) can
mehr more
modern modern
natürlich naturally
neu new
noch else, still yet
viel much
  viele many
Was sonst? What else?
warten (auf) (*acc.*) wait (for)
was für (*nom.*) what kind of

Lesson V

BASIC SENTENCES

Today I am going to show/show I/you pictures of my family.	(1)
Here is a picture of my father and his friend.	(2)
For twenty years now/since 20 years already/they have been friends.	(3)

(1) **Heute zeige ich Ihnen Bilder von meiner Familie.**

(2) **Hier ist ein Bild von meinem Vater und seinem Freund.**

(3) **Seit zwanzig Jahren schon sind sie Freunde.**

(1)

(2)

(3)

(4)

(5)

(6)

They are standing in front of our house. (4)

And this is a picture of my brothers, Karl and Helmut. (5)

Here are the two/the both/after work. (6)

Karl works for/in/a bank, (7)

and Helmut is employed as a salesman. (8)

Sie stehen vor unserem Haus.

Und dies ist ein Bild von meinen Brüdern, Karl und Helmut.

Hier sind die beiden nach der Arbeit.

Karl arbeitet in einer Bank,

und Helmut ist als Verkäufer angestellt.

(7)

(8)

(9)

(10)

(11)

Now comes a picture of my mother and my sister.	(9)	**Jetzt kommt ein Bild von meiner Mutter und meiner Schwester.**
My mother, by the way, is not "employed."	(10)	**Meine Mutter ist übrigens nicht „angestellt."**
She has enough work at home with the baby.	(11)	**Sie hat genug Arbeit zu Hause mit dem Kind.**
My sister helps her as much as possible.	(12)	**Meine Schwester hilft ihr so viel wie möglich.**
The baby, as you see, is still very small.	(13)	**Das Kind, wie Sie sehen, ist noch sehr klein.**
He doesn't go to school yet.	(14)	**Er geht noch nicht zur Schule.**
He doesn't even speak German.	(15)	**Er spricht nicht einmal Deutsch.**
And that's me/And that am I/!	(16)	**Und das bin ich!**
I don't work yet, either.	(17)	**Ich arbeite auch noch nicht.**
I just (merely) study at the university.	(18)	**Ich studiere bloß auf der Universität.**

(12)

(13)

(14)

(15)

(16)

(17)

(18)

VARIATIONS

These are my relatives.	Diese sind meine Verwandten.
parents.	Eltern.
children.	Kinder.
grandparents.	Großeltern.
This is my family.	Dies ist meine Familie.
son.	mein Sohn.
father.	mein Vater.
brother.	mein Bruder.
husband.	mein Mann.
mother.	meine Mutter.
sister.	meine Schwester.
daughter.	meine Tochter.
wife.	meine Frau.
grandmother.	meine Großmutter.
grandfather.	mein Großvater.
uncle.	mein Onkel.
aunt.	meine Tante.
My brother is only 5/years old/.	Mein Bruder ist nur fünf Jahre alt.
And who is this person?	Und wer ist dieser Mensch?
That's no person/human being/; that's an animal.	Das ist kein Mensch; das ist ein Tier.
That's our dog.	Das ist unser Hund.
cat.	unsere Katze.
He's an engineer.	Er ist Ingenieur.
a doctor.	Arzt.
lawyer.	Rechtsanwalt.
professor.	Professor.
teacher.	Lehrer.
businessman.	Geschäftsmann.
salesman.	Verkäufer.
student.	Student.

She's a secretary.	**Sie ist Sekretärin.**
nurse.	**Krankenschwester.**
teacher.	**Lehrerin.**
salesgirl.	**Verkäuferin.**
student.	**Studentin.**

What's that?	**Was ist das?**

That's a picture of a station.	**Das ist ein Bild von einem Bahnhof.**
my brother.	**meinem Bruder.**
your father.	**deinem Vater.**

Here's a photo of the harbor.	**Hier ist eine Aufnahme vom dem Hafen.**
	vom __ Hafen.
your mother.	**von Ihrer Mutter.**
his baby/child/.	**von seinem Kind.**

There's a picture of her husband.	**Da ist ein Bild von ihrem Man.**
our cat.	**unserer Katze.**
your dog.*	**eurem Hündchen.**

Are those pictures of those houses?	**Sind das Bilder von den Häusern?**

There is a picture of my sisters.	**Da ist ein Bild von meinen Schwestern.**
me.	**mir.**
you.	**dir.**
him (it).	**ihm.**
her (it).	**ihr.**
us.	**uns.**
you.	**euch.**
you.	**Ihnen.**
them.	**ihnen.**

Where does he work?	**Wo arbeitet er?**

---

* The diminutive ending (**-chen**) is affectionate; it does not necessarily imply that the dog is small. "Pooch" would be more nearly equivalent than "doggie" or "puppy."

He works in the station.	Er arbeitet in dem Bahnhof.
	im — Bahnhof.
a factory.	in einer Fabrik.
a store.	in einem Geschäft.
They work at his stores.	Sie arbeiten in seinen Geschäften.
Where do you live?	Wo wohnen Sie?
I live at my father's place.	Ich wohne bei meinem Vater.
at my mother's place.	meiner Mutter.
with my family.	meiner Familie.
with my friends.	meinen Freunden.
There's enough to do at our place.	Es gibt bei uns genug zu tun.
There's a lot to do at their place.	Es gibt bei ihnen viel zu tun.
There's not much to do at my place.	Bei mir gibt es nicht viel zu tun.
little	wenig
But at your place there's too much to do.	Bei euch gibt es aber zu viel zu tun.
Where/where to/are you going?	Wohin gehen Sie?
I'm going to your house.	Ich gehe zu Ihrem Haus.
I'm going to the hospital.	Ich gehe zu dem Krankenhaus.
	zum Krankenhaus.
I'm staying at home.	Ich bleibe zu Hause.
She's coming out of the station now.	Sie kommt jetzt aus dem Bahnhof.
She's coming out of the school now.	Sie kommt jetzt aus der Schule.
She's coming out of the city hall now.	Sie kommt jetzt aus dem Rathaus.
Are you coming with me?	Kommen Sie mit mir?
Is she coming with them?	Kommt sie mit ihnen?
I'm coming with my father.	Ich komme mit meinem Vater.
They're coming with their parents.	Sie kommen mit ihren Eltern.
Here's a picture of my little son.	Hier ist ein Bild von meinem kleinen Sohn.
his little daughter.	seiner kleinen Tochter.
her new baby.	ihrem neuen Kind.
our German relatives.	unseren deutschen Verwandten.
We're employed at the big station.	Wir sind in dem großen Bahnhof angestellt.
We're employed at that new bank.	Wir sind in der neuen Bank angestellt.

We're employed at this beautiful department store.

We're employed at the small hotels.

We're employed at those famous restaurants.

How long have you been here?

/Since when are you here?/

I've been here for one week.

                  one day.

                  one month.

Since that day I've been living   here.

                  working.

                  studying German.

No one except me is here.

No one except my father is there.

Except for her children, she has no family left/more/.

Opposite this church is the library.

Opposite the park is a school.

Opposite the hotel is a post office.

He is employed as a salesman.

They are employed as nurses.

Wir sind in diesem schönen Warenhaus angestellt.

Wir sind in den kleinen Hotels angestellt.

Wir sind in den berühmten Gaststätten angestellt.

Seit wann sind Sie hier?

Ich bin seit einer Woche hier.

           einem Tag

           einem Monat

Seit dem Tag wohne ich hier.

           arbeite ich.

           lerne   ich Deutsch.

Niemand außer mir ist hier.

Niemand außer meinem Vater ist dort.

Außer ihren Kindern hat sie keine Familie mehr.

Gegenüber dieser Kirche ist die Bibliothek.

Gegenüber dem Park ist eine Schule.

Gegenüber dem Hotel ist eine Post.

Er ist als Verkäufer angestellt.

Sie sind als Krankenschwestern angestellt.

STRUCTURE

A. The Dative Case after Prepositions

The dative case is used to indicate nouns or pronouns serving as objects of certain prepositions. Other uses of the dative will be taken up later.

The following prepositions govern the dative case at all times:

aus   bei   mit   nach   von   zu   seit   außer   gegenüber

B. Dative Forms of Dieser, the Ein- Words, and the Definite Article

TABLE V A

Gender	Nominative	Dative	Gender	Nominative	Dative
Masculine	**dieser**	**diesem**	Neuter	dieses	**diesem**
	der	**dem**		das	**dem**
	ein	**einem**		mein	**meinem**
Feminine	diese	**dieser**	Plural	diese	**diesen**
	die	**der**		die	**den**
	Ihre	**Ihrer**		deine	**deinen**

C. Dative Forms of Personal Pronouns

TABLE V B

Nominative			Dative		
	ich			mir	
	I			*me*	
	du			dir	
	you			*you*	
er	sie	es	ihm	ihr	ihm
he, it	*she, it*	*it*	*him*	*her*	*it*
				it	*it*
	wir			uns	
	we			*us*	
	ihr			euch	
	you			*you*	
Sie		sie	Ihnen		ihnen
you		*they*	*you*		*them*

D. Dative Endings of Attributive Adjectives

All dative attributive adjectives, when preceded by an **ein-** word, by the definite article, or by **dieser,** have the ending **-en.**

E. The Dative of Nouns

Most nouns have no special ending for the dative case *in the singular*. However, an optional ending of **-e** may be added to any one-syllable masculine or neuter (but *not* feminine) noun in the dative singular. Also, those masculine nouns which add **-n** or **-en** in the accusative singular will do the same in the dative singular.

All nouns, except those with **-s** plurals (e.g. Kinos, Hotels), *end in* **-n** *or* **-en** *in the dative plural.*

PATTERN PRACTICES

I. *Complete the statements by reversing subject and object:*

Ich helfe	ihm,		und	er	hilft	mir.
	ihr,			sie		
	Ihnen,			Sie	helfen	
Wir helfen	euch,			ihr	helft	uns.
	ihm,			er	hilft	
Er hilft	mir,			ich	helfe	ihm.
Sie	ihm,			er	hilft	ihr
	uns,			wir	helfen	ihr.
Ihr helft	ihm,			er	hilft	euch.
Du hilfst	mir,			ich	helfe	dir.
	ihr,			sie	hilft	dir.
Sie helfen	uns,			wir	helfen	Ihnen.

II. *Answer in the affirmative:*

Ist das ein Bild von	seinem	Vater?	Ja, das ist ein Bild von	seinem	Vater.
	ihrer	Mutter?		ihrer	Mutter.
	deinem	Bruder?		meinem	Bruder.
	ihrem	Kind?		ihrem	Kind.
	euren	Eltern?		unseren	Eltern.
	meiner	Großmutter?		Ihrer	Großmutter.
	unseren	Brüdern?		Ihren	Brüdern.
	deinem	Großvater?		meinem	Großvater.

III. *Answer in the negative:*

Haben Sie eine Aufnahme von der	Fabrik?	Nein, ich habe keine Aufnahme von der Fabrik.
	dieser Frau?	dieser Frau.
	dem Bahnhof?	dem Bahnhof.
	dem Rathaus?	
	dem Park?	
	dem Mann?	
	den Leuten?	
	der Post?	

IV. *Complete the statements, using the suggested nouns:*

Fritz geht zur Bibliothek,	(Bank)	aber ich gehe zur Bank.
zum Park,	(Post)	zur Post.
zum Bahnhof,	(Rathaus)	
zur Kirche,	(Laden)	
zur Schule,	(Universität)	
zum Warenhaus,	(Hauptstraße)	
zum Geschäft,	(Krankenhaus)	

V. *Answer in the negative, using the suggested nouns:*

Kommt sie aus der Post?	(Bibliothek)	Nein, sie kommt aus der Bibliothek.	
einem Kino?	(Fabrik)	einer Fabrik.	
dem Hotel?	(Bank)	der Bank.	
Kommen sie den Geschäften?	(Häuser)	sie kommen den Häusern.	
Kommst du dem Bahnhof?	(Gaststätte)	ich komme der Gaststätte.	
einem Hotel?	(Bahnhof)	einem Bahnhof.	
Kommen Sie den Gaststätten?	(Geschäften)	den Geschäften.	

VI. *Answer in the negative, using the suggested noun:*

Arbeitet er in diesem Laden?	(Fabrik)	Nein, er arbeitet in dieser Fabrik.	
Arbeiten Sie einer Schule?	(Universität)	ich arbeite einer Universität.	
dieser Gaststätte?	(Bank)	dieser Bank.	
Arbeitet sie einem Warenhaus?	(Laden)	sie arbeitet einem Laden.	
diesen Hotels?	(Krankenhaus)	diesen Krankenhäusern.	

Wohnt	er	bei seinem Vater?	(Mutter)	er wohnt bei seiner Mutter.
		seinem Bruder?	(Großvater)	seinem Großvater.
		seiner Großmutter?	(Schwester)	
Wohnst	du	deinem Bruder?	(Vater)	
		deinen Brüdern?	(Schwester)	
Wohnt	ihr	euren Großeltern?	(Eltern)	
		Schwestern?	(Bruder)	

VII. *Answer in the negative, using the suggested nouns:*

Studieren Sie seit einem Jahre	hier? (Monat)	Nein, ich studiere nur seit einem Monat hier.
einer Woche	(Tag)	einem Tage
einem Monat	(Woche)	einer Woche
vier Jahren	(Monat)	vier Monaten
drei Wochen	(Tag)	drei Tagen
fünf Monaten	(Woche)	fünf Wochen

VIII. *Answer in the negative, using the suggested nouns:*

Ist der Park gegenüber dem Geschäft?	(Bank)	Nein, er ist gegenüber der Bank.
dieser Fabrik?	(Bibliothek)	dieser Bibliothek.
der Schule?	(Laden)	dem Laden.
dem Rathaus?	(Krankenhaus)	dem Krankenhaus.
der Schule?	(Fabrik)	
einer Bank?	(Geschäft)	
den Hotels?	(Kino)	
den Fabriken?	(Laden)	
diesen Läden?	(Haus)	

IX. *Answer in the negative, using the correct dative form of the suggested nominative:*

Sie studieren mit ihr, nicht wahr?	(er)	Nein, ich studiere mit ihm.
Ihrem Freund	(mein Bruder)	meinem Bruder.
Bruder	(meine Schwester)	
diesem Studenten	(die Studentin dort)	
diesen Studenten	(die Studenten dort)	
den Amerikanern	(diese Deutschen)	
seiner Freundin	(meine Freundin)	

X. *Memorize the following rhyme:*

> **Aus, bei, mit, nach, von, zu, seit,**
> **Außer** und auch **gegenüber**
> Haben Dativ allezeit.

XI. *Complete the statement, using the suggested nouns:*

Dieser Arzt	hat nicht genug zu tun, (Rechtsanwalt)	aber der Rechtsanwalt hat zu viel zu tun.
Ingenieur	(Arzt)	Arzt
Diese Krankenschwester	(Studentin)	die Studentin
Sekretärin	(Lehrerin)	Lehrerin
Dieser Mann	(Junge)	
Professor	(Lehrer)	
Verkäufer	(Verkäuferin)	
Rechtsanwalt	(Geschäftsmann)	

XII. *Change the noun and its modifiers to the dative case following the preposition* **"von"**:

Hier ist	das	alte	Rathaus.	Das ist nur ein Bild vom __	alten	Rathaus.
	ein	schöner	Park.	von einem	schönen	Park.
	mein	kleiner	Sohn.	Ihrem	kleinen	Sohn.
	ein	kleines	Geschäft.	einem	kleinen	Geschäft.
	eine	neue	Bank.	einer	neuen	Bank.
sind __		neue	Hotels.	__	neuen	Hotels.
sind meine	alten		Hünde.	Ihren	alten	Hünden.
ist	der	neue	Rechtsanwalt.	vom __	neuen	Rechtsanwalt.
			Ingenieur.	__		Ingenieur.
	die	neue	Verkäuferin.	von der	neuen	Verkäuferin.
			Sekretärin.			Sekretärin.
			Lehrerin.			
sind die		neuen	Lehrerinnen.			
sind die		neuen	Studenten.			
ist	der	neue	Student.			

CLASS TALK. *Be prepared to show snapshots of the various members of your family and to tell a bit about each.*

VOCABULARY

als as
angestellt employed
die Arbeit -en work
der Arzt, ⸚e doctor
die Aufnahme, -n photo
aus (*dat.*) out
außer (*dat.*) except
bei (*dat.*) for, at
die beiden the two, both
bleiben stay
bloß just, merely
der Bruder, ⸚ brother
einmal:
   nicht einmal not even
die Eltern parents
die Familie, -n family
gegenüber (*dat.*) opposite
genug enough
der Geschäftsmann, Geschäftsleute businessman
die Großeltern grandparents
die Großmutter, ⸚ grandmother
der Großvater, ⸚ grandfather
der Hafen, ⸚ harbor
Haus:
   zu Hause at home
helfen (i) (*dat.*) help
heute today
der Hund, -e dog
das Hündchen, __ dog (affectionate), "pooch"
der Ingenieur, -e engineer
die Katze, -n cat
kommen come
die Krankenschwester, -n nurse

der Lehrer, __ teacher (man)
die Lehrerin, -nen teacher (woman)
der Mann, ⸚er husband
der Mensch, -en person
mit (*dat.*) with
möglich possible
die Mutter, ⸚ mother
nach (*dat.*) after
der Onkel, __ uncle
der Professor, -en professor
der Rechtsanwalt, ⸚e lawyer
die Schwester, -n sister
der Sekretär, -e secretary (man)
die Sekretärin, -nen secretary (woman)
so...wie... as...as...
der Sohn, ⸚e son
stehen stand
der Tag, -e day
die Tante, -n aunt
das Tier, -e animal
die Tochter, ⸚ daughter
tun (tue, tust, tut, tun) do
übrigens by the way
der Vater, ⸚ father
der Verkäufer, __ salesman
die Verkäuferin, -nen salesgirl
der Verwandte, -n relative
vor in front of
  vor unserem Haus in front of our house
wann? when?
wohin? where (to)?
zeigen show
zu to; too (excessively)

Lesson VI

BASIC SENTENCES

(1)

(2)

It's seven in the morning.	(1)
Mrs. Müller is making breakfast,	(2–3)
but Mr. Müller is still sleeping.	
He likes to sleep, and never wants to	(4)
get up in the morning.	

Es ist sieben Uhr morgens.
Frau Müller macht das Frühstück,
aber Herr Müller schläft noch.
Er schläft gern, und morgens will
er nie aufstehen.

(3)

(4)

(5)

(6)

(7)

(7)

(8-9)

"Heinrich!" she calls, "it's time to get up."   (5–6)   „Heinrich!" ruft sie, „es ist Zeit, aufzustehen."

Mr. Müller doesn't answer her.   (7)   Herr Müller antwortet ihr nicht.

He doesn't hear her.   (8–9)   Er hört sie nicht.

why difference

"Heinrich?" she asks, "are you getting up? It's late!" (10–11)

"Huh? What—who—why—oh. Yes, of course. (12)

I'm smoking a cigarette." (13)

„Heinrich?" fragt sie, „stehst du auf? Es ist spät!"

„So? Was—wer—warum—ach. Jawohl.

Ich rauche eine Zigarette."

(14)

(15)

(16-17)

But he's not smoking a cigarette.

He's asleep again.

"In /after/ five minutes—
Heinrich!" she calls, "breakfast is ready and on the table!"

(14)   **Aber er raucht keine Zigarette.**

(15)   **Er schläft wieder.**

(16–17) **Nach fünf Minuten—**
„Heinrich!" ruft sie, „das Frühstück ist bereit und auf dem
Tisch!"

"I'm bathing," he says.   (18)   „Ich bade," sagt er.

But Mrs. Müller knows her husband well.   (19)   **Aber Frau Müller kennt ihren Mann gut.**

(18)

(19)

She opens the door, goes into the bedroom,   (20–21–22)   **Sie macht die Tür auf, geht ins Schlafzimmer**
    and looks at him.   **und sieht ihn an.**

Mr. Müller isn't bathing.   (23)   **Herr Müller badet nicht.**

He's sleeping again.   (24)   **Er schläft wieder.**

(20)

(21)

(22)

(23)

(24)

VARIATIONS

What time is it?	Wieviel Uhr ist es?
It's one o'clock in the morning.	Es ist ein Uhr morgens.
two in the afternoon.	zwei nachmittags.
five	fünf
eight in the evening.	acht abends.
eleven at night.	elf nachts.
It's early.	Es ist früh.
late.	spät.
In the morning he gets up.	Morgens steht er auf.
forenoon works.	Vormittags arbeitet er.
afternoon studies.	Nachmittags studiert er.
evening bathes.	Abends badet er.
At night he sleeps.	Nachts schläft er.
In the daytime he works.	Tags arbeitet er.
All day long he works.	Tagsüber arbeitet er.
I know this man. (Tangible object.)	Ich kenne diesen Mann.
I know the answer. (Abstraction.)	Ich weiß die Antwort.
He doesn't want to say anything.	Er will nichts sagen.
We don't	Wir wollen nichts sagen.
He's supposed to get up.	Er soll aufstehen.
I'm	Ich soll
You're , Hans.	Du sollst , Hans.
He can never get up.	Er kann nie
We can almost never get up.	Wir können fast nie aufstehen.
I'm allowed to stay here.	Ich darf hier bleiben.
You're , Fritz.	Du darfst , Fritz.
He's	Er darf
We're	Wir dürfen
They're	Sie
You're , children.	Ihr dürft , Kinder.
I have to study now. (must)	Ich muß jetzt arbeiten.

You have to study now, Heinrich.	**Du mußt jetzt arbeiten, Heinrich.**
He has to	**Er muß**
We have to	**Wir müssen**
You , children.	**Ihr müßt , Kinder.**
They must	**Sie müssen**
They mustn't smoke here (aren't allowed to).	**Sie dürfen hier nicht rauchen.** (NOTE: *Not* **müssen nicht,** which never occurs in this sense!)
He mustn't smoke here.	**Er darf hier nicht rauchen.**
I like to work.	**Ich mag arbeiten.**
Do you feel like working, Hans?	**Magst du arbeiten, Hans?**
He _____ likes to work.	**Er _____ mag arbeiten.**
We _____ like	**Wir _____ mögen**
Mr. and Mrs. Müller like to work.	**Herr und Frau Müller mögen arbeiten.**
I'm going to open the window.	**Ich werde das Fenster aufmachen.**
Are you , Fritz?	**Wirst du , Fritz?**
He's going to open the window.	**Er wird das Fenster aufmachen.**
We're	**Wir werden**
You're	**Ihr werdet**
They're	**Sie werden**
What should I do?	**Was soll ich machen?**
Sleep.	**Schlafe!—Schlafen Sie!**
Make breakfast, Ilse!	**Mache Frühstück, Ilse!**
Make breakfast!	**Machen Sie Frühstück!**
Get up, Hans!	**Stehe auf, Hans!**
, Mr. Müller!	**Stehen Sie auf, Herr Müller!**
Come right away!	**Kommen Sie sofort!**
Bathe!	**Bade!**
	Baden Sie!
Eat breakfast!	**Frühstücke!**
	Frühstücken Sie!
Don't look at him!	**Sieh ihn nicht an!**
Please open the door!	**Bitte, machen Sie die Tür auf!**
close the window!	**das Fenster zu!**

What should we do?	**Was sollen wir machen?**
Sleep, children!	**Schlaft, Kinder!**
Go to sleep!	**Schlafen Sie!**
Make breakfast, children!	**Macht Frühstück, Kinder!**
Make breakfast!	**Machen Sie Frühstück!**
Get up, children!	**Steht auf, Kinder!**
Get up!	**Stehen Sie auf!**
Come right away, children!	**Kommt sofort, Kinder!**
Come right away!	**Kommen Sie sofort!**
Bathe, children!	**Badet, Kinder!**
Take a bath!	**Baden Sie!**
Eat breakfast, children!	**Frühstückt, Kinder!**
Eat breakfast!	**Frühstücken Sie!**
Don't look at him!	**Sehen Sie ihn nicht an!**
Look at him, children!	**Seht ihn an, Kinder!**
Let's sleep!	**Schlafen wir!**
Let's make breakfast!	**Machen wir Frühstück!**
get up!	**Stehen wir auf!**
bathe!	**Baden wir!**
eat breakfast!	**Frühstücken wir!**
Let's not look at him!	**Sehen wir ihn nicht an!**
He likes to live in New York.	**Er wohnt gern in New York.**
likes write German.	**schreibt gern Deutsch.**
work.	**arbeitet gern.**
read books.	**liest gern Bücher.**
speak German.	**spricht gern Deutsch.**
He understands his wife.	**Er versteht seine Frau.**
hears the man.	**hört den Mann.**
She knows the child.	**Sie kennt das Kind.**
sees the window.	**sieht das Fenster.**
loves her parents.	**liebt ihre Eltern.**
What is Mrs. Müller doing?	**Was macht Frau Müller?**

She's reading a book.	**Sie liest ein Buch.**
She is making breakfast.	**Sie macht das Frühstück.**
She is showing pictures.	**Sie zeigt Bilder.**
She is doing housework.	**Sie macht die Hausarbeit.**
She calls her husband.	**Sie ruft ihren Mann.**
She knows her husband well.	**Sie kennt ihren Mann gut.**
She looks at her husband.	**Sie sieht ihren Mann an.**
She says nothing.	**Sie sagt nichts.**
She opens the door.	**Sie macht die Tür auf.**
closes the window.	**das Fenster zu.**
She's helping her husband.	**Sie hilft ihrem Mann.**
forgives him.	**verzeiht ihm.**

She hears me.	She answers me.	**Sie hört mich.**	**Sie antwortet mir.**
you.	you.	**dich.**	**dir.**
him.	him.	**ihn.**	**ihm.**
her.	her.	**sie.**	**ihr.**
it.	it.	**es.**	**ihm.**
us.	us.	**uns.**	**uns.**
you.	you.	**euch.**	**euch.**
them.	them.	**sie.**	**ihnen.**
you.	you.	**Sie.**	**Ihnen.**

She's asking her husband something.	**Sie fragt ihren Mann etwas.**
telling	**Sie sagt ihrem Mann etwas.**
	erzählt
showing	**zeigt**
giving	**gibt**
reading	**liest ihrem Mann etwas vor.**
She's helping her husband.	**Sie hilft ihrem Mann.**
answering	**antwortet**
I'll do the housework later.	**Ich mache später die Hausarbeit.**
tomorrow.	**morgen**

STRUCTURE

A. Telling Time

The German word **Uhr** (*clock*) corresponds to the English expression "*o'clock*." Thus, **zwei Uhr** is the equivalent of "*two o'clock*." For telling time, the German uses the preposition **um** the way we use "*at*," so that **um elf Uhr** is the equivalent of "*at eleven o'clock*."

The table below shows how German divides an hour into quarters and halves. Note that where English would say "*half past*" the preceding hour, German says "*half of*" the following hour.

TABLE VI A

8:00 a.m.	acht Uhr morgens	8 Uhr
8:15 a.m.	Viertel nach acht	8^{15} Uhr
8:30 a.m.	halb neun	8^{30} Uhr
8:45 a.m.	Viertel vor neun *or* dreiviertel neun	8^{45} Uhr
9:00 a.m.	neun Uhr	9 Uhr
2:00 p.m.	zwei Uhr nachmittags	2 Uhr
2:05 p.m.	fünf nach zwei	2^{05} Uhr
2:15 p.m.	Viertel nach zwei	2^{15} Uhr
2:25 p.m.	fünfundzwanzig nach zwei	2^{25} Uhr
2:35 p.m.	fünfundzwanzig vor drei	2^{35} Uhr
2:50 p.m.	zehn vor drei	2^{50} Uhr

B. Stressed Adverbs

In English we sometimes use certain words along with verbs to give the verbs special meanings. These words always occur under primary or strong stress, and we will call them "*stressed adverbs*." In the sentence below, "*over*" is such a word.

He took his father's business over.

Notice the relationship of the word "*over*" to the word "*took*." We would say that the infinitive of this verb is "*to take over*," even though in the sentence above "*took*" and "*over*" are separated by "*his father's business*."

German has a similar construction:

TABLE VI B

Subject	Verb	Stressed adverb
Er	**steht**	**auf**
He	*is getting*	*up*

In German, a stressed adverb usually occurs at the end of an independent sentence or main clause. On the other hand, if the verb is an infinitive or a participle, the stressed adverb precedes and is attached to the beginning of the verb, as shown in the following table:

TABLE VI C

Er will nie	**aufstehen.**	*He never wants to get up.*
Sie kann die Tür	**aufmachen.**	*She can open the door.*
Wir wollen ihn	**ansehen.**	*We want to look at him.*

Other situations involving stressed adverbs will be taken up later.

C. The Verb sollen—*be supposed to*

Like **wollen** and **können, sollen** usually occurs with the infinitives of another verb.

TABLE VI D

Ich soll aufstehen.	**Wir sollen jetzt nicht rauchen.**	**Sie sollen das Fenster aufmachen.**
I'm supposed to get up.	*We're not supposed to smoke now.*	*You're supposed to open the window.*
Du sollst etwas sagen.	**Ihr sollt hier sein.**	
You're supposed to say something.	*You're supposed to be here.*	
Er soll nichts sagen.		**Sie sollen jetzt arbeiten.**
He's not supposed to say anything.		*They're supposed to work now.*

D. The Verb müssen—*have to; must*

A verb of the same type as **wollen, können,** and **sollen.** Note that the negative of **müssen** is equivalent to English "*don't (doesn't) have to*," NOT to English "*mustn't.*" (See Section E.)

TABLE VI E

Ich muß nicht aufstehen.	**Wir müssen das lesen.**
I don't have to get up.	*We have to read that.*
Du mußt nachts schlafen.	**Ihr müßt nicht arbeiten.**
You must sleep at night.	*You don't have to work.*

Sie müssen um acht Uhr aufstehen.
You have to get up at eight o'clock.

Sie muß etwas machen.	**Sie müssen morgens arbeiten.**
She must do something.	*They have to work in the morning.*

E. The Verb dürfen—*be allowed to; may*

Note that the negative of **dürfen** is the equivalent of English "*must not.*"

TABLE VI F

Ich darf hier lesen.	**Wir dürfen jetzt Englisch sprechen.**
I'm allowed to read here.	*We're allowed to speak English now.*
Du darfst nicht schlafen.	**Ihr dürft jetzt schlafen, Kinder.**
You mustn't sleep.	*You may sleep now, children.*

Sie dürfen hier nicht rauchen, Herr Müller.
You mustn't smoke here, Mr. Müller.

Er darf nichts sagen.	**Sie dürfen abends baden.**
He mustn't say anything.	*They're allowed to take baths at night.*

F. The Verb mögen—*like*

German has a number of ways to express the idea of liking. One is by using **mögen;** another way is explained in Section G, and a third way will be taken up later.

TABLE VI G

Ich mag studieren.	**Wir mögen schlafen.**	**Mögen Sie Bücher lesen?**
I like to study.	*We like to sleep.*	*Do you like to read books?*
Magst du frühstücken?	**Ihr mögt baden, nicht wahr?**	
Do you like to eat breakfast?	*You like to bathe, don't you?*	
Er mag nicht aufstehen.	**Sie mögen immer um sechs Uhr Abendbrot essen.**	
He doesn't like to get up.	*They always like to eat supper at six o'clock.*	

G. The Adverb gern(e)

Another way of expressing the idea of liking is by using the adverb **gern(e).** The final unstressed **e** is optional.

Er schreibt gern Deutsch.	**Er steht nicht gerne auf.**
He likes to write German.	*He doesn't like to get up.*

H. The Verb werden—*will*

This verb is often used to express the idea of future time in German, much as we use "*will*" in English. In the table below, note that **werden,** when used this way, occurs with an infinitive. Other uses of **werden** will be taken up later.

TABLE VI H

Ich werde morgen lesen.	**Wir werden nach Hause gehen.**	**Werden Sie die Bücher zumachen?**
I will read tomorrow.	*We'll go home.*	*Are you going to close the books?*
Wirst du um acht Uhr frühstücken?	**Ihr werdet nicht gehen wollen.**	
Will you eat breakfast at 8 o'clock?	*You won't want to go.*	
Er wird morgen nicht aufstehen.	**Sie werden nie hier arbeiten.**	
He won't get up tomorrow.	*They will never work here.*	

The idea of future time is also quite often expressed by simply using the present tense. Thus, the preceding table can be "expanded" to read as follows:

TABLE VI J

Ich werde morgen lesen.	**Wir werden nach Hause gehen.**
Ich lese morgen.	**Wir gehen nach Hause.**
I will read tomorrow.	*We'll go home.*
Wirst du um acht Uhr frühstücken?	**Ihr werdet nicht gehen wollen.**
Frühstückst du um acht Uhr?	**Ihr wollt nicht gehen.**
Will you eat breakfast at 8 o'clock?	*You won't want to go.*

Werden Sie die Bücher zumachen?
Machen Sie die Bücher zu?
Will you close the books?

Er wird morgen nicht aufstehen.	**Sie werden nie hier arbeiten.**
Er steht morgen nicht auf.	**Sie arbeiten nie hier.**
He won't get up tomorrow.	*They will never work here.*

I. Position of the Finite Verb

A "finite verb," as opposed to an infinitive, is a verb which goes with a particular subject noun, pronoun, or noun phrase.

In independent sentences and main clauses, the finite verb is the second element in the sentence (not necessarily the second word). THIS IS A KEY TO GERMAN WORD ORDER. In the examples below, note that when more than one word precedes the finite verb, the preceding words cannot be separated and still make sense.

TABLE VI K

Er	**steht**	morgens auf.	Er	**will**	nichts sagen.
Morgens	**steht**	er auf.	Nichts	**will**	er sagen.
Er	**badet**	um acht Uhr.	Sie	**machen**	das Fenster auf.
Um acht Uhr	**badet**	er.	Das Fenster	**machen**	Sie auf.

In **ja–nein** questions and in commands, the finite verb is always first.

Machen Sie das Fenster auf?
Are you opening the window?
Machen Sie das Fenster auf!
Open the window!

J. The Verbs antworten and helfen

Notice that **antworten** and **helfen** control DATIVE objects, rather than accusatives.

Sie antwortet mir.   **Wir helfen ihm.**
She answers me!   *We're helping him!*

K. Formal Commands

Commands to a person or persons addressed as **Sie** are usually made by using the **-en** form of the verb, followed by **Sie.** This will be discussed further in Chapter XVI.

Kommen Sie mit mir!   **Machen Sie Frühstück!**
Come with me!   *Make breakfast!*

L. Informal Commands

Commands to a person addressed as **du** consist of the verb stem of the **du-** form, either without an ending or with an **-e** ending, except for verbs whose stems end in **-d-** or **-t-**, where the **-e** ending is required. Such commands usually do not have the pronoun **du.**

Komm(e) mit mir!   **Bade!**   **Antworte ihm!**
Come with me!   *Take a bath!*   *Answer him!*

An exception to this occurs with verbs whose infinitive stem vowel is **a**, but whose **du-** form vowel is **ä**. In such verbs the vowel of the informal singular command is **a**. Thus:

Du schläfst jeden Tag.   BUT   **Schlaf!**
You sleep every day.   *Sleep!*

Commands to persons addressed as **ihr** consist of the **ihr-** form of the verb without a pronoun.

Kommt mit mir!   **Badet!**   **Antwortet ihm!**
Come with me!   *Take a bath!*   *Answer him!*

PATTERN PRACTICES

I. *Answer with the suggested time:*

Um wieviel Uhr stehen Sie auf?	(halb acht)	Ich stehe um halb acht auf.
steht er	(sieben Uhr)	Er steht um sieben Uhr auf.
stehen sie	(halb sechs)	Sie stehen um halb sechs auf.
steht ihr	(acht Uhr)	Wir stehen um acht Uhr auf.
steht sie	(neun Uhr)	Sie steht um neun Uhr auf.

II. *Answer with the suggested adverb, placing the latter first in your sentence:*

Arbeitet er abends?	(tagsüber)	Nein, tagsüber arbeitet er.
Schläft nachmittags?	(nachts)	nachts schläft
Studiert morgens?	(abends)	abends studiert
Steht nachmittags auf?	(morgens)	morgens steht er auf.
Arbeiten Sie morgens?	(nachmittags)	nachmittags arbeite ich.
Studieren nachmittags?	(abends)	abends studiere ich.
Baden nachts?	(morgens)	morgens bade
Rauchen morgens?	(nachts)	nachts rauche

III. *Change the given sentence as indicated:*

Er steht morgens auf.	Er steht morgens auf.
Ich	Ich stehe
Wir	Wir stehen
Du	Du stehst
Hans	Hans steht
früh	früh
spät	spät
nicht	nicht
macht das Fenster	macht das Fenster
Wir	Wir machen
Ilse	Ilse macht
Du	Du machst
Ich	Ich mache das Fenster auf.
Ihr	Ihr macht

Er				Er	macht	das Fenster auf.
	die Tür					die Tür
	die Fenster					die Fenster
Ich				Ich	mache	
	mein Buch					mein Buch
	meine Bücher					meine Bücher
Wir				Wir	machen	
	unser Buch					unser Buch
	Ihre Tür					Ihre Tür

IV. *Translate into English the sentences you have just formed.*

V. *Answer in the affirmative, using the adverb* **gern:**

Wollen Sie studieren?			Ja, ich studiere		gern.
	arbeiten?			arbeite	
	mir helfen?			helfe	Ihnen
Will	er		er	hilft	
	sie		sie		
Wollt	ihr		wir helfen		
Wollen Sie aufstehen?			ich stehe	——	gern auf.

VI. *Answer in the negative, using* **nicht gern:**

Studieren Sie?			Nein, ich studiere	nicht gern.
Stehen	Sie	morgens auf?	ich stehe morgens	nicht gern auf.
Arbeiten	Sie?		ich arbeite	nicht gern.
Arbeitet	sie?		sie arbeitet	
	ihr?		wir arbeiten	
Arbeiten	sie?		sie arbeiten	
Lesen	Sie?		ich lese	
Schreiben	Sie?		ich schreibe	

VII. *Complete the statement, using the suggested subject:*

Ich stehe	morgens auf,	(er)		und	er	steht	auch	morgens auf.
		(du)			du	stehst		
	früh	(ihr)			ihr	steht		früh
		(Sie)			Sie	stehen		
Er steht	spät	(ich)			ich	stehe		spät
		(wir)			wir	stehen		
		(Ilse)			Ilse	steht		

Ich studiere gern,   (er)

Sie arbeitet   (ich)

   spricht   (wir)

Ihr lest   (er)

Ich schlafe   (du)

VIII. *Answer in the affirmative:*

Hilft	er ihr?		Ja, er hilft	ihr.
	ihm?			ihm.
	mir?			Ihnen.
	Ihnen?			mir.
Antwortet er	mir?		antwortet	Ihnen.
	ihr?			ihr.
	ihnen?			ihnen.
	dir?			mir.
	euch?			uns.
Versteht	er sie?		versteht	sie.
	seine Frau?			seine Frau.
	sie ihren Mann?			ihren Mann.
	mich?			Sie.
	sie?			sie.
	ihn?			ihn.

IX. *Translate your answers to the above questions, then try to reproduce the original German.*

X. *Answer in the affirmative:*

Wollen	Sie mir	etwas erzählen?		Ja, ich will	Ihnen etwas erzählen.
Will	er			er	
	Ihnen				mir
		sagen?			sagen.
Kann	ich			Sie können	
Darf				dürfen	
Soll				sollen	
Werden	Sie mir			ich werde	Ihnen
Wird	er			er wird	
	sie ihr			sie	ihr
Müssen	Sie mir			ich muß	Ihnen
Muß	sie			sie	
Mußt	du ihnen			ich	ihnen
		____ antworten?			____ antworten.
Muß	ich	____		Sie müssen	____
	er	____		er muß	____

XI. *Answer in the negative:*

Wollen	Sie mir	die	Bilder dort zeigen?		Nein, ich will	Ihnen	die	Bilder dort nicht zeigen.
		das	Rathaus				das	Rathaus
		Ihre	Bücher				meine	Bücher
Kann	er	die	Stadt			er kann	die	Stadt
	sie	die	Bilder			sie	die	Bilder
Darf	er	den	großen Bahnhof zeigen?			er darf	den	großen Bahnhof nicht zeigen.
		einen	schönen Park				keinen	schönen Park zeigen.
Werden	Sie	ein	großes Rathaus			ich werde	kein	großes Rathaus zeigen.
Wirst	du	eine	berühmte Kirche					
Werden	sie							
Wird	er	eine	häßliche Fabrik					

Sollen Sie mir ein schönes Bild zeigen?			Wollt ihr mir ein schönes Bild zeigen?	
Soll	er		Werdet	
Sollt	ihr		Mußt	
			Könnt	

XII. *Translate the first ten questions and answers in the preceding exercise.*

XIII. *Complete the statement, using* **werden** *and the suggested subject:*

Ich	studiere jetzt,	(er)	aber er	wird	später studieren.
Wir	arbeiten	(du)	du	wirst	arbeiten.
Sie	lesen	(ich)	ich	werde	lesen.
Er	spricht	(ihr)	ihr	werdet	sprechen.
Ich	bade	(er)	er	wird	baden.
Ich	lese	(er)			lesen.
Wir	schlafen	(Irma)	Irma wird		schlafen.

XIV. *Complete the statements, using the present tense and the suggested subject:*

Ich werde	später in Heidelberg studieren,	(er)	aber er	studiert jetzt in Heidelberg.
	hier	arbeiten,	(Irma)	Irma arbeitet jetzt hier.
Sie werden	hier	lesen,	(ich)	
	hier	sein,	(ich)	
	hier	frühstücken,	(er)	
	etwas	erzählen,	(wir)	
Du wirst	mit Ihnen	arbeiten,	(ich)	

XV. *Translate the above exercise into English, then reproduce the German.*

XVI. *Answer in the negative, substituting a personal pronoun for the noun-object:* (NOTE: *Pay careful attention to the verbs which govern the dative!*)

Kennt sie ihren Mann gut?	Nein, sie kennt ihn nicht gut.
die Stadt	sie
die Kinder	sie

Weiß	er	die	Antwort?			Nein, er weiß	sie	nicht.	
Wissen	sie						sie wissen		
	Sie						ich weiß		
Werden	Sie	mir	die	Bilder	zeigen?	Nein, ich werde	sie	Ihnen nicht zeigen.	
Wird	er	mir					er wird	sie	Ihnen
Wirst	du	mir					ich werde	sie	Ihnen
Wird	sie	mir					sie wird	sie	Ihnen
		mir	das	Warenhaus				es	Ihnen
		mir	den	großen Park				ihn	Ihnen
		mir	ihr	Kind				es	Ihnen

Hilft	sie ____	ihrem	Manne?	sie hilft	ihm ____	nicht.
	____	den	Studentinnen dort?		ihnen ____	
	____	diesen	Amerikanern?		ihnen	
Verzeiht	sie ____	Hans?		sie verzeiht ihm ____ nicht.		
Verzeihen Sie Hans und mir?				ich verzeihe Ihnen ____ nicht.		
Antworten Sie Herrn Müller?				ich antworte ihm ____		

XVII. *Use each verb in a sentence and change the object pronoun as necessary:*

Model: Sie versteht mich.

(hilft)	Sie hilft mir.	(hört)
(ruft)	ruft mich.	(sagt etwas)
(zeigt Bilder)	zeigt mir Bilder.	(antwortet)
(sieht)	sieht mich.	(liebt)
(verzeiht)	verzeiht mir.	(erzählt etwas)
(kennt)	kennt mich.	(gibt etwas)
(fragt etwas)		
(versteht)		
(sieht an)		
(liest etwas vor)		

XVIII. *For each declarative statement, form the commands that go with the pronouns* **Sie, du,** *and* **ihr** *respectively and in that order:*

Er erzählt	mir	etwas.	Erzählen	Sie	mir	etwas!
			Erzähle	_____	mir	etwas!
			Erzählt	_____		
Er gibt	mir	eine Antwort.	Geben	Sie	mir	eine Antwort!
			Gib	_____	mir	eine Antwort
			Gebt	_____		
Er kommt	mit	mir.	Kommen	Sie	mit mir!	
			Komme	_____	mit mir!	
			Kommt	_____		
Er geht	nach	Hause.	Gehen	Sie		nach Hause!
			Gehe	_____		nach Hause!
			Geht	_____		
Er fragt	mich	etwas.	Fragen	Sie	mich	etwas!
			Frage	_____	mich	etwas!
			Fragt	_____		

Er steht   jetzt auf.
Er macht   die Tür zu.
Er macht   das Fenster auf.
Er liest   ein Buch.

XIX. *Form German questions from each of the commands above.*

VOCABULARY

abends in the evening	**dürfen (darf)** to be allowed to
ach! oh!	**fast** almost
sich an-sehen (ie) look at	**fast nie** almost never, hardly ever
die Antwort, -en answer	**das Fenster, —** window
antworten (*dat.*) answer someone	**fragen** (*acc.*) ask (somebody something)
auf on	**früh** early
auf-machen open	**das Frühstück** breakfast
auf-stehen get up	**frühstücken** eat breakfast
baden bathe	**für** (*acc.*) for
bereit ready	**geben (i)** give

gern:
  gern haben like
die Hausarbeit housework
hören hear
jawohl yes, of course
kennen know
lieben love
die Minute, -n minute
mögen (mag) like to
morgen tomorrow
morgens in the morning
müssen (muß) have to, must
nach:
  nach fünf Minuten in five minutes, five minutes later
nachmittags in the afternoon
nachts at night
rauchen smoke
rufen (*acc.*) call
sagen say
schlafen (ä) sleep
das Schlafzimmer, — bedroom
So? Huh? H'm?

sofort right away
sollen (soll) be supposed to
spät late
später later
tags in the daytime
tagsüber all day
der Tisch, -e table
die Tür, -en door
Uhr:
  Wieviel Uhr ist es? What time is it?
  Es ist sieben Uhr. It's seven o'clock.
vor-lesen:
  etwas jemandem vorlesen read something to someone
vormittags in the forenoon
warum? why?
werden (wird) (with *inf.*) be going to, will
wieder again
wissen (weiß) know
die Zeit, -en time
die Zigarette, -n cigarette
zu-machen close

Lesson VII

BASIC SENTENCES

Every day I get up at seven o'clock.	(1)	**Jeden Tag stehe ich um sieben Uhr auf.**
I don't like to get up,	(2)	**Ich stehe nicht gerne auf,**
but I do anyway /But nevertheless I get up/.	(3)	**aber trotzdem stehe ich auf.**

(1)

(2)

(3)

(4)

(5)

(6)

I brush my teeth,	(4)	**Ich putze mir die Zähne,**
get washed,	(5)	**wasche mich,**
shave,	(6)	**rasiere mich,**
comb my hair,	(7)	**kämme mir die Haare**
and get dressed.	(8)	**und ziehe mich an.**

(7)

(8)

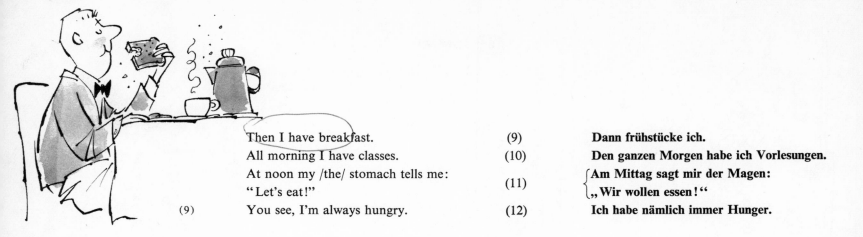

Then I have breakfast.	(9)	**Dann frühstücke ich.**
All morning I have classes.	(10)	**Den ganzen Morgen habe ich Vorlesungen.**
At noon my /the/ stomach tells me: "Let's eat!"	(11)	**⎰ Am Mittag sagt mir der Magen:** **⎱ „Wir wollen essen!"**
You see, I'm always hungry.	(12)	**Ich habe nämlich immer Hunger.**

(9)

(10)

(11)

(12)

why not "ich ruhe"

| After lunch I relax for a couple of hours; | (13–14) | **Nach dem Mittagessen ruhe ich mich ein paar Stunden aus;** |
| I read the newspaper or take a walk. | (15–16) | **ich lese die Zeitung oder gehe spazieren.** |

(13)

(15)

(14)

(16)

Then I do my homework until dinner.	(17)	**Dann mache ich meine Aufgaben bis zum Abendessen.**
In the evening I often study again,	(18)	**Abends arbeite ich oft wieder,**
but sometimes I meet my friends	(19)	**aber manchmal treffe ich meine Freunde,**
and we have a good time /amuse ourselves well/.	(20)	**und wir unterhalten uns gut.**
At about /towards/ eleven-thirty I go to bed,	(21)	**Gegen halb zwölf gehe ich zu Bett,**
close my eyes,	(22)	**mache die Augen zu**
and soon fall asleep.	(23)	**und schlafe bald ein.** why?

(17)

(18)

(19)

(20)

(21)

(22)

(23)

VARIATIONS

How often do you meet your friends?	**Wie oft treffen Sie Ihre Freunde?**
Every morning I meet my friends.	**Jeden Morgen treffe ich meine Freunde.**
Every noon she meets her friends.	**Jeden Mittag trifft sie ihre Freunde.**
Every afternoon he meets his friends.	**Jeden Nachmittag trifft er seine Freunde.**
Every evening we meet our friends.	**Jeden Abend treffen wir unsere Freunde.**
Every night you meet your friends.	**Jede Nacht triffst du deine Freunde.**
In the morning I get washed /wash myself/.	**Morgens wasche ich mich.**
they get washed.	** waschen sie sich.**
you get washed.	** wäschst du dich.**
he gets washed	** wäscht er sich.**
you get washed.	** waschen Sie sich.**
we get washed.	** waschen wir uns.**
you get washed.	** wascht ihr euch.**
I want to get washed.	**Ich will mich waschen.**
I wash my hands in the evening.	**Abends wasche ich mir die Hände.**
We wash our hands	** waschen wir uns die Hände.**
They wash their hands	** waschen sie sich die Hände.**
You wash your hands	** wäschst du dir die Hände.**
He washes his hands	** wäscht er sich die Hände.**
You wash your hands	** waschen Sie sich die Hände.**
She washes her hands	** wäscht sie sich die Hände.**
you wash your hands	** wascht ihr euch die Hände.**
I'm brushing /polishing/ my teeth.	**Ich putze mir die Zähne.**
He's brushing his teeth.	**Er putzt sich die Zähne.**
Hans and I are brushing our teeth.	**Hans und ich putzen uns die Zähne.**
I'm taking a shower /getting under the shower/.	**Ich stelle mich unter die Brause.**
He's taking a shower.	**Er stellt sich unter die Brause.**
Are you taking a shower?	**Stellst du dich unter die Brause?**
I am supposed to take a shower.	**Ich soll mich unter die Brause stellen.**
Now I'm shaving.	**Jetzt rasiere ich mich.**

Now they're shaving.	Jetzt rasieren sie sich.
Who's shaving now?	Wer rasiert sich jetzt?
I'm taking a bath.	Ich bade.
Are you taking a bath?	Badet ihr?
Is he taking a bath?	Badet er?
I'm combing my hair.	Ich kämme mir die Haare.
He's combing his hair.	Er kämmt sich die Haare.
We're combing our hair.	Wir kämmen uns die Haare.
She's combing her hair.	Sie kämmt sich die Haare.
I'm brushing my hair.	Ich bürste mir die Haare.
They're brushing their hair.	Sie bürsten sich die Haare.
Is she brushing her hair?	Bürstet sie sich die Haare?
I'm getting dressed /I dress myself/.	Ich ziehe mich an.
He's getting dressed.	Er zieht sich an.
They're getting dressed.	Sie ziehen sich an.
You're getting dressed, aren't you?	Du ziehst dich an, nicht wahr?
Who's getting dressed?	Wer zieht sich an?
I can't get dressed.	Ich kann mich nicht anziehen.
I'm getting undressed.	Ich ziehe mich aus.
I'm changing clothes.	Ich ziehe mich um.
I'll change clothes.	Ich werde mich umziehen.
I'm going to bed.	Ich gehe zu Bett.
I want to go to bed.	Ich will zu Bett gehen.
I'm falling asleep.	Ich schlafe ein.
I can't fall asleep.	Ich kann nicht einschlafen.
I'm waking up.	Ich wache auf.
I have to wake up.	Ich muß aufwachen.
I'm getting up.	Ich stehe auf.
I'm asking you something.	Ich frage Sie etwas.
And I'm answering you.	Und ich antworte Ihnen.
He's telling me something.	Er sagt mir etwas.
He's telling her something.	Er sagt ihr etwas.

They're telling us something.	Sie sagen uns etwas.
He's giving me something.	Er gibt mir etwas.
What's he giving me?	Was gibt er mir?
He's giving me a book.	Er gibt mir ein Buch.
He's bringing it to me.	Er bringt es mir.
She's giving them something.	Sie gibt ihnen etwas.
What's she giving them?	Was gibt sie ihnen?
She's giving them a pen.	Sie gibt ihnen eine Feder.
a pencil.	einen Bleistift.
She's bringing them to them.	Sie bringt sie ihnen.
I'm asking you a question.	Ich stelle Ihnen eine Frage.
I'm hungry.	Ich habe Hunger.
thirsty.	Durst.
I'm tired.	Ich bin müde.
sleepy.	schläfrig.
awake.	wach.
refreshed.	erfrischt.
What time is it?	Wieviel Uhr ist es?
/How late is it?/	Wie spät ist es?
What time do you have breakfast?	Um wieviel Uhr frühstücken Sie?
eat lunch?	essen Sie zu Mittag?
have (drink) coffee?	trinken Sie Kaffee?
eat supper?	essen Sie Abendbrot?
I eat breakfast at 8:00 a.m.	Ich frühstücke um acht Uhr morgens.
I eat lunch at noon.	Ich esse um zwölf Uhr zu Mittag.
I eat supper at about 6:00 p.m.	Ich esse Abendbrot gegen sechs Uhr abends.
It's three o'clock.	Es ist drei Uhr.
It's ten past three.	Es ist zehn nach drei.
It's a quarter past three.	Es ist Viertel nach drei.
It's twenty past three.	Es ist zwanzig nach drei.

It's half-past three (three-thirty).   **Es ist halb vier.**

It's twenty to four (3:40).   **Es ist zwanzig vor vier.**

It's a quarter to four (3:45).   **Es ist Viertel vor vier.**

After breakfast I take a walk.   **Nach dem Frühstück gehe ich spazieren.**

Before lunch I read.   **Vor dem Mittagessen lese ich.**

Until supper I study.   **Bis zum Abendbrot studiere ich.**

I study all morning.   **Ich studiere den ganzen Morgen.**

         afternoon.   **Nachmittag.**

         evening.   **Abend.**

         night.   **die ganze Nacht.**

She's going through the room.   **Sie geht durch das Zimmer.**

            station.   **den Bahnhof.**

            library.   **die Bibliothek.**

That's for my husband.   **Das ist für meinen Mann.**

         wife.   **meine Frau.**

         our children.   **unsere Kinder.**

I can't work without him.   **Ich kann ohne ihn nicht arbeiten.**

         her.   **sie**

         you.   **Sie**

         you, Franz.   **dich , Franz.**

Do you have something against my husband?   **Haben Sie etwas gegen meinen Mann?**

         his wife?   **seine Frau?**

         that shop?   **den Laden?**

         those banks?   **die Banken?**

He's going around the corner.   **Er geht um die Ecke.**

I get up at eight o'clock.   **Ich stehe um acht Uhr auf.**

         a quarter past eight.   **Viertel nach acht**

         half past eight.   **halb neun**

         a quarter to nine.   **dreiviertel neun**

STRUCTURE

A. Jeder—*each, every*

This word is made up of the stem **jed-** and the same endings used with **dieser.** Note, however, that as with its English equivalents, **jeder** is never used with plural nouns, and so has no plural forms.

B. Accusative Time Expressions

Time expressions using **der, dieser** and **jeder** are always in the accusative case, unless preceded by a preposition governing the dative. Thus, in the sentence

Jeden Morgen treffe ich meine Freunde.

Every morning I meet my friends.

jeden Morgen is in the accusative case. (**Morgen** is masculine.)

C. Reflexive Object Pronouns

In the English sentence

I'm washing myself.

"*myself*" is said to be a reflexive object pronoun, because it and the subject stand for the same individual. In the German sentence

Ich wasche mich.

mich is similarly called a reflexive object pronoun.

In German, reflexive object pronouns may be either accusative or dative. In either case, they are the same as the corresponding personal pronouns, except for the third person singular and plural, and **Sie.**

TABLE VII A

Personal pronoun	Reflexive object pronoun	
	Accusative	Dative
ich	mich	mir
du	dich	dir
er, sie, es	sich	sich
wir	uns	uns
ihr	euch	euch
Sie, sie	sich	sich

D. Reflexive Verbs

Reflexives are much more common in German than in English. These pronouns are associated with certain verbs whose name forms are usually listed along with the pronoun **sich** to show that they are reflexive, that is, they must be accompanied by a reflexive pronoun.

E. Double Objects

In the English sentence

She's giving him a pencil.

there are two objects, "*him*" and "*a pencil.*" We will call this a DOUBLE OBJECT. Note that the second object is more closely related to the verb than is the first. In English we use word order to express these verb-object relationships.

German, however, uses case to express this distinction. For this reason, a German double object almost always consists of an accusative and a dative. Thus,

She's giving | *him* | | *a pencil*
                1st object   2nd object

becomes in German

Sie gibt | ihm | | **einen Bleistift**
            Dative object   Accusative object

This is true also of reflexives.

Ich wasche | mich | **Ich wasche** | mir | **die Hände**
     Accusative object   Dative object   Accusative object

In a German double object the **accusative** object comes **last** if it is a noun, but **first** if it is a pronoun.

Sie gibt | ihm | **einen Bleistift**
        Dative object   Accusative noun object
She's giving him a pencil.

Sie gibt | ihn | ihm |
        Accusative pronoun object   Dative object
She's giving it (*the pencil*) *to him.*

This word order is determined by whether the *accusative* object is a *noun* or *pronoun*. The type of *dative* object used has no effect at all. (But see also Section F.)

F. Etwas and Nichts in Double Objects

Etwas ("*something*") and **nichts** ("*nothing*") are "special" pronouns, in that they show no case. If they occur in a double object, they are always the *second* element.

Sie gibt   mir   etwas

Dative object

She's giving me something.

Sie wollen   mir   nichts   sagen.

Dative object

They don't want to tell me anything.

G. The Accusative after Prepositions

Certain German prepositions must always be followed by the accusative case. The most important of these are:

durch	für	ohne	um	gegen
through	for	without	around about	towards against

PATTERN PRACTICES

I. *Restate each of the following, beginning with the time expression (adverb):*

Ich stehe morgens auf.	Morgens stehe ich auf.
Er trifft seine Freunde jeden Abend.	Jeden Abend trifft er seine Freunde.
Sie frühstückt um acht Uhr.	Um acht Uhr frühstückt sie.
Er liest die Zeitung den ganzen Abend.	Den ganzen Abend liest er die Zeitung.
Ich habe Vorlesungen den ganzen Nachmittag.	Den ganzen Nachmittag habe ich Vorlesungen.
Wir gehen abends spazieren.	Abends gehen wir spazieren.
Sie studieren gewöhnlich hier.	Gewöhnlich studieren sie hier.
immer	Immer
nie	Nie

II. *In each of the following, substitute the suggested subject and the corresponding reflexive pronoun, paying careful attention to case:*

Ich wasche mich.	(du)	Du	wäschst dich.
	(er)	Er	wäscht sich.

(Trudi)	Trudi	wäscht sich.
(wir)	Wir	waschen uns.
(ihr)	Ihr	wascht euch.
(Sie)	Sie	waschen sich.
(Herr und Frau Boll)	Herr und Frau Boll	waschen sich.
(Hand und ich)	Hans und ich	waschen uns.
(ich)	Ich	wasche mich.

Ich wasche mir die Hände. (er)	Er	wäscht sich die Hände.
(Sie)	Sie	waschen sich
(ihr)	Ihr	wascht euch
(wir)	Wir	waschen uns

Ich wasche mir die Hände. (Herr und Frau Schmidt)   Herr und Frau Schmidt waschen sich die Hände.

(ich)   Ich _____ wasche mir die Hände.

Ich putze mir die Zähne. (du)   Du putzt dir die Zähne.

(wir)

(Irma)

(Ihr)

(Hans)

Ich stelle mich under die Brause. (er)	Ich rasiere mich. (er)	Ich kämme mir die Haare. (Irmgard)
(wir)	(Sie)	(wir)
(ihr)	(wir)	(er)
(ich)	(sie)	(du)
	(ich)	(ich)

Ich bürste mir die Haare. (wir)	Ich ziehe mich aus. (ihr)	Ich ziehe mich um. (er)
(er)	(er)	(wir)
(Sie)	(du)	(du)
(ihr)	(ich)	(ich)
(ich)		(Sie)
(du)		

III. *Restate each of the sentences in the preceding exercise, using the suggested subject, and beginning with the time expression indicated:*

Ich wasche mich. (morgens)
(du)	Morgens wäschst du dich.
(er)	wäscht er sich.
(Trudi)	wäscht _____ sich Trudi.
(wir)	waschen wir uns.
(ihr)	wascht ihr euch.
(Herr und Frau Boll)	waschen _____ sich Herr und Frau Boll.
(Hans und Peter)	_____ Hans und Peter.
(ich)	wasche ich mich.

Ich wasche mir die Hände. (gewöhnlich)
(er)	Gewöhnlich wäscht er sich die Hände.
(Sie)	waschen Sie
(ihr)	wascht ihr euch
(wir)	waschen wir uns
(Herr und Frau Schmidt)	waschen _____ sich Herr und Frau Schmidt
(ich)	wasche ich mir

Ich putze mir die Zähne. (vor dem Frühstück)
(du)	Vor dem Frühstück putzt du dir die Zähne.
(wir)	putzen wir uns
(Irma)	putzt sich Irma
(ihr)	ihr euch
(Hans)	sich Hans

Ich stelle mich unter die Brause. (abends)
(er)	Abends stellt er sich unter die Brause.
(wir)	stellen wir uns
(ihr)	stellt ihr euch
(ich)	stelle ich mich

Ich rasiere mich. (gegen halb acht)
(er)	Gegen halb acht rasiert er sich.
(Sie)	rasieren Sie
(wir)	wir uns.
(sie)	sie sich.
(ich)	rasiere ich mich.

Ich kämme mir die Haare. (immer)	(Irmgard)	Ich ziehe mich an. (um Viertel vor acht)	(er)
	(wir)		(ihr)
	(er)		(Sie)
	(du)		(du)
	(ich)		(wir)
Ich bürste mir die Haare. (nie)	(wir)		(ich)
	(er)	Ich ziehe mich aus. (nachts)	(ihr)
	(Sie)		(er)
	(ihr)		(du)
	(ich)		(ich)
	(du)	Ich ziehe mich um. (nachmittags)	(er)
			(wir)
			(du)
			(ich)
			(Sie)

IV. *Change the following by adding the proper form of the suggested auxiliary verb* (*Do not change pronouns at all*):

Ich mache die Augen auf.	(können)	Ich kann die Augen aufmachen.
	(werden)	Ich werde
	(sollen)	soll
Er zieht sich morgens an.	(müssen)	Er muß sich morgens anziehen.
	(dürfen)	
	(werden)	
Du liest jetzt die Zeitung.	(können)	Du kannst jetzt die Zeitung lesen.
	(werden)	
	(wollen)	
Sie geben Ihnen eine Feder.	(wollen)	Sie wollen Ihnen eine Feder geben.
	(werden)	
	(müssen)	

V. *Translate your answers to each of the above.*

VI. *Make questions of the following by using the correct form of the suggested auxiliary verb:*

Sie zeigen uns Ihre schöne Stadt.	(wollen)	Wollen Sie uns Ihre schöne Stadt zeigen?
	(werden)	Werden
	(können)	Können
Er gibt mir seine neuen Bilder.	(müssen)	Muß er mir seine neuen Bilder geben?
	(dürfen)	Darf
	(werden)	Wird
Sie zeigt es ihrem Manne.	(werden)	Wird sie es ihrem Manne zeigen?
	(sollen)	Soll
	(wollen)	Will
Du bringst mir etwas.	(dürfen)	Darfst du mir etwas bringen?
	(können)	
	(werden)	
Wir stehen um halb fünf auf.	(sollen)	Sollen wir um halb fünf aufstehen?
	(müssen)	
	(werden)	
Ihr geht jetzt spazieren.	(können)	Könnt ihr jetzt spazieren gehen?
	(werden)	
	(müssen)	

VII. *Answer each of the above questions in the affirmative:*

Wir wollen Ihnen unsere schöne Stadt zeigen.
   werden
   können
Er muß dir seine neuen Bilder geben.
   darf
   wird
Sie wird es ihrem Manne zeigen.
   soll
   will

Ich darf   dir etwas bringen.
   kann
   werde
Sie sollen   um halb fünf aufstehen.
   müssen
   werden
Wir können jetzt spazieren gehen.
   werden
   müssen

VIII. *Translate each of the sentences you have just formed.*

IX. *Rewrite the following passage, using Hans as the subject.*

Jeden Tag soll ich um fünf Uhr aufstehen. Ich stehe gewöhnlich nicht gerne auf, aber trotzdem stehe ich auf. Ich soll mir die Zähne putzen, mich waschen, mir die Haare kämmen, mich rasieren und mich anziehen. Das mache ich nicht gerne. Es ist nämlich halb sechs. Dann will ich frühstücken, aber um sechs Uhr fünfzehn ist das Frühstück nie bereit. Den ganzen Vormittag habe ich Vorlesungen, und am Mittag habe ich wieder Hunger— und auch Durst. Ich esse gut, und dann will ich mich ausruhen und etwas lesen. Aber ich habe gar nichts zu lesen außer der Zeitung, und ich mag sie nicht. Was soll ich nun machen? Ich weiß, ich soll meine Aufgaben studieren, aber ich will meine Freunde treffen. Kennen Sie sie? Nein? Aber ich weiß, Sie kennen mich. Ich mache also keine Aufgaben, und treffe meine Freunde, Karl und Otto, und wir unterhalten uns gut. Und meine Aufgaben? Ja, wissen Sie, ich bin Student auf einer berühmten Universität, und dort darf man nicht vor Mitternacht studieren. Warum muß ich um fünf Uhr aufstehen? Was soll ich sonst machen? Ich will nämlich um acht Uhr ganz wach sein.

VOCABULARY

der **Abend, -e** evening
  jeden Abend every evening
  am Abend in the evening
das **Abendbrot** supper
an:
  am Mittag (etc.) at noon (etc.)
sich an-ziehen get dressed
die **Aufgabe, -n** homework, assignment
auf-wachen wake up
das **Auge, -n** eye
sich aus-ruhen relax
sich aus-ziehen get undressed
bald soon
das **Bett, -en** bed
bis zu (*dat.*) until
der **Bleistift, -e** pencil
die **Brause, -n** shower (-bath)
bringen bring
bürsten brush
  sich die Haare bürsten brush one's hair
dann then
durch (*acc.*) through
der **Durst** thirst
  Durst haben be thirsty

ein-schlafen (ä) fall asleep
erfrischt refreshed
essen (ißt) eat
  zu Mittag (zu Abend) essen eat lunch (dinner)
die **Feder, -n** pen
ganz whole, complete
  den ganzen Morgen all morning
gegen (*acc.*) at about, towards, against
das **Haar, -e** hair
halb zwölf eleven-thirty
die **Hand, ̈e** hand
der **Hunger** hunger
  Hunger haben be hungry
jeden Tag (Morgen, Mittag, Nachmittag, etc.) every day (morning, etc.)
der **Kaffee** coffee
kämmen comb
  sich die Haare kämmen comb one's hair
der **Magen, -** stomach
der **Mittag, -e** noon
das **Mittagessen, -** lunch
die **Mitternacht, ̈e** midnight
der **Morgen, -** morning
müde tired
der **Nachmittag, -e** afternoon

nämlich   . . .you see. . .
ohne (*acc.*)   without
paar:
  ein paar Stunden   a couple of hours
putzen   polish
  sich die Zähne putzen   brush one's teeth
sich rasieren   shave
schläfrig   sleepy
spät:
  Wie spät ist es?   What time is it? How late is it?
spazieren gehen   take a walk
stellen   put, place
  eine Frage stellen   ask a question
  sich unter die Brause stellen   take a shower
die Stunde, -n   hour
treffen (trifft)   meet
trinken   drink

trotzdem   nevertheless, anyway
Uhr:
  um wieviel Uhr   (at) what time
  um sieben Uhr   at seven o'clock
sich um-ziehen   change clothes
sich unterhalten (ä)   have a conversation; have a good time
viertel:
  Viertel vor   a quarter to
  Viertel nach   a quarter after
vor   before
die Vorlesung, -en   class, lecture
wach   awake
sich waschen (ä)   get washed
der Zahn, ⸚e   tooth
die Zeitung, -en   newspaper
das Zimmer, -   room

Lesson VIII

BASIC SENTENCES

Peter is in Germany this year

(1) **Peter ist dieses Jahr in Deutschland,**

because he wants to get to know (the) country and (the) people.

(2) **denn er will Land und Leute kennenlernen.**

Of course he goes to the University and studies several hours a day at home.

(3–4) **Natürlich geht er auf die Universität und arbeitet jeden Tag einige Stunden zu Hause.**

But after that he sometimes goes downtown and eats in a
   restaurant.

He likes to take walks,

and he likes to look at the shop windows.

(5–6)

(7)

(8)

**Aber danach *geht* er manchmal in die Stadt und ißt in einer
   Gaststätte.**

Er geht gern spazieren,

und er sieht sich gerne die Schaufenster an.

(5)

(7)

(6)

(8)

Often he sits on a bench in the park. (9) **Oft sitzt er auf einer Bank im Park.**

In the evening, once or twice a week, he goes to a movie. (10–11) **Abends, ein- oder zweimal die Woche, geht er ins Kino.**

(9)

(10)

(11)

Or he meets a friend and they go to a concert or a play together.   (12–13)

Oder er trifft einen Freund, und sie gehen zusammen ins Konzert oder ins Theater.

(12)

(13)

But sometimes they just stay home,   (14)

drink a glass of beer,   (15)

and talk about /have a conversation about/ their native countries.   (16)

Manchmal aber bleiben sie zu Hause,

trinken ein Glas Bier

und unterhalten sich über ihre Heimatländer.

(14)

(15)

(16)

VARIATIONS

Where are you going (short distance)?	**Wohin gehen Sie?**
Where are you going (longer distance)?	**fahren**
traveling?	**reisen**
I'm going into a night club.	**Ich gehe in ein Nachtlokal.**
I'm in a rathskeller.	**Ich bin in einem Ratskeller.**
I'm going into a lecture.	**Ich gehe in eine Vorlesung.**
I'm in a restaurant.	**Ich bin in einer Gaststätte.**
beer-hall.	**Bierstube.**
I'm going into the library.	**Ich gehe in die Bibliothek.**
I'm in the church.	**Ich bin in der Kirche.**
school.	**Schule.**
city.	**Stadt.**
I'm going into a hotel.	**Ich gehe in ein Hotel.**
I'm in a night club.	**Ich bin in einem Nachtlokal.**
I'm going into the store.	**Ich gehe ins Geschäft.**
I'm in the office	**Ich bin im Büro.**
at theater.	**Theater.**
movie theater.	**Kino.**
museum.	**Museum.**
coffee house.	**Café.**
hotel.	**Hotel.**
I'm going to the market.	**Ich gehe zu dem Markt.**
I'm at the market.	**Ich bin im Markt.**
I'm going (on my way) to work.	**Ich gehe zur Arbeit.**
I'm at the Opera.	**Ich bin in der Oper.**
university.	**Universität.**
I'm going to my seat /place/.	**Ich gehe auf meinen Platz.**
I'm ___ at my seat /place/.	**Ich bin auf meinem**

He goes up to the door.

/He places himself at the door/.

He's standing at the door.

I'm going to the bank.

I'm   at the bank.

I'm going to the /onto the/ country.

I'm in /on/ the country.

I'm going to (the) German class.

I'm in (at) (the)   German class.

I'm going (to the) back.	I'm in back.
home.	home.
outside.	outside.
inside.	inside.
up (stairs)	up (stairs).
down (stairs).	down (stairs).
(to the) left.	(to the) left.
(to the) right.	(to the) right.

I'm going to Germany.	I'm in Germany.
America.	America.
the United States.	the United States.
the U.S.A.	the U.S.A.
Europe.	Europe.

I'm going there.	I'm there. (here)
They're coming here.	They're here.
coming in.	inside.
going in.	inside.
coming out.	outside.
going out.	outside.
everywhere.	everywhere.
nowhere.	nowhere.

Er stellt sich an die Tür.

Er steht an der Tür.

Ich gehe zur   Bank.

Ich bin   in der

Ich gehe aufs   Land.

Ich bin   auf dem Land.

Ich gehe zur   Deutschstunde.

Ich bin   in der Deutschstunde.

Ich gehe nach hinten.	Ich bin hinten.
nach Hause.	zu Hause.
nach draußen.	draußen.
hinein.	drinnen.
nach oben.	oben.
nach unten.	unten.
nach links	links.
nach rechts.	rechts.

Ich fahre nach Deutschland.	Ich bin in Deutschland.
Amerika.	Amerika.
den Vereinigten Staaten.	den Vereinigten Staaten.
den USA.	den USA.
Europa.	Europa.

Ich gehe dahin.	Ich bin da.
Sie kommen hierher.	Sie sind hier.
herein.	drinnen.
gehen hinein.	drinnen.
kommen heraus.	draußen.
gehen hinaus.	draußen.
überall hin.	überall.
nirgendwo hin.	nirgends.

I usually walk. (go on foot)	Ich gehe gewöhnlich zu Fuß.
go by bus.	fahre mit dem (Omni)bus.
subway.	mit der U-Bahn.
train.	mit dem Zug.
airplane.	fliege mit dem Flugzeug.
ship.	fahre mit dem Schiff.
I'm putting my book on that table.	Ich lege mein Buch auf den Tisch dort.
My book is on that table.	Mein Buch liegt auf dem Tisch da.
It's lying on it.	Es liegt darauf.
I'm lying down on the bed.	Ich lege mich auf das Bett.
I'm lying on the bed.	Ich liege auf dem Bett.
He's sitting down on a bench.	Er setzt sich auf eine Bank.
He's sitting on a bench.	Er sitzt auf einer Bank.
He's coming into my room.	Er kommt in mein Zimmer herein.
He's in my room.	Er ist in meinem Zimmer.
He's sitting down in /into/ his easy chair.	Er setzt sich in seinen Sessel.
A dog runs in front of my car.	Ein Hund läuft vor meinen Wagen.
A dog is standing in front of my car.	Ein Hund steht vor meinem Wagen.
We're flying across the country.	Wir fliegen über das Land.
We're flying over the country.	Wir fliegen über dem Land.
His dog is running under the table.	Sein Hund läuft unter den Tisch.
Her cat is sitting under a table.	Ihre Katze sitzt unter einem Tisch.
Marie wants to sit down next to me.	Marie will sich neben mich setzen.
But Martha is already sitting next to me.	Aber Martha sitzt ja schon neben mir.
Heinrich gets (places himself) between his brothers.	Heinrich stellt sich zwischen seine Brüder.
Heinrich is standing between his brothers.	Heinrich steht zwischen seinen Brüdern.
He's sitting down behind me.	Er setzt sich hinter mich.
He always sits behind me.	Er sitzt immer hinter mir.
Where are you going?	Wohin gehst du?
I'm going downtown.	Ich gehe in die Stadt.

I'm going there.	**Ich gehe dahin.**
What are you writing with?	**Womit schreiben Sie?**
I'm writing with a pen.	**Ich schreibe mit einer Feder.**
I'm writing with it.	**Ich schreibe damit.**
What are you sitting on?	**Worauf sitzen Sie?**
I'm sitting on a bench.	**Ich sitze auf einer Bank.**
I'm sitting on it.	**Ich sitze darauf.**
What are you talking about?	**Worüber sprecht ihr?**
We're talking about books.	**Wir sprechen über Bücher.**
We're talking about them.	**Wir sprechen darüber.**
We're talking about our friends.	**Wir sprechen über unsere Freunde.**
We're talking about them.	**Wir sprechen über sie.** (NOTE: *not* **darüber**.)

STRUCTURE

A. Prepositions Governing Accusative and Dative Cases

in   auf   an   neben   hinter   vor   unter   über   zwischen

These prepositions are followed by an *accusative* if they indicate *direction* or *destination*, and by a *dative* if they indicate *location*.

Ich gehe in die Bibliothek.	(Accusative)
I'm going into the library.	(Direction)
Ich bin in der Bibliothek.	(Dative)
I'm in the library.	(Location)

B. Prepositional Contractions.

Certain prepositions can be combined with forms of the definite article to form contractions, as shown in the table:

TABLE VIII A

an	+	{das / dem}	=	{ans / am}	in	+	{das / dem}	=	{ins / im}	zu	+	{der / dem}	=	{zur / zum}
auf	+	das	=	aufs	von	+	dem	=	vom					
bei	+	dem	=	beim										

These contractions do not have to be made, but are used optionally.

A few other such contractions occur, but only rarely, usually in poetry.

C. Hin and Her

These are two special adverbs, in that they form compounds with other adverbs. In general, **hin** means motion *away* from the reference point, **her** means motion *toward* the reference point. The floorplan diagrams below illustrate the use of **heraus, hinaus, herein,** and **hinein.**

TABLE VIII B

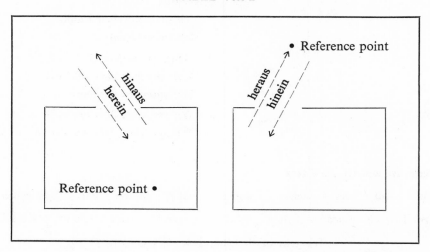

Notice that **-ein** means motion toward the interior of a closed space, and that **-aus** means motion out of the interior of a closed space. The **hin-** and **her-** compounds must be learned as vocabulary.

D. Da- and Wo- Compounds

Da and **wo** form adverbial compounds with most prepositions, as well as with **hin** and **her**. **Da** and **wo** are always the first elements of such compounds. If the preposition begins with a vowel, then **-r-** is used as a connector. Thus,

$$\textbf{da} + \textbf{über} = \textbf{darüber}$$
$$\textbf{wo} + \textbf{auf} \ = \textbf{worauf}$$

Wo- compounds are used as interrogatives; **da-** compounds are used in place of prepositional phrases. *However, neither set is ever used in reference to people!*

Worüber sprechen Sie?	Worüber sprechen Sie?
Wir sprechen über Bücher.	Wir sprechen über unsere Freunde.
Sprechen Sie über Bücher?	Sprechen Sie über Ihre Freunde?
Ja, wir sprechen darüber.	Ja, wir sprechen über sie.

PATTERN PRACTICES

I. *Answer in the affirmative:*

Gehen Sie in das Kino dort?   Ja, ich gehe in das Kino dort.

　　　　Ihr Zimmer hinein?   　　　mein Zimmer hinein.

　　　　diese alten Fabriken?   　　　diese alten Fabriken.

Setzen Sie sich auf das Bett?   setze mich auf das Bett.

Setzt sie　　diese Bank?   sie setzt sich　　diese Bank.

Stellt er sich vor die Tür?   er stellt sich vor die Tür.

　　　　das berühmte Rathaus?   　　　　das berühmte Rathaus.

　　　　den neuen Bahnhof?   　　　　den neuen Bahnhof.

　　　　die Amerikaner?   　　　　die Amerikaner.

Unterhalten Sie sich über berühmte Bücher?   wir unterhalten uns über berühmte Bücher.

　　　　ein berühmtes Buch?   　　　　ein berühmtes Buch.

Läuft Ihr Hund unter meinen Wagen?   mein Hund läuft unter Ihren Wagen.

Darf ich mich neben Sie setzen?   Sie dürfen sich neben mich setzen.

Darf er sich zwischen Sie setzen?   er darf sich zwischen uns setzen.

II. *Answer in the affirmative:*

Sind sie in der alten Kirche dort?   Ja, sie sind in der alten Kirche dort.

Bist du heute in der Stadt?   ich bin heute in der Stadt.

Wohnt er in einem berühmten Hotel?   er wohnt in einem berühmten Hotel.

Sitzt Herr Müller in dem großen Zimmer da?   Herr Müller sitzt in dem großen Zimmer da.

Liegt Ihr Buch auf meinem Platz?   mein Buch liegt auf Ihrem Platz.

Liegt er auf seinem breiten Bett?   er liegt auf seinem breiten Bett.

Sitzen sie auf einer Bank im Park?

Steht Fritz vor diesem alten Krankenhaus?

Wollen Sie vor diesen Gebäuden spazieren gehen?

Das Flugzeug fliegt über der Stadt, nicht wahr?

Sitzt Ihre Katze unter diesem Tisch?

Ist das Herr Glotz unter dem großen Baum dort?

Sitzt Josef zwischen seinen Brüdern?

Gibt es Bäume zwischen den Gebäuden?

Ist der Park neben den häßlichen Fabriken dort?

Wohnt er bei Ihnen nebenan?

III. *Answer the question of destination with a statement of presence:*

Geht er in das Kino dort?	Nein, er ist schon in dem Kino dort.
Wird er sich auf die kleine Bank setzen?	sitzt schon auf der kleinen Bank.
Werden Sie Ihr Buch auf den Tisch legen?	mein Buch liegt schon auf dem Tisch.
Kommt der Zug schon in den Bahnhof?	der Zug ist schon im Bahnhof.
Darf er sich vor Ihre Tür stellen?	Er steht schon vor meiner Tür.
Werden Sie sich neben Ihre Freunde setzen?	Ich sitze schon neben meinen Freunden.
Fährt er nach den Vereinigten Staaten?	Er ist schon in den Vereinigten Staaten.
Deutschland?	Deutschland.
Amerika?	Amerika.
den USA?	den USA.
Werden sie sich vor den kleinen Park stellen?	Sie stehen schon vor dem kleinen Park.
Will er sich auf ein Bett legen?	Er liegt schon auf einem Bett.

IV. *Now reverse question and answer in the preceding practice: Example:* Ist er schon in dem Kino dort? Nein, er geht in das Kino dort.

V. *Complete the following with a locative statement, using* **Peter** *as the subject:*

Ich gehe	nach Hause,	aber Peter ist schon zu Hause.
Wir fahren	nach Deutschland,	in Deutschland.
	in die Stadt,	der Stadt.

Ich	gehe	hinein,		drinnen.
	reise	auf das Land,		auf dem Lande.
	gehe	dahin,		da.
Sie	kommen	hierher,		hier.
		herein,		drinnen.
	gehen	hinein,		drinnen.
Ich	gehe	nach oben,		oben.
		unten,		unten.
	laufe	hinten,		hinten.
	gehe	rechts,		rechts.
		links,		links.

VI. *Now reverse the preceding practice. Example:* Peter ist schon zu Hause, aber ich gehe nach Hause.

VII. *Answer in the affirmative, using a* **da-** *compound whenever possible* (*never with people!*):

Schreiben Sie mit meiner Feder?	Ja, ich schreibe damit.
Sitzt er auf der kleinen Bank dort?	er sitzt darauf.
Legen Sie Ihre Bücher auf die Zeitungen?	ich lege meine Bücher darauf.
Fahren Sie mit den Leuten dort?	fahre mit ihnen.
Fliegt er mit dem Flugzeug?	er fliegt damit.
Fährt Zug?	fährt
Bus?	
Frühstückt er bei euch?	er frühstückt bei uns.
Liegt die Katze gewöhnlich unter diesem Tisch?	sie liegt gewöhnlich darunter.
Unterhalten Sie sich gewöhnlich über Ihre Freunde?	wir unterhalten uns gewöhnlich über sie.
das Theater?	darüber.

VIII. *Make your answer the reverse of the question:*

Ist er drinnen?	Nein, er ist draußen.
Gehen sie hinein?	sie kommen heraus.
Gehen Sie nach links?	ich gehe nach rechts.
hinten?	vorn.
oben?	unten.
Geht er dorthin?	er kommt hierher.
Sind sie überall?	sie sind nirgends.
Sprechen Sie immer mit ihnen?	ich spreche nie mit ihnen.
Schreiben Sie immer mit der Feder da?	schreibe nie damit.
diesem Bleistift?	damit.
Sprechen Sie oft mit den Leuten da?	ich spreche selten mit ihnen.
Ihren Eltern?	mit ihnen.

IX. *Complete the statements, using* **Herr Müller** *as the subject and employing the mode of transportation suggested:*

Ich fliege mit dem Flugzeug,	(Bus)	aber Herr Müller fährt mit dem Bus.
fahre Bus,	(Zug)	Zug.
Wagen,	(Fuß)	geht zu Fuß.
gehe zu Fuß,	(U-Bahn)	fährt mit der U-Bahn.
fahre mit der U-Bahn,	(Wagen)	dem Wagen.

X. *In your answer, use the* **da-** *compound corresponding to the* **wo-** *compound in the question:*

Wohin fahren Sie?	Ich fahre dahin.
Worüber sprecht ihr?	Wir sprechen darüber.
Worunter sitzt er?	Er sitzt darunter.
Womit schreiben Sie?	Ich schreibe damit.
Worauf liegt das alte Buch?	Es liegt darauf.

XI. *Read the following passage, adding endings for the blanks wherever you think it necessary. (Some of the blanks require no ending.)*

Dies_____ Jahr fahre ich nach Deutschland. Ich fliege mit dem Flugzeug. D_____ Schiff ist nicht schnell genug_____. Ich werd_____ mein_____ alt_____ Freunde in Heidelberg seh_____. Sie sind Student_____ auf d_____ Universität. Ich weiß_____, sie werd_____ mi_____ d_____ Stadt gerne zeigen. Ich will in ein_____ Kino, d_____ Bibliothek und d_____ Warenhaus_____ gehen, und in d_____ Park und in d_____ alt_____, eng_____ Straßen spazieren gehen. Und endlich will ich in ein_____ Vorlesung auf d_____ Universität gehen. Ich kann_____ schon d_____ Professor hören. „Gut_____ Morgen, mein_____ Damen und Herren. Unser_____ Vorlesung für heute ist...“

VOCABULARY

das Ballett ballet
die Bank, ̈e bench
bei (*dat.*) **nebenan** next to
das Bier, -e beer
die Bierstube, -n beer-hall
das Büro, -s office
das Café, -s coffee house
da-:
    damit, darauf with it, with them, on it; on them
denn because
die Deutschstunde, -n German class
draußen, nach draußen outside
einige several, a few
einmal (zweimal, *etc.*) once (twice, *etc.*)
fahren (ä) go
fliegen fly
das Flugzeug, -e airplane
    mit dem Flugzeug by airplane
der Fuß, ̈e foot
das Glas, ̈er glass
das Heimatland, ̈er native country
her-:
    heraus out
    herein in
hin-:
    hinaus out
    hinein in
hierher (to) here
hinten, nach hinten back, behind

hinter (*acc., dat.*) behind
ja schon already
kennen-lernen get to know
das Land, ̈er country
laufen (äu) run
legen lay, put
liegen lie (recline)
der Markt, ̈e market
das Museum, Museen museum
nach:
    nach Amerika (Deutschland, *etc.*) fahren go to America (Germany, *etc.*)
das Nachtlokal, -e nightclub
neben (*acc., dat.*) next to, near
nirgends nowhere
nirgendwo, nirgendwo hin nowhere
oben, nach oben up (stairs)
der Omnibus (der Bus), -se bus
    mit dem Omnibus (Bus) by bus
die Oper, -n opera
der Platz, ̈e seat, place
der Ratskeller, __ rathskeller
reisen travel
das Schaufenster, __ shopwindow
das Schiff, -e ship
    mit dem Schiff by ship
der Sessel, __ easy chair
sich setzen sit down
sitzen sit
sich stellen go up (to), place oneself (at)

die Stunde, -n hour, class, period
das Theater, __ theater
die U-Bahn (Untergrundbahn), -en subway
  mit der U-Bahn by subway
über (*acc., dat.*) about, over, across
überall, überall hin everywhere
unten, nach unten down (stairs)
die USA (*pl.*) the U.S.A.
wo-:
  womit? with what
  worauf? on what?
  worüber? over (about) what?

die Vereinigten Staaten (*pl.*) United States
der Wagen, __ car
der Zug, ⸚e train
  mit dem Zug by train
zusammen together
zwischen (*acc., dat.*) between

Lesson IX

BASIC SENTENCES

Yesterday I got up at seven o'clock.	(1)	**Gestern stand ich um sieben Uhr auf.**
I didn't like getting up,	(2)	**Ich stand nicht gerne auf,**
but I got up anyway.	(3)	**aber trotzdem stand ich auf.**

(1)

(2)

(3)

(4)

(5)

(6)

I brushed my teeth,	(4)	**Ich putzte mir die Zähne,**
washed,	(5)	**wusch mich,**
shaved,	(6)	**rasierte mich,**
combed my hair,	(7)	**kämmte mir die Haare**
and got dressed.	(8)	**und zog mich an.**

(7)

(8)

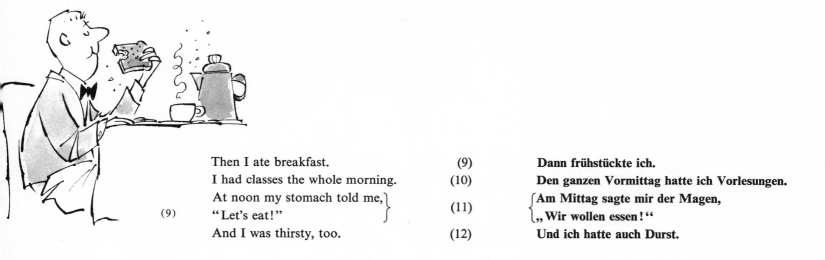

Then I ate breakfast.	(9)	Dann frühstückte ich.	
I had classes the whole morning.	(10)	Den ganzen Vormittag hatte ich Vorlesungen.	
At noon my stomach told me, "Let's eat!"	(11)	Am Mittag sagte mir der Magen, „Wir wollen essen!"	
And I was thirsty, too.	(12)	Und ich hatte auch Durst.	

(10)

(11)

(12)

After lunch I relaxed for a couple of hours.	(13–14)	**Nach dem Mittagessen ruhte ich mich ein paar Stunden aus.**
I read the (news) paper and took a walk.	(15–16)	**Ich las die Zeitung und ging spazieren.**

(13)

(14)

(15)

(16)

Then I did my assignments until dinner.	(17)	**Dann machte ich meine Aufgaben bis zum Abendessen.**
I didn't study again in the evening,	(18)	**Am Abend arbeitete ich nicht wieder,**
but met my friends,	(19)	**sondern traf meine Freunde,**
and we had a good time.	(20)	**und wir unterhielten uns gut.**

(17)

(18)

(19)

(20)

At eleven-thirty I went to bed,	(21)	**Um halb zwölf ging ich zu Bett,**
closed my eyes,	(22)	**machte die Augen zu**
and soon fell asleep.	(23)	**und schlief bald ein.**

(21)

(22)

(23)

VARIATIONS

I wake up. (I'm waking up.)	I woke up. (I was waking up.)	Ich wache auf.	Ich wachte auf.
I get up. (I'm getting up.)	I got up. (I was getting up.)	stehe auf.	stand auf.
I wash. (I'm washing.)	I washed. (I was washing.)	wasche mich.	wusch mich.
I brush my teeth. (I'm brushing my teeth.)	I brushed my teeth. (I was brushing my teeth.)	putze mir die Zähne.	putzte mir die Zähne.
I take a bath. (I'm taking a bath.)	I took a bath. (I was taking a bath.)	bade.	badete.
I take a shower. (I'm taking a shower.)	I took a shower. (I was taking a shower.)	stelle mich unter die Brause.	stellte mich unter die Brause.
I shave. (I'm shaving.)	I shaved. (I was shaving.)	rasiere mich.	rasierte mich.
I comb my hair. (I'm combing my hair.)	I combed my hair. (I was combing my hair.)	kämme mir die Haare.	kämmte mir die Haare.
I brush my hair. (I'm brushing my hair.)	I brushed my hair. (I was brushing my hair.)	bürste mir die Haare.	bürstete mir die Haare
I get dressed. (I'm getting dressed.)	I got dressed. (I was getting dressed.)	ziehe mich an.	zog mich an.
I eat. (I'm eating.)	I ate. (I was eating.)	esse.	aß.
I drink coffee. (I'm drinking coffee.)	I drank coffee. (I was drinking coffee.)	trinke Kaffee.	trank Kaffee.
I go to bed. (I'm going to bed.)	I went to bed. (I was going to bed.)	gehe zu Bett.	ging zu Bett.
I sleep. (I'm sleeping.)	I slept. (I was sleeping.)	schlafe.	schlief.

I am here.	I was here.	bin hier.	war hier.
I am hungry.	I was hungry.	habe Hunger.	hatte Hunger.
I woke up.	I got up.	Ich wachte auf.	Ich stand auf.
You woke up.	You got up.	Du wachtest	Du standst
He woke up.	He got up.	Er wachte	Er stand
We woke up.	We got up.	Wir wachten	Wir standen
You woke up.	You got up.	Ihr wachtet	Ihr standet
They woke up.	They got up.	Sie wachten	Sie standen

I was here.	Ich war hier.
You were here.	Du warst
He was here.	Er war
We were here.	Wir waren
You were here.	Ihr wart
They were here.	Sie waren

The days of the week are:

Sunday, Monday, Tuesday, Wednesday,
    Thursday, Friday, Saturday.

Die Tage der Woche sind:

Sonntag, Montag, Dienstag, Mittwoch, Donnerstag,
    Freitag, Samstag (Sonnabend).

The seasons are:

    spring
    summer
    fall
    winter.

Die Jahreszeiten sind:

    der Frühling
    der Sommer
    der Herbst
    der Winter.

The months are:

January, February, March, April, May, June, July, August,
    September, October, November, December.

Die Monate sind:

Januar, Februar, März, April, Mai, Juni, Juli, August,
    September, Oktober, November, Dezember.

When were you doing that?
    (did you do)

Wann machten Sie das?

Yesterday.
Today.
The day before yesterday.

Gestern.
Heute.
Vorgestern.

Yesterday morning.	**Gestern früh.**
afternoon.	**nachmittag.**
evening.	**abend.**
This morning.	**Heute morgen.**
afternoon.	**nachmittag.**
evening.	**abend.**
On Sunday.	**Sonntag.**
In January.	**Im Januar.**
In the Spring.	**Im Frühling.**
Last week.	**Vorige Woche.**
month.	**Vorigen Monat.**
year.	**Voriges Jahr.**
A week ago.	**Vor einer Woche.**
month	**einem Monat.**
year	**einem Jahr.**
A long time ago.	**Vor langer Zeit.**
A short time ago; recently.	**Kürzlich; neulich.**
Once (once, long ago).	**Einst.**
Previously, formerly /earlier/.	**Früher.**
I worked here a month ago.	**Vor einem Monat arbeitete ich hier.**
We were reading that a year ago.	**Vor einem Jahr lasen wir das.**
What was he saying?	**Was sagte er?**
She wrote me a letter every day.	**Sie schrieb mir jeden Tag einen Brief.**
They spoke for a whole hour.	**Sie unterhielten sich eine ganze Stunde lang.**
There was always a lot to do.	**Es gab immer viel zu tun.**
We never saw them.	**Wir sahen sie nie.**
He lived here two years ago.	**Vor zwei Jahren wohnte er hier.**
We always liked to help him.	**Wir halfen ihm immer gerne.**
He seldom came into the city.	**Er kam selten in die Stadt.**
She knew her husband well.	**Sie kannte ihren Mann gut.**
He called something to us.	**Er rief uns etwas zu.**

He gave me something more every day.	**Er gab mir jeden Tag noch etwas.**
We drank a glass of beer yesterday.	**Wir tranken gestern ein Glas Bier.**
I like her /She is pleasing to me/.	**Sie gefällt mir.**
I like him.	**Er gefällt mir.**
We like them.	**Sie gefallen uns.**
They like you.	**Du gefällst ihnen.**

STRUCTURE

A. Weak and Strong Verbs

English verbs form their past tenses in several ways, of which two are most common:

(1) Adding an ending to the name form or stem. This ending may have the sound /-d/, /-id/, or /-t/, although spellings do not always correspond.

TABLE IX A

Name form	Past tense	Ending sound	Name Form	Past Tense	Ending sound
ask	ask-ed	/t/	try	trie-d	/d/
help	help-ed	/t/	need	need-ed	/id/
saw	saw-ed	/d/	wait	wait-ed	/id/

Note that, regardless of spelling, *the stem vowel sound is the same* in the past tense as it is in the name form. We call such verbs *weak verbs*.

(2) Changing the stem vowel, but adding no ending. However, the lack of an ending in the past tense is grammatically significant, since it helps to signal past time. We will call such a phenomenon a zero-ending, and represent it with the symbol -Ø

TABLE IX B

Name form	Past tense	Name form	Past tense
rise	rose-Ø	come	came-Ø
sing	sang-Ø	run	ran-Ø
slide	slid-Ø		

The nature of the vowel change is rarely predictable, and in learning English we must learn each of these past tenses separately. We call such verbs *strong verbs*.

For a non-native speaker of English, it is often hard to tell whether a verb is weak or strong simply from knowing the name form. Thus the past tense of "fly" is "flew" if we are talking about airplanes, but "flied" if we are talking about baseball. Thus, we must learn each English verb as being weak or strong or both.

German verbs are similar to English ones in this regard.

B. German Weak Verbs—Past Tense

German weak verbs can be defined as verbs which always have endings (other than -Ø) in all tenses. Most weak verbs have no vowel change. The few which have one must be learned as vocabulary. As in the present tense, the type of ending is determined by the final sound of the stem. Past tenses of typical German weak verbs are found in the following table.

TABLE IX C

Name form	Pronoun	Added to stem	Past tense form
mach-en	ich, er, sie, es	-te	mach-te
	du	-test	mach-test
	wir, Sie, sie	-ten	mach-ten
	ihr	-tet	mach-tet
arbeit-en	ich, er, sie, es	-ete	arbeit-ete
	du	-etest	arbeit-etest
	wir, Sie, sie	-eten	arbeit-eten
	ihr	-etet	arbeit-etet
bad-en	ich, er, sie, es	-ete	bad-ete
	du	-etest	bad-etest
	wir, Sie, sie	-eten	bad-eten
	ihr	-etet	bad-etet

In general, **-et-** occurs in the past tense of all weak verbs whose 3rd person singular present tense ending is **-et.** This happens whenever the final stem consonant is **-d** or **-t,** or after certain consonant combinations ("clusters"), as for example **-gn-,** as we shall see.

TABLE IX D

Name form	Present form	Past form
bad-en	er bad-et	er bad-ete
arbeit-en	er arbeit-et	er arbeit-ete
regn-en	es regn-et	es regn-ete

C. German Strong Verbs—Past Tense

German strong verbs can be defined as verbs which have -Ø- endings in the 1st and 3rd person singular of the past tense. Coincidentally, the stem vowel of the past tense of a strong verb is different from that of its name form; sometimes the stems of strong verbs have consonant changes as well. All these changes must be learned as vocabulary, just as they must be in English. Past tenses of typical German strong verbs are found in the following table.

TABLE IX E

Name form	Pronouns	Ending	Past tense form
schlaf-en	ich, er, sie, es	-Ø	schlief-Ø
	du	-st	schlief-st
	wir, Sie, sie	-en	schlief-en
	ihr	-t	schlief-t
trink-en	ich, er, sie, es	-Ø	trank-Ø
	du	-st	trank-st
	wir, Sie, sie	-en	trank-en
	ihr	-t	trank-t
geh-en	ich, er, sie, es	-Ø	ging-Ø
	du	-st	ging-st
	wir, Sie, sie	-en	ging-en
	ihr	-t	ging-t

D. The Past Tense of Sein

TABLE IX F

ich, er, sie, es du	war-Ø war-st	wir, Sie, sie ihr	war-en war-t

E. The Past Tense of Haben

TABLE IX G

ich, er, sie, es du	hat-te hat-test	wir, Sie, sie ihr	hat-ten hat-tet

F. The Verb Gefallen—(to) please

Germans often use this verb where we would use the verb "like." In this case the German subject is the equivalent of the English object, and vice versa. Note that, like **antworten** and **helfen, gefallen** requires a dative object.

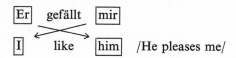

/He pleases me/

PATTERN PRACTICES

I. *Answer in the affirmative:*

Frühstückte er	gestern?		Ja, er	frühstückte gestern.		
Arbeitete				arbeitete		
Las				las		
Badete				badete		
Machten	Sie gestern Ihre Aufgabe?		ich machte	gestern meine Aufgabe.		
Gingen		zu Bett?		ging	zu	Bett.
Schliefen		ein?		schlief	ein.	
Waren		in Berlin?		war	in	Berlin.

II. *Complete the statement in the past tense, using the suggested subject:*

Ich wachte gestern um halb acht auf, (Hans)   und Hans wachte auch gestern um halb acht auf.

Wir standen gestern um halb neun   (er)   er   stand   auch gestern um halb neun.

Ich badete am Nachmittag,   (du)   du   badetest auch am Nachmittag.

Er zog sich früh an,   (wir)   wir   zogen uns auch früh an.

Meine Freunde waren gestern in
    Heidelberg,   (ich)   ich   war auch gestern in Heidelberg.

Ich blieb vorige Woche zu Hause,   (Herr und Frau Müller) Herr und Frau Müller blieben auch vorige Woche zu
                                                              Hause.

Er sprach vorigen Monat mit mir,   (sie)   sie   sprach auch vorigen Monat mit mir.

Vorigen Sonntag kam ich nach Hause   (er)   er   kam auch vorigen Sonntag nach Hause.

Er ging gestern ins neue Kino,   (wir)   wir   gingen auch gestern ins neue Kino.

Sie schrieb ihm gestern einen Brief, (ihr)   ihr   schriebt ihm auch gestern einen Brief.

III. *Complete the statement, using the past tense and the suggested subject:*

Ich bin heute in Heidelberg,   (Hans)   aber Hans war gestern in Heidelberg.

Er lernt jetzt seine Aufgabe,   (ich)   ich lernte gestern meine Aufgabe.

Sie stehen heute früh auf,   (wir)   wir standen gestern früh auf.

Marie schreibt jetzt ihrem Vater einen Brief, (ich) ich schrieb gestern meinem Vater einen Brief.

Heute arbeiten Sie in diesem Laden,   (ich)   gestern arbeitete ich in diesem Laden.

Heute liest er das berühmte Buch,   (Sie)   gestern lasen Sie das berühmte Buch.

Wir gehen heute in die Stadt,   (du)   du gingst gestern in die Stadt.

Heute gibt es viel zu tun,   (nichts)   gestern gab es nichts zu tun.

IV. *Change the statements to the past tense, reversing subject and object:*

Sie kennt ihn sehr gut.   Er kannte sie sehr gut.

Er trifft mich.   Ich traf ihn.

Sie helfen uns.   Wir halfen Ihnen.

Er schreibt mir einen Brief.

Sie antwortet uns.

Ich rufe sie.

Wir sehen dich.

Hören Sie ihn?

V. *Translate the last two pattern practices into English.*

VI. *Restate each of the following, substituting a personal pronoun for the noun-subject:*

Der schöne Park dort gefällt mir.	Er gefällt mir.
Diese neue Universität gefällt ihnen.	Sie gefällt ihnen.
Diese Aufgabe gefällt ihm nicht.	Sie gefällt ihm nicht.
Die beiden Zeitungen gefallen uns sehr.	Sie gefallen uns sehr.
Ihm gefällt der Frühling.	Ihm gefällt er.
Euch gefiel der Winter.	Euch gefiel er.
Dir gefiel immer der Sommer.	Dir gefiel er immer.
Mir gefiel der Winter nur selten.	Mir gefiel er nur selten.
Meine neuen Bücher gefielen ihr sehr.	Sie gefielen ihr sehr.
Gefällt Ihnen die neue Bibliothek?	Gefällt sie Ihnen?

VII. *Answer in the affirmative, using the verb* **gefallen,** *a pronoun as a subject, and the tense of the statement given:*

Sieht	er	die	Bibliothek?	Ja, sie	gefällt	ihm.
Sehen	Sie	diese	Straßen?		sie	gefallen	mir.
Sieht	sie	unsere	Schule?			gefällt	ihr.
Sahen	Sie	den	Sessel?		er	gefiel	mir.
	sie	die	Kinder dort?		sie	gefielen	ihnen.
Seht	ihr	meine	Bücher?			gefallen	uns.
Hast	du	das	Büro?		es	gefällt	mir.
Habt	ihr	das	Zimmer?				uns.
Kennen	Sie	unsere	Stadt?		sie		mir.
Kanntest	du	seine	Freundin?			gefiel	
Kannte	er	meine	Mutter?				ihm.
		ihren	Vater?		er		

VIII. *Translate the preceding exercise into English; then reproduce the original German.*

IX. *Reverse subject and object in each of the following, keeping the same tense:*

Er	gefällt	ihnen.		Sie	gefallen	ihm.
		mir.		Ich	gefalle	
	gefiel	ihr.		Sie	gefiel	
Sie	gefallen	ihnen.			gefallen	Ihnen.
Sie	gefiel	ihm.		Er	gefiel	ihr.
Ihm		sie.		Ihr		er.
Euch	gefällt	er.				
Uns	gefallen	sie.				
Wir	gefielen	ihnen.				
Ich	half	ihm.				
Sie	antwortet	uns.				
Er	anwortete					
Sie	hilft	euch.				
Ihr	halft	ihr.				
Du	hilfst	uns.				
Wir	antworteten	ihm.				

X. *Translate the preceding exercise into English; then reproduce the original German.*

XI. *Reverse the subject and object in each of the following, keeping tense constant:*

Er	will	mir	etwas	sagen.		Ich	will	ihm	etwas	sagen.
Ich	werde	ihm	etwas	geben.		Er	wird	mir	etwas	geben.
Sie	können	uns	etwas	zeigen.		Wir	können	Ihnen	etwas	zeigen.
Du	mußt	mir	etwas	sagen.						
Ich	kann	Ihnen	nichts	geben.						
Ihr	dürft	ihnen	etwas	geben.						
Er	kann	ihnen	selten	antworten.						
Du	wirst	ihr	nichts	geben.						

XII. *Translate the above exercise into English; then reproduce the original German.*

XIII. *Complete the statement in the past tense, using* **Fritz** *as the subject and the preposition* **vor** *("ago") with the period of time given:*

Ich	wohne	seit	einem	Jahr	in Heidelberg,	aber Fritz wohnte vor einem Jahr in Heidelberg.
Sie	trinken		einer	Stunde	ihr Bier,	trank einer Stunde sein Bier.
Wir	sind		drei	Monaten	hier,	war drei Monaten hier.
Du	fährst		vier	Tagen	nach Berlin,	fuhr vier Tagen nach Berlin.
Ich	treffe		zwei	Monaten	meine Freunde hier,	traf zwei Monaten seine Freunde hier.
Wir	unterhalten	uns seit einem Tag hier,				unterhielt sich vor einem Tag hier.

XIV. *Complete the statements in the past tense, using* **wir** *as the subject and* **gestern** *as the adverb of time:*

Sie bringt heute ihre Bilder,	aber wir brachten gestern unsere Bilder.
Er ist heute in Heidelberg,	waren gestern in Heidelberg.
Sie ruht sich heute aus,	ruhten uns gestern aus.
Du gehst heute ins Kino da,	gingen gestern ins Kino da.
Sie sitzen heute auf dieser kleinen Bank,	saßen gestern auf dieser kleinen Bank.
Sie kommt heute um acht Uhr,	kamen gestern um acht Uhr.
Ihr werdet morgen euren Eltern helfen,	halfen gestern unseren Eltern.

XV. *Respond in the past tense:*

Wollen Sie mit ihm sprechen?	Ich sprach gestern mit ihm.
mit mir zu Hause bleiben?	blieb mit Ihnen zu Hause.
in dieser neuen Gaststätte essen?	aß in dieser neuen Gaststätte.
ein bißchen Bier trinken?	trank ein bißchen Bier.
jetzt arbeiten?	arbeitete gestern.
sich rasieren?	rasierte mich gestern.
sich unter die Brause stellen?	stellte mich gestern unter die Brause.
baden?	badete gestern.

XVI. *Change to the past:*

Ich verstehe alles.	Ich verstand...	Ich bürste mir die Haare	Ich bürstete...
wiederhole.	wiederholte...	tue nichts.	tat...
habe Durst.	hatte...	zeige Ihnen Bilder.	
schlafe ein.	schlief...	fliege nach Deutschland.	
lege meine Bücher auf den Tisch.	legte...	kämme mir die Haare.	
mache die Tür auf.	machte...	ziehe mich an.	
reise nach Europa.	reiste...	wache auf.	
setze mich.	setzte...	frage ihn etwas.	
putze mir die Zähne.	putzte...	laufe langsam.	
liege auf dem Bett.	lag...	sage nichts.	
erzähle ihm etwas.	erzählte...	rauche Zigaretten.	
warte hier.	wartete...	liebe meine Eltern.	
wasche mich.	wusch...		

XVII. *Give a real or fictional account of yesterday's activities in 200 German words.*

VOCABULARY

der Brief, -e   letter
Dienstag   Tuesday
Donnerstag   Thursday
einst   once, one day, long ago
Freitag   Friday
früh:
   gestern früh   yesterday morning
früher   earlier, previously, formerly, before
der Frühling, -e   spring
gefallen, gefiel* (ä) (*dat.*)   please
gestern   yesterday
der Herbst   fall, autumn
heute morgen (*etc.*)   this morning (*etc.*)
in:
   im Januar (*etc.*)   in January (*etc.*)
   im Frühling (*etc.*)   in spring (*etc.*)
die Jahreszeit, -en   season, time of year
kürzlich   recently, not long ago

lang   long
   eine ganze Stunde lang   for a whole hour
Mittwoch   Wednesday
Montag   Monday
neulich   recently
Samstag   Saturday
der Sommer, —   summer
Sonnabend   Saturday
Sonntag   Sunday
vor:
   vor einer Woche (*etc.*)   a week (*etc.*) ago
vorig:
   vorige Woche, vorigen Monat, voriges Jahr, *etc.*   last week, last
      month, last year, *etc.*
vorgestern   day before yesterday
der Vormittag, -e   forenoon (morning)
der Winter   winter
Zeit:
   vor langer Zeit   a long time ago
die Zeitschrift, -en   magazine

---

* Henceforth verb entries will include the past tense of strong verbs.

Lesson X

BASIC SENTENCES

When I was in Heidelberg last year,	(1)	**Als ich voriges Jahr in Heidelberg war,**
I found the climate of Heidelberg (to be) pretty (rather) mild.	(2)	**fand ich das Klima Heidelbergs ziemlich mild.**
In general, it was like (similar to) the climate of Pennsylvania.	(3)	**Im allgemeinen war es dem Klima Pennsylvaniens ähnlich.**

(1)

(2)

(3)

(4)

The winter was long,
it got (became) pretty cold,
and the ground was completely covered with snow.
It (the sky) was often cloudy,
and the weather was raw (wet-cold).

(4) **Der Winter war lang,**
(5) **es wurde ziemlich kalt,**
(6) **und der Boden war ganz mit Schnee bedeckt.**
(7) **Der Himmel war oft bewölkt,**
(8) **und das Wetter war naßkalt.**

(5)

(6)

(7)

(8)

(9)

(10)

(11)

Spring came in April, and we were looking forward to it.	(9–10) **Der Frühling kam im April, und man freute sich darauf.**
In Heidelberg spring was the most beautiful season.	(11) **In Heidelberg war der Frühling die schönste Jahreszeit.**

In June it began to get warm,	(12)	**Im Juni begann es, warm zu werden,**
but during the summer it hardly ever got really hot.	(13)	**aber während des Sommers wurde es fast niemals wirklich heiß.**
Sometimes there was a thunderstorm,	(14)	**Manchmal gab es ein Gewitter,**
but it (that) didn't last long.	(15)	**aber das dauerte nicht lange.**

(12)

(13)

(14)

(15)

Autumn was very pleasant at first, (16)

and in November it rained a lot. (17)

In December autumn was /already/ over (past) (18)

and winter was back (was there again). (19)

Der Herbst war am Anfang sehr angenehm, (16)

aber im November regnete es viel. (17)

Im Dezember war der Herbst schon vorbei, (18)

und der Winter war wieder da. (19)

(19)

(16)

(17)

(18)

VARIATIONS

The climate of Heidelberg	is mild.	Das Klima Heidelbergs	ist mild.
(H's climate)			
Germany	is severe.	Deutschlands	ist streng.
the North		des Nordens	
our town		unserer Stadt	
this country		dieses Landes	
the United States		der Vereinigten Staaten	

The man's first name /The first name of the man/ is Peter.	Der Vorname des Mannes ist Peter.
The woman's first name is Liese.	Der Vorname der Frau ist Liese.
The parents' family name is Schulz.	Der Familienname der Eltern ist Schulz.
The young woman's first name is Gudrun.	Der Vorname des Fräuleins ist Gudrun.
My friend's first name is Klaus. (male friend)	Der Vorname meines Freundes ist Klaus.
My friend's first name is Ute. (female friend)	Der Vorname meiner Freundin ist Ute.
Are you going to school in spite of the rain?	Gehen Sie trotz des Regens zur Schule?
Because of the weather I am not going to school.	Wegen des Wetters gehe ich nicht zur Schule.
Is it pleasant here in spite of the climate?	Ist es hier trotz des Klimas angenehm?
Because of the cold climate it is not pleasant here.	Wegen des kalten Klimas ist es hier nicht angenehm.
In spite of the beautiful spring I'm driving to Hamburg.	Trotz des schönen Frühlings fahre ich nach Hamburg.
Because of the beautiful spring I am not driving to Hamburg.	Wegen des schönen Frühlings fahre ich nicht nach Hamburg.
Is he outside in spite of the sun?	Ist er trotz der Sonne draußen?
Because of the warm sun he is not outside.	Wegen der warmen Sonne ist er nicht draußen.
How's the weather today?	Wie ist das Wetter heute?
What's the weather today?	Was für Wetter gibt es heute?
The weather is nice today.	Es ist schön heute.
It's nasty out.	Es ist unangenehm draußen.
hot	heiß
warm	warm
cool	kühl
cold	kalt
cloudy	Der Himmel ist bewölkt.

It's raining out.	Es regnet draußen.
snowing	schneit
freezing	friert
The sun in shining. (*Or*, the sun is out)	Die Sonne scheint.
moon is shining.	Der Mond scheint.
stars are shining /glowing/.	Die Sterne leuchten.
It's getting /becoming/ cold.	Es wird kalt.
It suddenly got dark.	Es wurde plötzlich dunkel.
light /bright/.	hell.
The temperature is going up /climbing/.	Die Temperatur steigt.
down /falling/.	fällt.
Winter is beginning.	Der Winter beginnt.
It's beginning to get cold.	Es beginnt, kalt zu werden.
Autumn is ending.	Der Herbst geht zu Ende.
Autumn is over.	Der Herbst ist vorbei.
It stopped raining.	Es hörte auf zu regnen.
The ground is covered with snow.	Der Boden ist mit Schnee bedeckt.
ice.	Eis
We're going to have a thunderstorm.	Wir werden ein Gewitter haben.
In the north it snows a lot.	Im Norden schneit es viel.
south it's warm.	Süden ist es warm.
east it's cold.	Osten ist es kalt.
west it rains.	Westen regnet es.
Let's go south!	Fahren wir nach dem Süden!
When did you do that? I did it...	Wann machten Sie das? Ich machte das...
yesterday.	gestern.
yesterday morning.	gestern früh.

last week.	vorige Woche.
month.	vorigen Monat.
year.	voriges Jahr.
Sunday.	vorigen Sonntag.
January.	Januar.
Spring.	Frühling.
a few days ago.	vor einigen Tagen.
months	einem Monat.
a long time ago.	vor langer Zeit.
once (one day, long ago).	einst.
today.	heute.
this morning.	heute morgen.
week.	diese Woche.
month.	diesen Monat
year.	dieses Jahr.
Sunday.	diesen Sonntag.
March.	diesen März.
spring.	diesen Frühling.
on Sunday.	am Sonntag.
in March.	im März.
in the spring.	im Frühling.
I'm going to do that...	Ich mache das...
tomorrow.	morgen.
tomorrow morning.	morgen früh.
next week.	nächste Woche.
month.	nächsten Monat.
year.	nächstes Jahr.
Sunday.	nächsten Sonntag.
March.	März.
spring.	Frühling.

right away.	sofort.

in a few days.	in einigen Tagen.
a month.	einem Monat.
some day.	eines Tages.
during the summer.	während des Sommers.
at the end of fall.	am Ende des Herbstes.
at the beginning of winter.	am Anfang des Winters.
spring.	Frühlings.

How long did it last? It lasted...	Wie lange dauerte es? Es dauerte...
all morning (long).	den ganzen Morgen.
week.	die ganze Woche.
month.	den ganzen Monat.
year.	das ganze Jahr.
day Sunday.	den ganzen Sonntag.
during January.	während des ganzen Januars.
spring.	Frühlings.

STRUCTURE

A. The Genitive Case

The German genitive case corresponds roughly to the English possessive case, which we usually indicate by adding the sound /s/ or /z/ (spelled -'s) to singular nouns and names. The German genitive is also governed by certain prepositions. A German noun in the genitive is the possessor, not the thing which is possessed.

B. Noun Endings

German *names* of all genders and *masculine* and *neuter singular nouns* have genitive case endings. Feminine singular and plural nouns (other than names) have no genitive case ending.

(See Table XA on page 200.)

TABLE X A

Noun type	Typical nominative	Ending	Genitive
Most one-syllable singular masculine and neuter	Tag Kind	-es -es	**Tages** **Kindes**
Most polysyllabic singular masculine and neuter	Bahnhof Mädchen	-s -s	**Bahnhofs** **Mädchens**
Masc. and neut. singular nouns ending in -s	Haus Rathaus	-es -es	**Hauses** **Rathauses**
Masc. nouns with acc. and dat. -en endings	Student Deutscher	-en -en	**Studenten** **Deutschen**
Masc. nouns with acc. and dat. -n endings	Herr	-n	**Herrn**
Names	Karl Ilse	-s -s	**Karls** **Ilses**

C. Genitive Forms of the Definite Article and Dieser

TABLE X B

Gender and number	Nominative	Genitive ending	Genitive form
Masc. and neut. sing	der Tag dieser Student das Kind dieses Mädchen	-es	**des Tages** **dieses Studenten** **des Kindes** **dieses Mädchens**
Fem. sing. and all plurals	die Frau die Herren diese Stadt diese Leute	-er	**der Frau** **der Herren** **dieser Stadt** **dieser Leute**

D. Genitive Endings of the Ein- Words

TABLE X C

Gender and number	Nominative	Genitive ending	Genitive form
Masc. and neut. sing.	ein Herr Ihr Haus	-es	**eines Herrn** **Ihres Hauses**
Fem. sing. and all plurals	eine Bank unsere Kinder	-er	**einer Bank** **unserer Kinder**

E. Genitive Endings of Attributive Adjectives

Attributive adjectives preceded by genitive forms of the definite article, **dieser, jeder,** or any of the **ein-** words have the ending **-en.**

F. Summary of Noun-modifier Endings

TABLE X D

Case	Singular			Plural
	Masc.	**Fem.**	**Neut.**	
Nom.	dies-**er** gut-**e** Mann kein-**Ø** gut-**er** Mann	dies-**e** gut-**e** Frau kein-**e** gut-**e** Frau	dies-**es** gut-**e** Kind kein-**Ø** gut-**es** Kind	dies-**e** gut-**en** Kinder kein-**e** gut-**en** Kinder
Acc.	d-**en** alt-**en** Platz ein-**en** alt-**en** Platz	d-**ie** alt-**e** Fabrik ein-**e** alt-**e** Fabrik	d-**as** alt-**e** Haus ein-**Ø** alt-**es** Haus	d-**ie** alt-**en** Plätze kein-**e** alt-**en** Plätze
Dat.	jed-**em** jung-**en** Studenten unser-**em** jung-**en** Studenten	jed-**er** jung-**en** Studentin unser-**er** jung-**en** Studentin	jed-**em** jung-**en** Mädchen unser-**em** jung-**en** Mädchen	dies-**en** jung-**en** Studenten unser-**en** jung-**en** Studenten
Gen.	dies-**es** deutsch-**en** Herrn kein-**es** deutsch-**en** Herrn	dies-**er** deutsch-**en** Stadt kein-**er** deutsch-**en** Stadt	dies-**es** deutsch-**en** Hotels kein-**es** deutsch-**en** Hotels	dies-**er** deutsch-**en** Städte kein-**er** deutsch-**en** Städte

In the table above, note the occurrence of **-en** as an adjective ending. In attributive adjectives following the definite article, **dieser, jeder,** or any of the **ein-** words, the ending **-en** occurs whenever the preceding article-type word and/or the following noun is other than its base (nominative singular) form. If the article-type word is a base form and has an ending, the following adjective ends in **-e.** If the article-type word has a **-Ø** ending, the adjective will have the ending that **dieser** would have in the same slot.

G. The Genitive Case after Prepositions

The genitive case usually follows certain German prepositions, of which **wegen, während** and **trotz** are three. Some others will be encountered later.

PATTERN PRACTICES

I. *Answer in the affirmative, using the genitive case:*

Ist das Klima	in Heidelberg	mild?	Ja, das Klima	Heidelbergs	ist mild.
	in Deutschland			Deutschlands	
	im Norden			des Nordens	
	im Süden			des Südens	
	im Osten			des Ostens	
	im Westen	heiß?		des Westens	heiß.
	in unserer Stadt			unserer Stadt	
	in diesem Land			dieses Landes	
	in den Vereinigten Staaten			der Vereinigten Staaten	
	in Pennsylvanien			Pennsylvaniens	

II. *Answer in the affirmative, using the preposition* **während:**

Ist es im Sommer	in Heidelberg warm?	Ja, es ist während des Sommers	in Heidelberg warm.
im Herbst	kühl?	des Herbstes	kühl.
im Winter	kalt?	des Winters	kalt.
im Frühling	angenehm?	des Frühlings	angenehm.
am Morgen	heiß?	des Morgens	heiß.
am Abend	kalt?	des Abends	kalt.
am Nachmittag	warm?	des Nachmittags.	warm.

III. *Answer in the negative, using the preposition* **wegen**:

Gehen Sie trotz des Wetters zur Schule?   Nein, wegen des Wetters gehe ich nicht zur Schule.

Bleiben Sie hier trotz des langen Winters?   des langen Winters bleibe ich nicht hier.

Ist es hier trotz des kalten Klimas angenehm?   des kalten Klimas ist es hier nicht angenehm.

Gehen Sie trotz des bewölkten Himmels schwimmen?   des bewölkten Himmels gehe ich nicht schwimmen.

Sind Sie hier trotz des heißen Sommers zufrieden?   Nein, wegen des heißen Sommers bin ich hier nicht zufrieden.

Fahren Sie trotz des schönen Frühlings nach Hamburg?   Nein, wegen des schönen Frühlings fahre ich nicht nach Hamburg.

Ist er trotz der warmen Sonne draußen?   Nein, wegen der warmen Sonne ist er nicht draußen.

IV. *Answer in the negative, using the adjective suggested:*

Ist es warm	draußen?	(kühl)	Nein, es ist nicht warm	draußen, sondern kühl.
heiß		(kalt)	heiß	kalt.
kalt		(heiß)	kalt	heiß.
dunkel		(hell)	dunkel	hell.
schön		(schlecht)	schön	schlecht.
angenehm		(kalt)	angenehm	kalt.
hell		(dunkel)	hell	dunkel.
kühl		(warm)	kühl	warm.

V. *Answer in the negative, using the time expression suggested:*

Machten Sie das gestern morgen?	(gestern abend)	Nein, ich machte das gestern abend.
Lasen gestern abend?	(gestern morgen)	las gestern morgen.
Schrieben heute?	(gestern)	schrieb gestern.
Studierten letztes Jahr?	(letzte Woche)	studierte letzte Woche.
Taten letzte Woche?	(letzten Monat)	tat letzten Monat.
Waren Sie vor einigen Tagen dort?	(vor einem Monat)	war vor einem Monat dort.
gestern abend dort?	(heute morgen)	heute morgen dort.
am Sonntag dort?	(am Montag)	am Montag dort.
Sie im Januar dort?	(im März)	im März dort.
im Frühling dort?	(im Winter)	im Winter dort.

VI. *Answer in the negative, using the time expression suggested:*

Werden Sie das heute machen?	(morgen)	Nein, ich werde das morgen machen.
nächste Woche	(nächsten Monat)	nächsten Monat machen.
nächsten Monat lesen?	(nächstes Jahr)	nächstes Jahr lesen.
in einigen Tagen sehen?	(in einem Monat)	in einem Monat sehen.
nächsten Sonntag hören?	(nächsten Montag)	nächsten Montag hören.
— am Dienstag arbeiten?	(am Mittwoch)	— am Mittwoch arbeiten.
das im Sommer tun?	(im Winter)	

Werden Sie während des Frühlings hier sein?	(während des Herbstes)
am Ende des Herbstes	(am Anfang des Herbstes)
diese Woche in der angenehmen Gaststätte essen?	(nächste Woche)
nächsten Sonntag ins Theater gehen?	(diesen Sonntag)

VII. *Answer the question, using the genitive case and the name suggested:*

Heißt	der	Mann	Wolfgang?	(Peter)	Nein, der Vorname des		Mannes	ist Peter.
Heißt			Heinrich?	(Klaus)				Klaus.
	die	Frau	Hetta?	(Liese)		der	Frau	Liese.
			Amalie?	(Grete)				Grete.
	das	Fräulein	Sonja?	(Gertrud)		des	Fräuleins	Gertrud.
Heißen	Ihre	Freunde	Böcker?	(Steiner)	der Familienname	meiner	Freunde	Steiner.
Heißt	Ihr	Freund	Willy?	(Hans)				
	Ihre	Freundin	Maria?	(Ute)				
Heißt	die	Gaststätte,	„Am Rhein"?	("Die Rote Mühle")				
Heißt	der	Herr	Weil?	(Strauß)				
Heißt	der	Student	Mieter?	(Böll)				

VIII. *Answer with the genitive of the suggested noun:*

Ist das Ihr	Name?	(der Junge)	Nein, das ist der Name des Jungen.
Ihr	Buch?	(diese Dame)	das Buch dieser Dame.
unsere	Bibliothek?	(die Universität)	die Bibliothek der Universität
Ihre	Zeitung?	(das Mädchen dort)	die Zeitung des Mädchens dort.
Ihr	Haus?	(der Arzt)	das Haus des Arztes.
Ihre	Katze?	(die Leute dort)	die Katze der Leute dort.
Ihr	Hund?	(mein Bruder)	der Hund meines Bruders.
Ihr	Zimmer?	(unsere Eltern)	das Zimmer unserer Eltern.
Ihr	Mann?	(meine Schwester)	der Mann meiner Schwester.
Ihre	Aufgabe?	(die Studentin dort)	die Aufgabe der Studentin dort.
Ihre	Arbeit?	(meine Sekretärin)	
Ihre	Aufname?	(mein Vater)	
Ihr	Wagen?	(meine Familie)	
Ihr	Platz?	(der Professor)	
Ihr	Familienname?	(meine Verwandten)	

IX. *Write a composition describing the climate of the place where you are from.*

VOCABULARY

ähnlich (*dat.*) like, similar to
allgemein general
  im allgemeinen in general
als (*conj.*) when (fixed time in past)
der Anfang, -s, ̈e* beginning
  am Anfang at first, at the beginning
angenehm pleasant
auf-hören stop, cease
bedecken cover
beginnen, a begin
bewölkt cloudy
der Boden, -s, ̈ ground
dauern last

dunkel dark
das Eis, -es ice
das Ende, -s, -n end
  zu Ende gehen come to an end, end
  am Ende at the end
fallen, ie, (ä) go down, fall
finden, a find
sich freuen be glad
  sich freuen auf look forward to
frieren, o freeze
das Gewitter, -s, — thunderstorm
heiß hot
hell light, bright

---

* From here on, the genitive singular will be listed (after the nominative singular but before the nominative plural) for all masculine and neuter nouns.

der Himmel, -s, — sky
in:
   in einem Monat in a month
kalt cold
das Klima, -s climate
kühl cool
lange for a long time
   Wie lange? (For) how long?
leuchten glow
mild mild
der Mond, -s moon
morgen früh tomorrow morning
nächst next
   nächste Woche, nächsten Monat, *etc.* next week, next month, *etc.*
naßkalt raw (wet-cold)
niemals never
der Norden, -s north
   im Norden in the north
   nach dem Norden (to the) northward
der Osten, -s east
plötzlich sudden(ly)
der Regen, — rain
regnen rain

scheinen, ie shine
der Schnee, -s snow
schneien snow
die Sonne, -n sun
steigen, ie climb, go up
der Stern, -s, -e star
streng severe
der Süden, -s south
Tag:
   eines Tages some day
die Temperatur, -en temperature
trotz (*gen.*) in spite of
vorbei over, past, finished
während (*gen.*) during
warm warm
wegen (*gen.*) because of
werden, wurde, (wird) get, become
der Westen, -s west
das Wetter, -s weather
wirklich real
ziemlich rather, "pretty," quite
zufrieden satisfied

Lesson XI

BASIC SENTENCES

Hans and I went/are gone/to a party last night.   (1)

One (fellow) played/has played/(the) piano,   (2)

and we sang/have sung/some songs.   (3)

(1) Hans und ich sind gestern abend zu einer Party gegangen.

(2) Einer hat Klavier gespielt,

(3) und wir haben ein paar Lieder gesungen.

(1)

(2)

(3)

They asked me to sing an American song, (4)

and so I did/and I have done it, too/. (5)

I certainly don't sing like a bird/I certainly have no bird-voice/, (6)

but they liked the song (the song pleased them) anyhow. (7)

(4) Sie haben mich gebeten, ein amerikanisches Lied zu singen,

(5) und ich hab's auch getan.

(6) Ich habe ja keine Vogelstimme,

(7) aber trotzdem hat ihnen das Lied gefallen.

(4)

(5)

(6)

(7)

(8)

(9)

(10)

Then we danced a little. (8)

I danced with a very pretty girl (9)

who had studied English. (10)

Of course I asked her for a date; (11)

I invited her to a play. (12)

Dann haben wir ein bißchen getanzt.

Ich habe mit einem sehr hübschen Mädchen getanzt,

das Englisch studiert hatte.

Natürlich hab' ich sie um eine Verabredung gebeten;

ich habe sie eingeladen, mit ins Theater zu gehen.

(11)

(12)

At eleven o'clock I went home.   (13)   **Um elf Uhr bin ich nach Hause gegangen.**

I really had a good time.   (14)   **Ich hatte mich wirklich sehr gut unterhalten.**

(13)

(14)

VARIATIONS

What has he done?   **Was hat er getan?**

He's played the piano.   **Er hat Klavier gespielt.**

He's studied his assignment.   **Er hat seine Aufgabe gelernt.**

He's had a good time.   **Er hat sich gut unterhalten.**

He's combed his hair.   **Er hat sich die Haare gekämmt.**

What did you do?   **Was haben Sie getan?**

We sang some songs.	Wir haben ein paar Lieder gesungen.
We drank a glass of wine.	Wir haben ein Glas Wein getrunken.
I wrote a letter.	Ich habe einen Brief geschrieben.
I spoke with him.	Ich habe mit ihm gesprochen.
I washed my hands.	Ich habe mir die Hände gewaschen.
We didn't understand him.	Wir haben ihn nicht verstanden.
I invited him.	Ich habe ihn eingeladen.
What has he done?	Was hat er getan?
He's eaten lunch.	Er hat zu Mittag gegessen.
He's drunk a glass of milk.	Er hat ein Glas Milch getrunken.
He's asked for his mail.	Er hat um seine Post gebeten.
He hasn't invited me.	Er hat mich nicht eingeladen.
He's slept already.	Er hat schon geschlafen.
What did you do?	Was hast du getan?
I went to the movies.	Ich bin ins Kino gegangen.
I went swimming.	Ich bin schwimmen gegangen.
I didn't go into the water.	Ich bin nicht ins Wasser gegangen.
I stayed at home.	Ich bin zu Hause geblieben.
I wasn't there very long.	Ich bin nicht lange da gewesen.
What did he do?	Was hat er getan?
He went out.	Er ist ausgegangen.
He ran downtown.	Er ist in die Stadt gelaufen.
He walked home.	Er ist zu Fuß nach Hause gegangen.
He fell asleep.	Er ist eingeschlafen.
He got/became/tired.	Er ist müde geworden.
You had already sung a song, hadn't you?	Sie hatten schon ein Lied gesungen, nicht wahr?
	Du hattest
	Ihr hattet
I had made a date with her.	Ich hatte mich mit ihr verabredet.
I had sung a song.	Ich hatte ein Lied gesungen.
I had opened the window.	Ich hatte das Fenster aufgemacht.

We had had a good time.
We had danced a little.
We had chatted a little.

What had he done?
He had traveled to America.
He had become an engineer.
He had run home.

What had you done?
I had gone downtown.
I hadn't been here very long.
They hadn't been very pleasant.
We hadn't stayed at home.
I had become very tired.

We had come here too early.
We had a party.

I had made a date with a girl friend.

We invited   some people.
    sang   a few   songs
    told   a few   stories.
               jokes.
    chatted.
    laughed a lot.
    played cards.
    ate something.
    drank wine.
        only milk.
    talked about politics.

We spent an enjoyable   evening.
        interesting
      a   comfortable

Wir hatten uns gut unterhalten.
Wir hatten ein bißchen getanzt.
Wir hatten ein bißchen geplaudert.

Was hatte er getan?
Er war nach Amerika gefahren.
Er war Ingenieur geworden.
Er war nach Hause gelaufen.

Was hatten Sie getan?
Ich war in die Stadt gefahren.
Ich war nicht sehr lange da gewesen.
Sie waren nicht sehr angenehm gewesen.
Wir waren nicht zu Hause geblieben.
Ich war sehr müde geworden.

Wir waren zu früh hierher gekommen.
Wir haben eine Party gehabt.

Ich hatte mich mit einer Freundin verabredet.

Wir haben einige Leute eingeladen.
        ein paar Lieder gesungen.
           Geschichten erzählt.
           Witze erzählt.
    geplaudert.
    viel gelacht.
    Karten gespielt.
    etwas gegessen.
    Wein getrunken.
    nur Milch getrunken.
    über Politik gesprochen.

Wir haben einen lustigen   Abend verbracht.
      interessanten
      gemütlichen

We visited a few friends.	Wir haben einige Freunde besucht.
watched a movie.	uns einen Film angeschaut.
football game.	uns ein Fußballspiel angeschaut.
played football.	Fußball gespielt.
went swimming.	Wir sind schwimmen gegangen.
didn't go into the water.	nicht ins Wasser gegangen.
The game wasn't very exciting.	Das Spiel ist nicht sehr aufregend gewesen.
I didn't go out.	Ich bin nicht ausgegangen.
stayed at home.	zu Hause geblieben.
wrote letters.	habe Briefe geschrieben.
listened to records.	mir Schallplatten angehört.
the radio.	Radio gehört.
music.	mir Musik angehört.
watched a television program.	mir eine Fernsehsendung angeschaut.
watched television.	mir Fernsehen angeschaut.
I had worked long hours.	Ich hatte lange Stunden gearbeitet.
studied my assignment.	meine Aufgabe gelernt.
I got tired toward ten o'clock.	Ich bin gegen zehn Uhr müde geworden.
fell asleep soon.	bald eingeschlafen.
I liked her.	Sie hat mir gefallen.
We liked them.	Sie haben uns gefallen.

STRUCTURE

A. The Perfect Participle

In English we have a special verb form that "goes with" forms of the verb "*have*" to form so-called perfect tenses. This special form is called the perfect participle.

>*He has <u>gone</u> home already.*
>*We have <u>talked</u> with him many times.*

In the sentences above, "*gone*" and "*talked*" are perfect participles. German also has perfect participles which are used in a similar way.

The German perfect participle is composed of three elements:

(1) A STEM. For weak verbs, the stem is the same as the infinitive stem, with certain exceptions which must be learned. For strong verbs, the stem is the same as the infinitive stem, but often has a different vowel which, like the past tense vowel, must be learned along with the verb.

(2) AN ENDING. For weak verbs the ending is the same as the **er/sie/es** form of the present tense, that is, **-t** or **-et.** For strong verbs the ending is **-en.**

(3) A MINIMAL STRESS PATTERN. This consists of a weak stress followed by a strong one. There may be two or more syllables in the participle but the weak-strong pattern must be somewhere in it. Most infinitive stems do not contain such a pattern, so it must be created in the participle by adding a weak-stressed syllable, **ge-** to the beginning of the participle. Note the occurrence of the **ge-** in the examples below.

TABLE XI A

Weak verbs		Strong verbs	
Infinitive	Perfect participle	Infinitive	Perfect participle
ARbeit-en	geARbeit-et	SING-en	geSUNG-en
MACH-en	geMACH-t	FAHR-en	geFAHR-en
WOHN-en	geWOHN-t	STEH-en	geSTAND-en
raSIER-en	raSIER-t	verSTEH-en	verSTAND-en
stuDIER-en	stuDIER-t	HELF-en	geHOLF-en

(NOTE: Verbs ending in ieren do not take ge)

NOTE: The perfect participle of **sein** is **ge-WES-en.**

B. Perfect Participles with Stressed Adverbs

A stressed adverb never loses its strong stress. If one occurs with the perfect participle of a verb, it will be placed immediately before the participle (adverb and verb are actually written as one word). In such cases the stress pattern mentioned in Section A is nullified, although the syllable **ge-** will be there if the participle would ordinarily have one. This is true because such structures are actually phrases, rather than words, and in German a phrase cannot contain more than one strong stress. Thus:

Infinitive	*Perfect Participle*
EIN-lad-en	EIN-gelad-en
AUF-mach-en	AUF-gemach-t
AN-komm-en	AN-gekomm-en

C. German Perfect Auxiliaries

English forms perfect tenses by using the perfect participle with the auxiliary verb "*have*." German, however, has two such auxiliaries, **haben** and **sein,** which are used as follows:

1. **sein** when the principal verb cannot be followed by an object (i.e. an intransitive verb) *and* is a verb whose meaning

indicates motion or change of condition on the part of the subject. The verbs **sein** and **bleiben** also use **sein** as their perfect auxiliary.

2. **haben** in all other cases.
(See also Section D below.)

D. The Present Perfect and Pluperfect Tenses

These German tenses are formed by using the perfect participle of the principal verb with the proper present tense form of **haben** or **sein** (present perfect), or with a past tense form of **haben** or

sein (pluperfect). The participle almost always occurs at the end of its sentence or clause. Note carefully the English equivalents of the examples below and in the Variations.

Present Perfect

Wir haben Karten gespielt.	*We played cards. (We've played cards.)*
Ich habe Wein getrunken.	*I drank wine. (I've drunk wine.)*
Ich habe mir die Hände gewaschen.	*I washed my hands. (I've washed my hands.)*
Er is zu Hause geblieben.	*He stayed at home. (He's stayed at home.)*
Hans ist nicht ausgegangen.	*Hans didn't go out. (Hans hasn't gone out.)*
Bist du in Berlin gewesen?	*Were you in Berlin? (Have you been in Berlin?)*

Pluperfect

Wir hatten Karten gespielt.	*We had played cards.*
Ich hatte Wein getrunken.	*I'd drunk wine.*
Ich hatte mir die Hände gewaschen.	*I had washed my hands.*
Er war zu Hause geblieben.	*He had stayed at home.*
Hans war nicht ausgegangen.	*Hans hadn't gone out.*
Warst du in Berlin gewesen?	*Had you been in Berlin?*

E. Bitten and Fragen—*ask*

Bitten is used in the sense of English "*request*" or "*ask for,*" while **fragen** is used in the sense of English "*inquire.*" **Bitten** is often used with the preposition **um,** just as we use "*for*" in the expression "*ask for.*"

Sie hat ihren Mann etwas gefragt.	*She asked her husband something.*
Sie hat ihren Mann um etwas gebeten.	*She asked her husband for something.*

PATTERN PRACTICES

I. *Answer in the affirmative:*

Hat er Klavier gespielt?	Ja, er hat Klavier gespielt.
Fußball	Fußball
gut	gut
Haben Sie sich gut unterhalten?	ich habe mich gut unterhalten.
schon rasiert?	mich schon rasiert.
schon die Haare gekämmt?	mir schon die Haare gekämmt.
die Hände gewaschen?	die Hände gewaschen.
Hast du Wein getrunken?	ich habe Wein getrunken.
Bier	Bier
Milch	Milch
Hat sie Wasser getrunken?	sie hat Wasser getrunken.
ein paar Lieder gesungen?	ein paar Lieder gesungen.
ein bißchen getanzt?	bißchen getanzt.
geplaudert?	geplaudert.
Habt ihr ein bißchen gearbeitet?	wir haben ein bißchen gearbeitet.
schon lange	schon lange
mit ihnen gesprochen?	mit ihnen gesprochen.
zu Mittag gegessen?	zu Mittag gegessen.
zu Abend	zu Abend
um sieben Uhr gefrühstückt?	um sieben Uhr gefrühstückt.

II. *Answer in the negative:*

Ist er nach Amerika gefahren?	Nein, er ist nicht nach Amerika gefahren.
Deutschland	Deutschland
in die Stadt gegangen?	in die Stadt gegangen.
auf sein Zimmer	auf sein Zimmer

Sind Sie nach Hause gelaufen?			Nein, ich bin nicht nach Hause gelaufen.		
sie Ingenieure geworden?			sie sind keine Ingenieure geworden.		
Ärzte			Ärzte		
Lehrer			Lehrer		
Studenten			Studenten		
Bist du lange dort gewesen?			ich bin nicht lange dort gewesen.		
in der Stadt			in der Stadt		
Bist du lange dort gewesen?			Nein, ich bin nicht lange dort gewesen.		
hier			hier		
zu Hause			zu Hause		
bei der Arbeit			bei der Arbeit		
in der Schule			in der Schule		

III. *Complete the statements, using* **wir** *as the subject, and using the present perfect tense:*

Sie spielen	jetzt Karten,		aber wir haben schon Karten			gespielt.
	Fußball,			Fußball		
trinken	Wein,			Wein		getrunken.
	Milch,			Milch		
	Bier,			Bier		
	Wasser,			Wasser		
essen	zu Abend,			zu Abend		gegessen.
Er hört sich	Schallplatten an,		uns	schon Schallplatten angehört.		
erzählt __	Geschichten,		__	Geschichten schon erzählt.		
schaut sich	einen Film an,		uns	einen Film schon angeschaut.		
lernt __	seine Aufgabe,		__	unsere Aufgabe schon gelernt.		

IV. *Complete the statements, using the present perfect and* **er** *as the subject:*

Wir geben	heute eine	Party,	aber er hat gestern eine Party gegeben.	
sprechen	über	Politik,	über Politik gesprochen.	
plaudern	mit	ihr,	mit ihr geplaudert.	

Sie	arbeitet heute	lange	Stunden,	aber er hat gestern	lange Stunden gearbeitet.
	geht	aus,		ist	ausgegangen.
		ins	Wasser,		ins Wasser gegangen.
		schwimmen,			schwimmen gegangen.
		spazieren,			spazieren gegangen.
Du	verbringst	einen lustigen Abend,		hat	einen lustigen Abend verbracht.
		einen gemütlichen Abend,			einen gemütlichen Abend verbracht.
	besuchst	ein paar Freunde,			ein paar Freunde besucht.

V. *Answer in the negative, using the present perfect:*

Gehen	Sie heute	ins Kino?	Nein, ich bin gestern ins Kino	gegangen.
		schwimmen?		schwimmen
Fahren	Sie	nach Berlin?		nach Berlin	gefahren.
		Heidelberg?		Heidelberg
		Hause?		Hause
		in die Stadt?		in die Stadt
Bleiben	Sie	hier?		hier geblieben.
		zu Hause?		zu Hause geblieben.
Werden	Sie morgen	in Berlin sein?		in Berlin gewesen.
		zu Hause		zu Hause
Wird	er	morgen zu Hause sein?	er ist gestern zu Hause gewesen.
	sie		sie ist
		hierher kommen?	
	er	seine Aufgabe lernen?	
		eine Party geben?	
		zu Hause bleiben?	
		einen langen Brief schreiben?	

VI. *Answer in the affirmative, using the present perfect:*

| Waschen | Sie sich die Hände? | Ich habe mir | die Hände schon gewaschen. |
| Kämmen | die Haare? | | die Haare | gekämmt. |

Stellen	Sie sich unter die Brause?	Ich habe mich schon unter die Brause gestellt.
Waschen	sich?	gewaschen.
Trinken	— Milch?	schon — Milch getrunken.
	— Wein?	— Wein
Gehen	spazieren?	bin spazieren gegangen.
	schwimmen?	schwimmen
Spielen	Fußball?	
	Klavier?	
Frühstücken Sie?		
Essen	Sie etwas?	

VII. *Complete the statements in the pluperfect, using the suggested subject and* **vorgestern** *as the time adverb:*

Ich	habe	gestern meine Aufgabe gelernt,	(er)	aber er	hatte vorgestern seine Aufgabe	gelernt.
Hans hat		früh zu Mittag gegessen,	(Lena)	Lena hatte	früh zu Mittag	gegessen.
Du	bist	in Heidelberg gewesen,	(wir)	wir waren	in Heidelberg	gewesen.
Ich	habe	das alte Lied gesungen,	(ihr)	ihr hattet	das alte Lied	gesungen.
Wir	sind	in die Stadt gegangen,	(Sie)	Sie waren	in die Stadt	gegangen.
Sie	hat	mit ihm gesprochen,	(er)	er hatte	mit ihm	gesprochen.
Wir	haben	Fußball gespielt,	(du)	du hattest	Fußball	gespielt.
Er	hat ihr	die Stadt gezeigt,	(ihr)	ihr hattet ihr	die Stadt	gezeigt.

VIII. *Answer in the negative, using the pluperfect:*

Lernte er gestern seine Aufgabe?	Nein, er hatte schon vorgestern seine Aufgabe gelernt.
Waren Sie gestern in Heidelberg?	ich war in Heidelberg gewesen.
Gingen sie gestern in die Stadt?	sie waren in die Stadt gegangen.
Spieltest du gestern Fußball?	ich hatte Fußball gespielt.
Sprach er gestern mit euch?	er hatte mit uns gesprochen.
Hörte er sich gestern Schallplatten an?	er hatte sich Schallplatten angehört.
Erzählten Sie gestern eine Geschichte?	ich hatte — eine Geschichte erzählt.
Sahst du gestern diese häßlichen Gebäude?	diese häßlichen Gebäude gesehen.
Wart ihr gestern in der Kirche?	wir waren in der Kirche gewesen.

IX. *In your response, reverse the subject and object, keeping tense constant:*

Hat er Sie eingeladen, mit ins Kino zu gehen?	Nein, ich habe ihn eingeladen, mit ins Kino zu gehen.
Hattet ihr Herrn Schulz gebeten, euch das Buch zu geben?	Herr Schulz hatte uns gebeten, ihm das Buch zu geben.
Haben Sie ihm mit seiner Aufgabe geholfen?	er hat mir mit meiner Aufgabe geholfen.
Hast du ihm zugehört?	zugehört.
Hat sie euch geantwortet?	wir haben ihr geantwortet.
Sieht er uns?	sehen ihn.
Wollen Sie ihm die Stadt zeigen?	er will mir die Stadt zeigen.
Dürfen	darf
Müssen	muß
Sollen	soll
Werden	wird

X. *Answer with the present perfect:*

Wann soll er dahin fliegen?	Er ist schon dahin geflogen.	Wann soll er sich rasieren?
hier sitzen?	hat hier gesessen.	sich setzen?
hier wohnen?	hat hier gewohnt.	sich anziehen?
da studieren?	hat da studiert.	sich ausruhen?
dahin reisen?		

XI. *Answer with the present perfect:*

Wann sollen wir tanzen?	Wir haben schon getanzt.	Wann sollen Sie fragen?
soll er aufstehen?	Er ist aufgestanden.	soll es regnen?
soll sie	Sie ist	soll er aufwachen?
sollen wir laufen?	wir sind gelaufen.	soll sie
soll er baden?		soll es frieren?
soll es schneien?		
sollen wir beginnen?		
soll er		
sollen sie schlafen?		

XII. *Answer with the present perfect:*

Wann wird er es finden?	Er hat es schon gefunden.
soll er	

rauchen?		geraucht.
zeigen?		gezeigt.
bringen?		gebracht.
aufmachen?		aufgemacht.
ihr helfen?	ihr	geholfen.
ihr verzeihen?	ihr	verziehen.
sie treffen?	sie	getroffen.
es lesen?		
ihr antworten?		
es wiederholen?		
es tun?		
sie rufen?		

XIII. *Write a German composition, contrasting yesterday's real or imaginary activities with those of the preceding day. Make use of the past tense (imperfect), present perfect, and pluperfect tense to bring out these contrasts. Your composition should be at least 200 words in length. Keep thinking in German; avoid translating English thoughts into German.*

VOCABULARY

aufregend exciting
sich an-hören listen to
sich an-schauen watch, look at
aus-gehen, ging aus, ist ausgegangen go out
besuchen visit, attend
bitten, a, e* to ask
   bitten (*acc.*) **zu** (*infin.*) ask someone to do something
   bitten (*acc.*) **um** ask someone for something
einer, eine, ein(e)s one
ein-laden, u, a, ä invite

das Fernsehen, -s television
   sich Fernsehen anschauen watch television
die Fernsehsendung, -en television program
der Film, -s, -e movie
der Fußball, -s, ⸚e football
das Fußballspiel, -s, -e football game
gemütlich comfortable, pleasant, nice
die Geschichte, -n story; history
hübsch pretty
interessant interesting

---

* Henceforth we list the stem vowel of the perfect participle as the third entry (after the vowel of the past tense) for strong verbs.

ja   certainly
die Karte, -en   card
  Karten spielen   play cards
das Klavier, -s, -e   piano
lachen   laugh
das Lied, -s, -er   song
lustig   enjoyable
die Milch   milk
die Musik   music
die Party, -s   party
plaudern   chat
die Politik(s)   politics
die Post   mail

das Radio, -s, -s   radio
die Schallplatte, -n   phonograph record
singen, a, u   sing
spielen   play
tanzen   dance
die Verabredung, -en   date, appointment
verbringen, verbrachte, verbracht   spend (time)
die Vogelstimme, -n   voice like a bird
das Wasser, -s   water
der Wein, -es, -e   wine
der Witz, -es, -e   joke
zu-hören (*dat.*)   listen to

Lesson XII

BASIC SENTENCES

Although Johannes' sister teaches English and French,	(1)	**Obwohl Johannes' Schwester Englisch und Französisch lehrt,**
he himself isn't very good at languages.	(2)	**ist er selbst in Sprachen nicht sehr gut.**
He studied English for five years at school,	(3)	**Er hat Englisch fünf Jahre lang in der Schule gelernt,**
but he couldn't retain anything.	(4)	**aber er konnte nichts behalten.**

But since he wanted to go to (attend) the University,	(5)	**Da er aber die Universität besuchen wollte,**
he had to pass the exams in foreign languages.	(6)	**mußte er die Prüfungen in Fremdsprachen bestehen.**
So he went to his sister,	(7)	**Also ging er zu seiner Schwester,**
and she gave him lessons/instruction/.	(8)	**und sie gab ihm Unterricht.**

Well, can you guess/just guess/ what came of that?

(9) {Nun, raten Sie mal, was daraus geworden ist?

He just barely/with difficulty and hardship/passed the examinations.

(10) Er hat die Prüfungen mit Mühe und Not bestanden.

On the other hand, he was always good in mathematics,

(11) Dagegen war er in Mathematik immer gut

and in the natural sciences—physics, chemistry and biology.

(12) und in den Naturwissenschaften—Physik, Chemie und Biologie.

(9)

(10)

(11)

(12)

In these subjects his grades were always good.	(13)	**In diesen Fächern waren seine Noten immer gut.**
When he graduated from secondary school,/when he was finished/	(14)	**Als er mit der Oberschule fertig war,**
he was admitted to the University.	(15)	**wurde er zur Universität zugelassen.**
Now he's studying very hard.	(16)	**Jetzt arbeitet er sehr viel.**
You have to apply yourself, you know/One must be very industrious/,	(17–18)	**Man muß nämlich sehr fleißig sein,**
in order to become a physicist.		**um Physiker zu werden.**

(13)

(14)

(15)

(16)

(17-18)

VARIATIONS

Can you tell me what he's doing?
        he did?
           can do?
I can't tell you what he's doing.
        he did.
         will do.
Tell me what you studied in high school.
Tell me what courses you're taking/you've registered for/.
I'm studying mathematics.
What kind of mathematics—Arithmetic, Geometry, or Trigonometry?
I'm studying differential calculus.
I'm learning a lot.
You have to study hard in order to become a physicist.
He has to study hard in order to become a doctor.

Können Sie mir sagen, was er tut?
                getan hat?
                tun kann?
Ich kann Ihnen nicht sagen, was er tut.
                getan hat.
                tun wird.
Sage mir, was du auf der Mittelschule gelernt hast.
Sage mir, welche Fächer du belegt hast.
Ich studiere Mathematik.
Was für Mathematik—Arithmetik, Geometrie oder Trigonometrie?
Ich studiere Differentialrechnung.
Ich lerne viel.
Man muß schwer arbeiten, um Physiker zu werden.
Er muß viel arbeiten, um Arzt zu werden.

He had to study hard in order to become a lawyer.	**Er mußte viel arbeiten, um Rechtsanwalt zu werden.**
We had to study hard in order to become engineers.	**Wir mußten fleißig arbeiten, um Ingenieure zu werden.**
They had to study hard in order to become teachers.	**Sie mußten fleißig arbeiten, um Lehrer zu werden.**
You had to study, Hans.	**Du mußtest arbeiten, Hans.**
children.	**Ihr mußtet arbeiten, Kinder.**
Were you able to work?	**Konnten Sie arbeiten?**
No, I couldn't work.	**Nein, ich konnte nicht arbeiten.**
Was Hans able to work?	**Konnte Hans arbeiten?**
We weren't able to work.	**Wir konnten nicht arbeiten.**
Were you able to work, Peter?	**Konntest du arbeiten, Peter?**
children?	**Konntet ihr arbeiten, Kinder?**
Nobody was able to work.	**Niemand konnte arbeiten.**
What subjects did you want to study?	**Welche Fächer wollten Sie studieren?**
We wanted to study philosophy.	**Wir wollten Philosophie studieren.**
art.	**Kunst**
music.	**Musik**
geology.	**Geologie**
geography.	**Erdkunde**
German literature.	**deutsche Literatur**
psychology.	**Psychologie**
I wanted to study medicine.	**Ich wollte Medizin studieren.**
nursing.	**Krankenpflege**
law.	**Jura**
history.	**Geschichte**
engineering.	**Ingenieurwesen**

He didn't want to study mathematics.	**Er wollte keine Mathematik studieren.**
music.	**Musik**
geology.	**Geologie**
engineering.	**kein Ingenieurwesen**
education.	**keine Pädagogik**
English.	**kein Englisch**
German literature.	**keine deutsche Literatur**
English literature.	**englische Literatur**

What did you want to be?   **Was wollten Sie werden?**

I wanted to be a doctor,   **Ich wollte Arzt werden,**

but now I'm interested in   **aber jetzt interessiere ich mich für**

music.	**Musik.**
art.	**Kunst.**
mathematics.	**Mathematik.**
politics.	**Staatskunde.**
nursing.	**Krankenpflege.**

We wanted to be engineers,   **Wir wollten Ingenieure werden,**

but now we're teaching at a university.   **aber jetzt lehren wir an einer Universität.**

                 high school.   **aber jetzt unterrichten wir an einer Oberschule.**

Where were you supposed to go?   **Wohin solltest du gehen?**

I was supposed to go to a lecture.   **Ich sollte in eine Vorlesung gehen.**

           to school.   **zur Schule**

We were supposed to go to the University.   **Wir sollten auf die Universität gehen.**

                German class.   **zur Deutschstunde**

I didn't know that he's a professor.   **Ich wußte nicht, daß er Professor ist.**

           studying German.   **Deutsch studiert.**

           his major is physics.   **sein Hauptfach Physik ist.**

Did you know that he got an A/a one/?   Wußten Sie, daß er eine 1 bekommen hat?
                          a good grade?   eine gute Note
                          a poor grade?   eine schlechte Note
                          passed the exam?   die Prüfung bestanden hat?
                          flunked the exam?   in der Prüfung durchgefallen ist?

We were allowed to   take the course.   Wir durften   das Fach belegen.
I wasn't allowed to   Ich durfte nicht
He wasn't allowed to   Er durfte nicht

I like German because it's easy.   Ich mag Deutsch, weil es leicht ist.
I don't like French, because it's hard.   Ich mag Französisch nicht, weil es schwer ist.

Because it's easy, I like German.   Weil es leicht ist, mag ich Deutsch.
Because it's hard, I don't like French.   Weil es schwer ist, mag ich Französisch nicht.

Although he studies a lot, he doesn't get good grades.   Obwohl er viel arbeitet, bekommt er keine guten Noten.
Although he works hard, he's never tired.   Obwohl er schwer arbeitet, ist er nie müde.

He doesn't get good grades, although he studies a lot.   Er bekommt keine guten Noten, obwohl er schwer arbeitet.
He's never tired, although he works hard.   Er ist nie müde, obwohl er schwer arbeitet.

If he studies a lot, he gets good grades.   Wenn er viel arbeitet, bekommt er gute Noten.

If he works hard, he's tired.   Wenn er schwer arbeitet, ist er müde.

He gets good grades if he studies a lot.   Er bekommt gute Noten, wenn er viel arbeitet.

He's tired if he works hard.   Er ist müde, wenn er schwer arbeitet.

STRUCTURE

A. Indirect Statements and Questions; Subordinate Word Order

Note the subject-verb relationship in the English question

What $\boxed{\text{is}}$ $\boxed{\text{he}}$ doing?
verb subj.

Now, if we begin the same question with an introductory phrase, such as "*Can you tell me...*," this relationship is changed.

Can you tell me what he is doing?
subj. verb

Such a question is called an *indirect question*. A possible reply to this question has the same subject-verb relationship.

No, I can't tell you what he is doing.
subj. verb

Notice that this sentence contains two subjects and two verbs, and that the whole sentence consists of two "thought-groups," each having a subject and a verb.

(1) No, I can't tell you   (2) what he is doing.
subj. verb   subj. verb

Such thought-groups are called *clauses*. In the sentence above, clause (1) can stand by itself as a sentence, and is called the *main clause*. Clause (2) cannot stand by itself and is called a *subordinate clause*. A sentence consisting of a main clause and a subordinate clause is called a *complex sentence*. German also has complex sentences, similarly defined. In a German subordinate clause the *finite verb* is almost always the *last element*. (This does not violate our rule about the finite verb in second place, since subordinate clauses are not sentences.) In a German complex sentence, the two clauses are separated by a pause in speech, and by a comma in writing. Notice carefully the placement of the finite verbs in the indirect statements and questions which follow.

Können Sie mir sagen, was er tut?
Ich kann Ihnen nicht sagen, was er tut.
Können Sie mir sagen, was er getan hat?
Ich kann Ihnen nicht sagen, was er getan hat.

In German this arrangement with the finite verb at the end of the subordinate clause is called *subordinate word order*.

B. Coordinating and Subordinating Conjunctions

Conjunctions are words used to connect clauses or parts of clauses. Typical English conjunctions are "*and*," "*or*," "*but*," "*if*," "*whenever*," and "*although*." In speaking of conjunctions which connect clauses, we distinguish between two types:

COORDINATING CONJUNCTIONS such as "*and*" and "*but*," which must be placed *between* the clauses they connect.

SUBORDINATING CONJUNCTIONS such as "*because*" and "*if*," which can be placed *either between* the clauses or *before* the first clause.

In the following English examples, notice that the clauses connected by subordinating conjunctions can be reversed:

> *I like to swim <u>because</u> it's good exercise.*
> *<u>Because</u> it's good exercise, I like to swim.*

whereas the two clauses in this sentence cannot be reversed:

> *I like to swim, <u>and</u> it's good exercise.*

German also has coordinating and subordinating conjunctions. Typical coordinating conjunctions are **und, oder, aber, sondern,** and **denn.** Typical subordinating conjunctions are **weil, wenn, obwohl,** and **daß.** German subordinating conjunctions are always followed by subordinate word order; that is, they begin subordinate clauses. The German examples which follow parallel the English sentences just given.

> **Ich mag Deutsch, weil es leicht ist.**
>
> **Weil es leicht ist, mag ich Deutsch.**
>
> **Ich mag Deutsch, und es ist leicht.**

In the German complex sentence the placement of the finite verbs is of utmost importance. In almost all cases, the finite verb of the subordinate clause is the last element in its clause, as we have said. The *main finite verb* (i.e. the finite verb of the main clause) is as usual the second element in the sentence.

> **Ich mag Deutsch, weil es leicht ist.**

In this sentence **mag** is the main finite verb, and is obviously in second place. Now if we reverse the clauses,

> **Weil es leicht ist, mag ich Deutsch**

mag is still the main finite verb and is *still in second place in the sentence!* The subordinate clause cannot be broken up and therefore must be regarded as one element of the sentence as a whole. If we think of this sentence as a set of "slots," we will see that the second "slot" is always occupied by the main finite verb.

TABLE XII A

1	2	3	4
Ich	mag	Deutsch,	weil es leicht ist.
Weil es leicht ist,	mag	ich	Deutsch.
Deutsch	mag	ich,	weil es leicht ist.

Notice that the other elements in the sentence seem to be able to *change places, but* **mag,** *the main finite verb, remains fixed. The main finite verb of a German simple or complex sentence is the anchor and the pivot of the entire sentence.* Study carefully the examples of complex sentences in this and in the following lessons and notice how the main finite verb acts in this function.

C. Past-Present Verbs

We have been meeting a group of German verbs which have -Ø endings in the **ich** and **er** forms of the present tense. These verbs are **dürfen, können, mögen, müssen, sollen, wissen,** and **wollen.** The present tense singular of these verbs closely resembles the past tense singular of the strong verbs; the present tense forms were once past tense forms. For this reason these verbs are often called the *past-present* verbs.

D. The Past Tense of Past-Present Verbs

The past-present verbs have the same past tense endings as the weak verbs, but all of them except **sollen** and **wollen** have stem changes.

TABLE XII B

Name form	Present and Past forms	Examples
dürf-en	ich, er, sie, es darf-Ø	Er darf etwas schreiben. *He may write something.*
	ich, er, sie, es durf-te	Er durfte etwas schreiben. *He was allowed to write something.*
	du darf-st du durf-test	
	wir, Sie, sie dürf-en wir, Sie, sie durf-ten	
	ihr dürf-t ihr durf-tet	

TABLE XII B (continued)

Name form	Present and Past forms	Examples
können	ich, er, sie, es kann-Ø ich, er, sie, es konn-te	Ich kann das nicht tun. *I can't do that.* Ich konnte das nicht tun. *I couldn't do that.*
	du kann-st du konn-test	
	wir, Sie, sie könn-en wir, Sie, sie konn-ten	
	ihr könn-t ihr konn-tet	
mög-en	ich, er, sie, es mag-Ø ich, er, sie, es moch-te	Ich mag ihn. *I like him.* Ich mochte ihn. *I liked him.*
	du-mag-st du moch-test	
	wir, Sie, sie mög-en wir, Sie sie moch-ten	
	ihr mög-t ihr moch-tet	
müss-en	ich, er, sie, es muß-Ø ich, er, sie, es muß-te	Ich muß nach Hause gehen. *I have to go home.* Ich mußte nach Hause gehen. *I had to go home.*
	du muß-t du muß-test	
	wir, Sie, sie müss-en wir, Sie, sie muß-ten	
	ihr muß-t ihr muß-tet	

TABLE XII B (continued)

Name form	Present and Past forms	Examples
wiss-en	ich, er, sie, es weiß-Ø ich, er, sie, es wuß-te	Sie weiß die Antwort. *She knows the answer.* Sie wußte die Antwort. *She knew the answer.*
	du-weiß-t du wuß-test	
	wir, Sie, sie wiss-en wir, Sie, sie wuß-ten	
	ihr wiss-t ihr wuß-tet	
soll-en	ich, er, sie, es soll-Ø ich, er, sie, es soll-te	Ich soll essen. *I'm supposed to eat.* Ich sollte essen. *I was supposed to eat.*
	du soll-st du soll-test	
	wir, Sie, sie soll-en wir, Sie, sie soll-ten	
	ihr soll-t ihr soll-tet	
woll-en	ich, er, sie, es will-Ø ich, er, sie, es woll-te	Er will nicht aufstehen. *He doesn't want to get up.* Er wollte nicht aufstehen. *He didn't want to get up.*
	du will-st du woll-test	
	wir, Sie, sie woll-en wir, Sie, sie woll-ten	
	ihr woll-t ihr woll-tet	

The perfect participles and the present perfect and pluperfect tenses of these verbs will be discussed later.

E. Um. . .zu. . .*in order to. . .*

In this German expression, **zu** is always followed by the name form of a verb. While **zu** may be the next word after **um,** any number of words may come between them. Notice that **um** is not regarded as a preposition in this expression, and therefore has no object; rather, **um** can be said to be in this case a special conjunction. The expression including **um, zu** and the name form of a verb is always separated in writing from the rest of the sentence by a comma. Such phrases, however, do not usually occur at the beginning of a question.

> **Man muß nämlich sehr fleißig sein, um Physiker zu werden.**
> **Um Physiker zu werden, muß man nämlich sehr fleißig sein.**
> **Muß man viel arbeiten, um Ingenieur zu werden?**

PATTERN PRACTICES

I. *Change each question to an indirect question, using* **Können Sie mir sagen** *as an introductory phrase:*

Warum ist er in Sprachen nicht sehr gut?	Können Sie mir sagen, warum er in Sprachen nicht sehr gut ist?
Wer gab ihm Unterricht?	wer ihm Unterricht gab?
Warum mußte er die Prüfungen bestehen?	warum er die Prüfungen bestehen mußte?
Wann durfte er auf die Universität gehen?	wann er auf die Universität gehen durfte?
Wie lange hat er Englisch studiert?	wie lange er Englisch studiert hat?
Wer will Physiker werden?	wer Physiker werden will?
Was lernen Sie auf der Mittelschule?	was Sie auf der Mittelschule lernen?

II. *Answer the following questions using* **um zu** *plus the suggested infinitive:*

Warum ist er zur Gaststätte gegangen?	(essen)	Er ist zur Gaststätte gegangen, um zu essen.
Warum ist er in die Bibliothek gegangen?	(lesen)	Er ist in die Bibliothek gegangen, um zu lesen.
Warum kamen Sie nach Hause?	(helfen)	Ich kam nach Hause, um zu helfen.
Warum wäscht er sich die Hände?	(essen)	Er wäscht sich die Hände, um zu essen.
Warum geht ihr auf die Universität?	(studieren)	Wir gehen auf die Universität, um zu studieren.
Warum muß sie früh aufstehen?	(sich anziehen)	Sie muß früh aufstehen, um sich anzuziehen.
Warum muß er aufstehen?	(sich rasieren)	Er muß früh aufstehen, um sich zu rasieren.

III. *Answer the following in the negative:*

Durfte er in die Schule gehen?	Nein, er durfte nicht in die Schule gehen.
Konnte er Physiker werden?	Nein, er konnte kein Physiker werden.
Mochte er den Professor?	Nein, er mochte den Professor nicht.
Mußte er die Prüfungen in Fremdsprachen bestehen?	Nein, er mußte keine Prüfungen in Fremdsprachen bestehen.
Sollte er die Differentialrechnung studieren?	Nein, er sollte keine Differentialrechnung studieren.
Wollte er Rechtsanwalt werden?	Nein, er wollte kein Rechtsanwalt werden.
Konnte er schwimmen gehen?	Nein, er konnte nicht schwimmen gehen.
Durfte er ins Kino gehen?	Nein er durfte nicht ins Kino gehen.

IV. *Answer in the past tense with* **früher:**

Muß er arbeiten?	Nein, aber er mußte früher arbeiten.
Darfst du hier rauchen?	Nein, aber ich durfte früher hier rauchen.
Kann sie zur Schule gehen?	
Mag er Brot?	
Soll er zur Bibliothek gehen?	
Will er Ingenieur werden?	
Darfst du ins Kino gehen?	

V. *Change the subject in the following sentences and substitute pronouns for the object whenever possible:*

Er konnte Deutsch lesen,	(ich)	und ich konnte es auch lesen.
Wir mußten fleißig arbeiten,	(du)	und du mußtest auch fleißig arbeiten.
Ich sollte Frühstück essen,	(ihr)	
Sie wollten Französisch sprechen,	(wir)	
Du wolltest Physiker werden,	(er)	
Ihr durftet zur Universität gehen,	(Sie)	
Sie wußte die richtige Antwort,	(er)	
Wir wußten, was er wollte,	(du)	

VI. *Change all the above sentences to the present tense and translate.*

VII. *Combine each of the following pairs of sentences using the suggested conjunction:*

Ich mag Deutsch. Es ist leicht.	(weil)	Ich mag Deutsch, weil es leicht ist.
Er wollte Arzt werden. Es war sehr schwer.	(obwohl)	Er wollte Arzt werden, obwohl es sehr schwer war.
Du weißt, er hat eine 1 bekommen.	(daß)	Du weißt, daß er eine 1 bekommen hat.
Ich weiß nicht. Er kommt.	(wann)	Ich weiß nicht, wann er kommt.
Ich lese Französisch. Ich gehe in die Bibliothek.	(wenn)	Ich lese Französisch, wenn ich in die Bibliothek gehe.
Wir wissen. Er ist Rechtsanwalt.	(daß)	Wir wissen, daß er Rechtsanwalt ist.

VIII. *Begin each of the preceding sentences with the subordinate clause:* z.B.* **Weil es leicht ist, mag ich Deutsch.**

IX. *Answer each of the following questions, using the suggested verb:*

Warum lernten Sie Deutsch?	(wollen)	Ich lernte Deutsch, weil ich es wollte.
Warum gingen Sie in die Vorlesung?	(müssen)	Ich ging in die Vorlesung, weil ich es mußte.
Warum arbeiteten Sie fleißig?	(wollen)	Ich arbeitete fleißig, weil ich es wollte.
Warum standen Sie so früh auf?	(sollen)	Ich stand so früh auf, weil ich es sollte.
Warum fuhren Sie so schnell?	(dürfen)	Ich fuhr so schnell, weil ich es durfte.
Warum lesen Sie kein Französisch?	(können)	Ich lese kein Französisch, weil ich es nicht kann.

X. *Translate the above sentences.*

XI. *Write about school: what courses you have taken and are now taking; what subjects you are good at, your grades, and so on.*

VOCABULARY

die Arithmetik Arithmetic
behalten, ie, a (ä) retain, remember
das Beispiel, -s, -e example
    zum Beispiel (abbr. z.B.) for example, e.g.
bekommen, a, o receive, get
belegen take (a course), register for
bestehen, bestand, bestanden pass (a course)
die Biologie biology
die Chemie chemistry

da since (= because), as, inasmuch as
dagegen on the other hand
daß that (*conj.*)
die Differentialrechnung differential calculus
durch-fallen, ie, ist a, (ä) fail, flunk
eine eins a "one," an A (mark in school)
englisch English (*adj.*)
die Erdkunde geography
das Fach, -es, ⸚er subject, field of study

---

* z.B.=zum Beispiel, "for example."

fertig   finished; ready
    mit...fertig sein   be finished with...
fleißig   industrious
das Französisch   French (language)
die Fremdsprache, -n   foreign language
die Geologie   geology
die Geometrie   geometry
das Hauptfach, -s, ⁓er   major subject (course of study)
das Ingenieurwesen, -s   engineering
sich interessieren für   be interested in
(die) Jura (*pl.*)   (study of) law
die Krankenpflege   nursing
die Kunst, ⁓e   art
lehren   teach
leicht   easy
die Literatur, -en   literature
mal   once
die Mathematik (*singular*)   mathematics
die Medizin   medicine (the subject; also "medicament")
die Mittelschule, -en   high school
mit Mühe und Not   with difficulty and hardship
die Naturwissenschaft, -en   natural science
die Note, -n   grade, mark
nun   well (*interj.*)

die Oberschule, -n   high school
obwohl   although
die Pädagogik   education
die Philosophie, -n   philosophy
die Physik (*singular*)   physics
der Physiker, -s   physicist
die Prüfung, -en   exam
die Psychologie   psychology
raten, ie, a, (ä)   guess
das Recht, -s, -e   law
schwer   hard (difficult)
selbst   oneself (himself, myself, *etc.*)
die Sprache, -n   language
die Staatskunde   politics
die Trigonometrie   Trigonometry
um...zu...   in order to...
der Unterricht   instruction
unterrichten   instruct, teach
weil   because
welcher, welche, welches?   which? what?
wenn   if
zu-lassen, ie, a (ä)   admit (permit entrance)
    zugelassen werden   be admitted (to a University)

Lesson XIII

BASIC SENTENCES

What must you do in order to speak German perfectly/ without errors/?	**(1)** **Was muß man machen, um Deutsch ohne Fehler zu sprechen?**
Naturally, the best thing is to be born in Germany/if one is born in Germany/.	**(2)** **Natürlich ist es am besten, wenn man in Deutschland geboren ist.**
However, even though you haven't/one hasn't/even seen Germany, it is still possible.	**(3–4)** **Aber selbst wenn man Deutschland nicht einmal gesehen hat, ist es doch möglich.**

You have to/one has to/find good teachers and study many years/long years/. (5)

Peter began German only a couple of years ago, at the university. (6)

His teacher had him study a great deal/very much/, but he loved it from the beginning /liked to do it/. (7) (8)

(5) Man muß gute Lehrer finden und lange Jahre arbeiten.

(6) Peter hat <u>erst vor ein paar Jahren</u> begonnen, auf der Universität Deutsch zu lernen.

(7) Sein Lehrer ließ ihn sehr viel arbeiten,

(8) aber von Anfang an machte er es gern.

(5)

(6)

(7)

(8)

(9)

(10)

(11-12)

(12-a)

He had already studied other languages, (9)	**Er hatte schon andere Sprachen gelernt,**
and German was therefore not at all difficult for him. (10)	**und daher war Deutsch gar nicht schwer für ihn.**
When he arrived in Germany, he already spoke it pretty (11–12)	**Als er in Deutschland ankam, sprach er es schon**
fluently, and understood everything,	**ziemlich fließend und verstand alles,**
if people (one) didn't speak too fast. (12a)	**wenn man nicht zu schnell sprach.**

Since then he's been speaking only German, and hasn't (13–14) **Seitdem spricht er nur Deutsch und spricht kein Wort Englisch** spoken a word of English (any more). **mehr.**

Now he speaks almost without an American accent/without (15) **Jetzt spricht er beinahe ohne amerikanischen Akzent.** American accent/.

(13)

(14)

(15)

VARIATIONS

That is hot	coffee.	Das ist heißer	Kaffee
	hard work.		schwere	Arbeit.
	poor beer.		schlechtes Bier.

Those are similar mistakes.

Das sind ähnliche Fehler.

Without hot coffee　　　it is impossible.
　　　hard work
　　　pleasant weather
　　　good teachers

Ohne heißen　　　Kaffee　ist es unmöglich.
　　　schwere　　　Arbeit
　　　angenehmes Wetter
　　　gute　　　　Lehrer

With hot　　　coffee　everything is possible.
　　hard　　work
　　pleasant weather
　　good　　teachers

Mit heißem　　　Kaffee　ist alles möglich.
　　schwerer　　　Arbeit
Bei angenehmem Wetter
Mit guten　　　Lehrern

During bad weather
　　　hot

Bei schlechtem Wetter
　　　heißem

Do you like to swim in cold water?

Schwimmen Sie gern in kaltem Wasser?

No, I don't like to swim in cold water.

Nein, ich schwimme nicht gern in kaltem Wasser.

You can/one can/drink good beer in German restaurants.

Man kann in deutschen Gaststätten gutes Bier trinken.

You find wonderful old wines here in the cellar.

Man findet wunderbare alte Weine hier im Keller.

However, children have to drink good milk.

Kinder müssen aber gute Milch trinken.

Does he speak fluent German?

Spricht er fließend Deutsch?

No, he speaks poor German.

Nein, er spricht schlecht Deutsch.

He answered in fluent German.

Er hat in fließendem Deutsch geantwortet.

I always stay here during pleasant weather.

Bei angenehmem Wetter bleibe ich immer hier.

You can hear beautiful music in this restaurant.

Man kann in dieser Gaststätte schöne Musik hören.

Peter is studying modern literature, German history and German art.

Peter studiert moderne Literatur, deutsche Geschichte und deutsche Kunst.

Are you very thirsty?

Haben Sie großen Durst?

Are you very hungry?	**Haben Sie großen Hunger?**
Naturally she has short hair.	**Natürlich hat sie kurzes Haar.**
He got to know his friend last week.	**Er hat vorige Woche seinen Freund kennengelernt.**

In order to learn German well,
    you must/you have to, one must/
        have good German lessons.
        try to practice every day.
        go often to the laboratory.
        look up new words in a dictionary.
        study German grammar.
        study German pronunciation.
        converse a lot.
        ask the professor questions.
        think in German.
        learn many sentences by heart.
        repeat over and over again
        /always again repeat/.

Um Deutsch gut zu lernen,
    muß man
        gute Deutschstunden haben.
        versuchen, sich jeden Tag zu üben.
        oft ins Laboratorium gehen.
        neue Wörter in einem Wörterbuch nachschlagen.
        deutsche Grammatik lernen.
        deutsche Aussprache lernen.
        sich viel unterhalten.
        dem Professor Fragen stellen.
        Deutsch denken.
        viele Sätze auswendig lernen.
        immer wieder wiederholen.

You speak slowly but correctly.
      without bad mistakes.
      fluent German.
      without an American accent.
      without great difficulty
            /difficulties/.
      with difficulty
            /difficulties/.

Sie sprechen langsam aber richtig.
      ohne große Fehler.
      fließend Deutsch.
      ohne amerikanischen Akzent.
      ohne große Schwierigkeiten.

      mit Schwierigkeiten.

Our teacher had us practice diligently.
        repeat over and over.
        /always again repeat/
        talk a lot.

Unser Lehrer ließ uns fleißig üben.
        immer wieder wiederholen.

        viel sprechen.

He explained everything to us.	Er erklärte uns alles.
I have learned French.	Ich habe Französisch gelernt.
Spanish.	Spanisch
Italian.	Italienisch
Greek.	Griechisch
Latin.	Latein
Hebrew.	Hebräisch
Russian.	Russisch
What does this word mean?	Was bedeutet dieses Wort?
sentence	dieser Satz?
expression	dieser Ausdruck?
Can you translate this into English?	Können Sie das ins Englische übersetzen?
It's hard to learn German,	Es ist schwer, Deutsch zu lernen,
if one was not born in Germany.	wenn man nicht in Deutschland geboren ist.
one has not studied (did not study) there.	wenn man nicht da studiert hat.
When we arrived there (had arrived there), we wanted to eat dinner.	Als wir da angekommen waren, wollten wir zu Abend essen.
When we had seen our friends, we wanted to eat dinner.	Als wir unsere Freunde gesehen hatten, wollten wir zu Abend essen.
Whether we will study other languages, I can't say.	Ob wir andere Sprachen lernen werden, kann ich nicht sagen.
Whether we will go to Berlin, I can't say.	Ob wir nach Berlin fahren werden, kann ich nicht sagen.
Because our instructor had explained everything to us, it was easy for us.	Weil unser Lehrer uns alles erklärt hatte, war es uns leicht.
Because we had practiced hard, it was easy for us.	Weil wir uns fleißig geübt hatten, war es uns leicht.

STRUCTURE

A. Attributive Adjectives without Articles

Quite often a noun will occur with an attributive adjective but with no article or article-like words preceding it. In such a case the adjective has the same ending that **dieser** would have in the same slot, except that in the genitive masculine and neuter the ending is **-en** instead of **-es.**

TABLE XIII A

Case	Singular			Plural
	Masc.	*Fem.*	*Neut.*	
Nom.	heiß-er Kaffee	{ weiß-e Milch }	{ kalt-es Wasser }	{ alt-e Leute }
Acc.	heiß-en Kaffee			
Dat.	heiß-em Kaffee	{ weiß-er Milch }	kalt-em Wasser	alt-en Leuten
Gen.	heiß-en Kaffees		kalt-en Wassers	alt-er Leute

(handwritten margin notes: "Objects", "objects of prep.", "possessive")

B. Multiple Adjectives

We have noticed how the ending of an attributive adjective is affected by a preceding article or article-like word. Attributive adjectives have no such effect on one another, as can be seen in the following examples.

Ich kenne diese jungen amerikanischen Leute gut.
Ich mag gutes deutsches Bier immer sehr gern.

C. More Subordinating Conjunctions

The following conjunctions, which are used in this lesson, are subordinating:

wenn: *if; when; whenever*   **nachdem:** *after*

als: *when (in the sense of: at that*   **obwohl:** *although*
          moment in the past when)   **weil:** *because*

D. Alles in Double Objects

Like **nichts** and **etwas**, **alles** is always the last element in a double object.

Er erklärte uns alles.   *He explained everything to us.*

PATTERN PRACTICES

I. *Answer in the affirmative, using the adjective to modify the noun:*

Ist	dieser Kaffee	heiß?		Ja, das ist	heißer	Kaffee.
Ist	diese Arbeit	schwer?		Ja, das ist	schwere	Arbeit.
Ist	das Deutsch	schlecht?		Ja, das ist	schlechtes	Deutsch.
	die Milch	gut?			gute	Milch.

Sind die	Lehrer	gut?		Ja, das sind	gute	Lehrer.
Ist der	Wein nicht	wunderbar?		ist	wunderbarer	Wein.
das	Wetter	angenehm?			angenehmes	Wetter.
Sind die	Gebäude	modern?		sind	moderne	Gebäude.
Ist die	Musik	schön?		ist	schöne	Musik.
das	Wasser	kalt?		ist	kaltes	Wasser.

II. *Add to the statement given, using the expression* **"ohne ____ ist es unmöglich"**:

Mit schneller	Arbeit	ist es möglich,		aber ohne schnelle	Arbeit	ist es unmöglich.
Bei schönem	Wetter				schönes	Wetter
Mit guten	Lehrern				gute	Lehrer
kaltem	Wasser				kaltes	Wasser
schwerer	Arbeit				schwere	Arbeit
guten	Büchern				gute	Bücher
alten	Freunden				alte	Freunde
alten	Freundinnen				alte	Freundinnen

III. *Answer in the affirmative, using the expression* **"Um Deutsch richtig zu lernen, muß man"** . . .

Soll man gute Deutschstunden haben?	Um Deutsch richtig zu lernen, muß man gute Deutschstunden haben.
sich jeden Tag üben?	Um sich jeden Tag üben.
oft ins Laboratorium gehen?	Um oft ins Laboratorium gehen.
neue Wörter in einem Wörterbuch nachschlagen?	
deutsche Grammatik lernen?	
sich viel unterhalten?	
Deutsch denken?	
viele Sätze auswendig lernen?	

IV. *Change the given statement into a* **"wenn"** *clause:*

Ich übe mich jeden Tag.	Wenn ich mich jeden Tag übe, ist alles gut.
Man spricht fließend Deutsch.	man fließend Deutsch spricht,
Ich verstehe alles.	ich alles verstehe,
Wir haben gute Deutschstunden.	

Sie sprechen nicht zu schnell.

Ich habe diesen Satz verstanden.

Er fährt jeden Sommer nach Deutschland.

Man hat schon andere Sprachen gelernt.

V. *Change the given statement into a dependent clause, using the conjunction in parentheses* (*keeping the tense constant*):

Ich war um sechs Uhr da angekommen. (als)	Als ich um sechs Uhr da angekommen war, gab es noch viel zu tun.
Er hatte seine Freunde gesehen. (nachdem)	Nachdem er seine Freunde gesehen hatte, gab es noch viel zu tun.
Man studierte moderne Literatur. (nachdem)	Nachdem man moderne Literatur studierte, gab es noch viel zu tun.
Wir werden andere Sprachen lernen. (obwohl)	Obwohl wir andere Sprachen lernen, gibt es noch viel zu tun.
Wir fahren nach Berlin. (wenn)	Wenn wir nach Berlin fahren, wird es noch viel zu tun geben.
Unser Lehrer hat uns nicht alles erklärt. (weil)	Weil unser Lehrer uns nicht alles erklärt hat, gibt es noch viel zu tun.
Wir wollen Deutsch sprechen. (weil)	Weil wir Deutsch sprechen wollen, gibt es noch viel zu tun.
Wir haben uns nicht fleißig geübt. (weil)	Weil wir uns nicht fleißig geübt haben, gibt es noch viel zu tun.

VOCABULARY

der Akzent, -s, -e accent
an:
  am besten best
ander other
Anfang:
  von Anfang an from the beginning
an-kommen, a, ist o arrive
der Ausdruck, -s, ⁓e expression
die Aussprache, -n pronunciation
auswendig lernen learn by heart
bedeuten mean
bei:
  bei schlechtem Wetter in (during) bad weather
beinahe almost
daher therefore
denken, dachte, gedacht think
doch still, yet, even, so, nevertheless
erklären explain

erst first
  erst vor ein paar Jahren (*etc.*) just (only) a couple of years ago
der Fehler, -s, __ error, mistake
fließend fluent
geboren born
die Grammatik grammar
(das) Griechisch Greek (language)
groß:
  Ich habe großen Durst/Hunger I'm very thirsty/hungry
(das) Hebräisch Hebrew (language)
immer wieder wiederholen repeat over and over again
(das) Italienisch Italian (language)
der Keller, -s, __ cellar
kurz short
langsam slow
lassen, ie, a, (ä) have (something done), have (someone do something)
das Laboratorium, -s, Laboratorien laboratory
(das) Latein Latin (language)

nach-schlagen, u, a, (ä)   look up (a word in a dictionary)
ob   whether
richtig   correct
(das) Russisch   Russian (language)
der Satz, -es, ¨e   sentence
schnell   fast
die Schwierigkeit, -en   difficulty
schwimmen, a, o   swim
seitdem   since then

(das) Spanisch   Spanish (language)
sich üben   practice
übersetzen   translate
der Unterschied, -(e)s, -e   difference
versuchen   try, attempt
das Wort, -es, ¨er, *or,* **-e**   word
das Wörterbuch, -s, ¨er   dictionary
wunderbar   wonderful

Lesson XIV

BASIC SENTENCES

Whenever you think of Heidelberg,
you think of the University.

That is quite natural,

for it is one of the universities
of which everyone has heard.

(1) **Wenn man an Heidelberg denkt,**
(2) **denkt man an die Universität.**
(3) **Das ist ganz natürlich,**
(4) **denn es ist eine der Universitäten,**
    von denen jeder gehört hat.

(1)

(2)

(3)

(4)

But there are also (in addition) many other kinds of sights in the region around Heidelberg.	(5–6) Aber es gibt auch noch mancherlei andere Sehenswürdigkeiten in der Umgebung Heidelbergs.
Through the city flows the Neckar,	(7) Durch die Stadt fließt der Neckar,
which has charmed many students and poets.	(8) der viele Studenten und Dichter entzückt hat.
Everyone who visits Heidelberg	(9) Jeder, der Heidelberg besucht,
ought to see the castle.	(10) sollte sich das Schloß ansehen.

(5)

(6)

(7)

(8)

(9)

(10)

It is/lies/on the mountain,
and from there (out) you can look
out over the whole valley.

(11) **Es liegt auf dem Berg,**

(12) **und von da aus kann man das ganze Tal übersehen.**

(11)

(12)

The castle has been partially rebuilt/one has in part rebuilt the castle/,

and some of the rooms are just as beautiful today
as (they were) three hundred years ago.

(13)   **Man hat das Schloß zum Teil wiederaufgebaut,**

(14)   **{ und manche Zimmer sind heute noch ebenso schön
wie vor dreihundert Jahren.**

(13)

(14)   **1660 ~ HEUTE**

VARIATIONS

Where's the university that's so famous?
Where's the river that's around here?
Where's the castle that's so old?
Where are the students who live here?

Wo ist die Universität, die so berühmt ist?
Wo ist der Fluß, der in der Nähe ist?
Wo ist das Schloß, das so alt ist?
Wo sind die Studenten, die hier wohnen?

There's the lake	that you saw yesterday.	
region		
building		

There are the co-eds that you saw yesterday.

There was a village whose beauty I remember.

There was a building which was amazingly old.

There was a city whose name I have forgotten.

There were some poets whose names were well-known.

There's the river	that I've spoken about.	
church		
mountain range		

There are the flowers

Goethe was one of these poets.

Sigrid was one of the girls in the class.

It was one of the valleys in the area.

He has two sons: one is a lawyer and the other (one) is a doctor.

They have two daughters: one is a nurse and the other is a co-ed.

There are two houses: one is pretty but the other is especially unattractive.

On this side of the river there is a footpath.

On this side of the city there are fields.

On this side of the valley the air is clean (pure).

On this side of the lakes there are many trees standing.

On that (the other) side of the city there are several good hotels.

On the other side of the field there are a few trees standing.

On the other side of the lake there are/lie/high mountains.

On the other side of the mountains the climate is especially cold.

Within the city there are many hotels.

Within the castle there are many rooms.

Inside the station there are many people.

Da ist der See,	**den Sie gestern gesehen haben.**	
die Gegend,	**die**	
das Gebäude,	**das**	

Da sind die Studentinnen, die Sie gestern gesehen haben.

Es war ein Dorf, an dessen Schönheit ich mich erinnere.

Es war ein Gebäude, das erstaunlich alt war.

Es war eine Stadt, deren Namen ich vergessen habe.

Es waren einige Dichter, deren Namen wohlbekannt waren.

Da ist der Fluß,	**von dem**	**ich gesprochen habe.**
die Kirche,	**der**	
das Gebirge,	**dem**	

Da sind die Blumen, **denen**

Goethe war einer dieser Dichter.

Sigrid war eins der Mädchen in der Klasse.

Es war eins der Täler in der Gegend.

Er hat zwei Söhne: einer ist Rechtsanwalt, und der andere ist Arzt.

Sie haben zwei Töchter: eine ist Krankenschwester, und die andere ist Studentin.

Es sind zwei Häuser: eins ist schön, aber das andere ist besonders unansehnlich.

Diesseits des Flusses gibt es einen Fußweg.

Diesseits der Stadt gibt es Felder.

Diesseits des Tals ist die Luft rein.

Diesseits der Seen stehen viele Bäume.

Jenseits der Stadt gibt es einige gute Hotels.

Jenseits des Feldes stehen ein paar Bäume.

Jenseits des Sees liegen hohe Berge.

Jenseits der Berge ist das Klima besonders kalt.

Innerhalb der Stadt gibt es viele Hotels.

Innerhalb des Schlosses gibt es viele Zimmer.

Im Bahnhof sind viele Leute.

Many families live in these houses.	**Es wohnen viele Familien in diesen Häusern.**
Many children are playing outside the school.	**Es spielen viele Kinder außerhalb der Schule.**
Outside the city there are a few farms.	**Außerhalb der Stadt gibt es ein paar Höfe.**
Just outside the hotel you can see a new shop.	**Gleich außerhalb des Hotels kann man einen neuen Laden sehen.**
This street leads past the zoo.	**Diese Straße führt an dem Tiergarten vorbei.**
The road leads past the university.	**Die Straße führt an der Universität vorbei.**
The road goes into the city.	**Die Landstraße führt in die Stadt.**
through a forest.	**geht durch einen Wald.**
The forest is nearby.	**Der Wald ist in der Nähe.**
far away.	**weit entfernt.**
There are many kinds of sights to see here.	**Hier gibt es mancherlei Sehenswürdigkeiten.**
all kinds of	**allerlei**

STRUCTURE

A. Relative Pronouns and Relative Clauses

In English we have a set of words called relative pronouns. These pronouns begin subordinate clauses but never occur at the beginning of a sentence, and they always refer back to some other noun or pronoun in the same sentence. The English relative pronouns are "*who*," "*whom*," "*whose*," "*which*," and "*that*." They may be used as subjects, objects, or possessors. Note the uses of the relative pronouns in the following example:

> *Is that the man who was here yesterday?* (subject)
> *There's the school that I attended.*   (object)
> *Are you the girl whose book I found?*   (possessor)

German relative pronouns are similarly defined and similarly used. They introduce subordinate clauses and agree with their antecedents in gender and number. In form, they closely resemble the definite article, except that in the dative plural and in all genitive forms an extra syllable, **-en,** is added.

TABLE XIV A

Case	Singular			Plural
	Masc.	*Fem.*	*Neut.*	
Nom.	der	die	das	die
Acc.	den	die	das	die
Dat.	dem	der	dem	**denen**
Gen.	**dessen**	**deren**	**dessen**	**deren**

Study carefully the sentences having relative clauses which are found in the Variations.

B. More Genitive Prepositions

In addition to the ones we have already learned, the following prepositions take a genitive case:

diesseits—*on this side of*   **innerhalb**—*inside of*
jenseits—*on that* (*the other*) *side of*   **außerhalb**—*outside of*

C. Ein as a Pronoun

Notice the use of the word "*one*" in the English sentences below:

John has a book and I have one, too.
They have two sons; one is a doctor.

The German equivalents of these sentences are:

Johannes hat ein Buch, und ich habe auch eins.
Sie haben zwei Söhne; einer ist Arzt.

In English we sometimes use the words "*one*" and "*some*" to distinguish a particular thing from a group of similar things. German uses **ein** for this purpose. In this use, **ein** has the endings of **dieser;** the genitive is rarely used. The plural word **einige,** corresponds to English "*some.*"

TABLE XIV B

Case	Singular			Plural
	Masc.	*Fem.*	*Neut.*	
Nom.	ein-er	{ein-e}	{ein-(e)s}	{ein-ige}
Acc.	ein-en			
Dat.	ein-em	ein-er	ein-em	ein-igen

Study carefully the illustrative sentences in the Variations. In all cases, **ein** has the same gender as the noun to which it refers.

D. Noch ein—*another one*

Any of the pronominal forms of **ein** found in Section C can be preceded by the adverb **noch,** to make the German equivalent of "*another one.*"

Ich habe eine Feder, und Peter hat noch eine.
I have a pen and Peter has another one.

Ich habe einige Bücher, und Johannes hat noch einige.
I have some books and Johannes has some more.

E. D— andere— "*the other one*"

The German equivalent of English "*the other one*" is the definite article followed by the adjective **ander-** ("*other*"). Notice that, while **ander-** does not in this case precede a noun, it still has the endings of an attributive adjective.

Sie haben zwei Töchter; eine ist Sekretärin, und die andere ist Krankenschwester.
They have two daughters; one is a secretary and the other one is a nurse.

Ich habe einen der Bleistifte; bitte, bringen Sie mir den anderen!
I have one of the pencils; please bring me the other one.

F. Es as an Impersonal Pronoun—*there*

Recall that **es gibt** is equivalent to "*there is*" or "*there are.*" **Es** can be similarly used with other verbs, in very much the same way we use "*there*" in English.

> **Viele Leute wohnen in diesem Hause.**
>
> *Many people are living in this house.*
>
> **Es wohnen viele Leute in diesem Haus.**
>
> *There are many people living in this house. (There live...)*

Except for the expression **es gibt, es** can be used with a singular or a plural verb form, depending on the noun used. This use of **es** is optional in German, just as the corresponding use of "*there*" is optional in English.

PATTERN PRACTICES

I. *Complete the statements with the clause* "**d- so berühmt ist**":

In der Umgebung ist der Fluß,	der so berühmt ist.
die Kirche,	die
das Hotel,	das
die Universität,	die
die Straße,	die
der Wald,	der
der Neckar,	
das Schloß,	
der Berg,	
das Tal,	
sind die Sehenswürdigkeiten,	

II. *Complete the statement with the phrase* "**d- ich gestern gesehen habe**":

Da ist der See,	den ich gestern gesehen habe.
die Gegend,	die
das Dorf,	das
der Fluß,	den
die Studentin,	die
sind die Leute,	
ist der Berg,	
sind die Höfe,	
Felder,	
ist das Schloß,	

III. *Answer in the negative, using the appropriate pronoun and the adverb* **"noch nicht"**:

Haben Sie	den Fluß	gesehen,	der	so schön ist?	Nein, ich habe ihn noch nicht gesehen.
	die Kirche		die	sind?	sie
	die Hotels		die	sind?	sie
	den Platz		der	ist?	ihn
	das Fräulein		das		sie
	die Universität		die		sie

Haben Sie	die Gegend	gesehen,	die	so schön ist?	Nein, ich habe sie noch nicht gesehen.
	den Neckar		der		ihn
	das Gebäude		das		
	das Schloß		das		
	den Berg		der		
	das Tal		das		
	die Täler		die so schön sind?		

IV. *Answer with the phrase* **"d- Namen ich vergessen habe"**:

Es war	eine	Blume,	deren Namen ich vergessen habe.
	ein	Fluß,	dessen
		See,	dessen
waren	einige	Leute,	deren
war	ein	Berg,	dessen
		Schloß,	dessen
	eine	Gaststätte,	
	ein	Student,	
	ein	Dorf,	
waren	einige	Studentinnen,	
war	ein	Tal,	

V. *Answer with the phrase* **"von d- ich gesprochen habe"**:

Dort ist	der Fluß,	von dem	ich gesprochen habe.
	die Schule,	der	
	der See,	dem	
	der Berg,		
	die Bierstube,		
sind die	Plätze,		
ist	das Nachtlokal,		
	die Deutsche,		
sind die	Deutschen,		
	die Täler,		
ist	das Gebirge,		
sind die	Stundenten,		
	die Studentinnen,		

VI. *Complete the statements with the phrase* **"und hier ist noch ein-"**:

Dort ist ein Bus,	und hier ist noch einer.	Dort sind einige Schallplatten,	und hier sind noch einige.
eine Zeitung,	eine.	Läden,	einige.
ein Café,	eins.	Damen,	einige.
ein junger Mann,	einer.	ist ein Ratskeller,	ist einer.

VII. *Answer with the phrase* **"von denen ein- besonders schön ist"**:

Das sind die Berge,	von denen einer besonders schön ist.	Das sind die Täler,
Kirchen,	eine	Gärten,
Schlösser,	eins	Studentinnen,
Bäume,	einer	Gebäude,
Blumen,	eine	
Flüsse,	einer	
Damen,		

VIII. *In your answer, use* **"jenseits"** *and the appropriate pronoun:*

Gibt es	eine	Kirche	diesseits des Flusses?
	ein	Gebäude	diesseits der Kirche?
	einen	Garten	diesseits des Gebäudes?
	einen	Wald	diesseits der Stadt?
	ein	Tal	diesseits des Waldes?
	einen	Berg	diesseits des Tals?
	ein	Dorf	diesseits des Berges?

Nein, aber jenseits des Flusses gibt es eine.
der Kirche gibt es eins.

IX. *Answer in the negative, affirming the opposite of the question:*

Stehen die Bäume vor dem Haus?

Ist die Stadt in der Nähe?

Ist das Rathaus diesseits des Parks?

Liegt die Stadt diesseits des Waldes?

Fahren sie dahin?

Liegen die Berge weit entfernt?

Steht das Krankenhaus hinter den Hotels?

Liegt das Schloß in der Stadt?

Nein, sie stehen hinter dem Haus.

sie ist weit entfernt.

es ist jenseits des Parks.

sie liegt jenseits des Waldes.

sie kommen hierher.

sie liegen in der Nähe.

es steht vor den Hotels.

es liegt außerhalb der Stadt.

X. *Tell a visitor about the sights in and around your home town.*

VOCABULARY

allerlei all sorts of
auch noch in addition, yet another
außerhalb (*gen.*) outside
bekannt known
  wohlbekannt well-known
der Berg, -es, -e mountain
besonders especially
die Blume, -n flower
denken:
  denken an (*acc.*) think of (about) someone or something
der, die, das who, which, that (relative pronouns)
der Dichter, -s, ___ poet

diesseits (*gen.*) on this side of
das Dorf, -es, ⁻er village
ebenso...wie... just as...as...
entfernt:
  weit entfernt far away
entzücken charm
sich erinnern an (*acc.*) remember
erstaunlich amazing, astonishing
das Feld, -es, -er field
fließen, o, ist o flow
der Fluß, -es, ⁻e river
führen lead

der Fußweg, -s, -e footpath
das Gebirge, -s mountain range
die Gegend, -en region
gleich just, right, directly
hoch, hoher, hohe, hohes high
der Hof, -es, ⸚e farm
innerhalb (*gen.*) within, inside of
jeder everyone
jenseits (*gen.*) on that (the other) side of
die Klasse, -n class
die Landstraße, -n road
die Luft air
manche many
mancherlei many kinds of
die Nähe nearness; vicinity
  in der Nähe nearby
rein pure
das Schloß, -es, ⸚er castle
das Schönheit, -en beauty

der See, -s, -n lake
die Sehenswürdigkeit, -en sight (tourist attraction)
sein:
  es ist there is
  es sind there are
das Tal, -s, ⸚er valley
der, das Teil, -s, -e part, share
  zum Teil in part, partly
der Tiergarten, -s, ⸚ zoo, zoological garden
über-sehen, a, e, (ie) see out over
die Umgebung, -en surrounding region
unansehnlich unattractive (to look at)
vergessen, a e, (i) forget
vorbei:
  an __ vorbei past __
der Wald, -(e)s, ⸚er forest
wenn whenever
wieder-auf-bauen rebuild, reconstruct

Lesson XV

BASIC SENTENCES

I'm glad that/fortunately/I brought my winter coat with me, because it's especially cold here this winter.

I've even/to be sure/had to buy a hat, a pair of gloves, overshoes and a scarf.

(1) **Glücklicherweise habe ich meinen Wintermantel mitgebracht,**

(2) **weil es diesen Winter hier besonders kalt ist.**

(3) **Zwar habe ich einen Hut, ein Paar Handschuhe, Gummischuhe und einen Schal kaufen müssen.**

(1)

(2)

(3)

You positively/unconditionally/need these clothes,   (4)   **Man braucht diese Kleidungsstücke unbedingt,**

in order not to freeze.   (5)   **um nicht zu frieren.**

I'll be glad
                                                                (6)   {**Ich freue mich,**
when it gets warm again.
                                                                        wenn es wieder warm wird.

Then I'll need only my sweater.   (7)   **Dann brauch' ich nur den Pullover.**

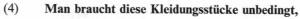

(4)

(5)

(6)

(7)

If we go on outings this summer,

perhaps I'll wear "Lederhosen"/short leather pants/ and knee-
   socks,

as is the custom in Bavaria.

(8)   **Wenn wir diesen Sommer Ausflüge machen,**

(9)   **werde ich vielleicht Lederhosen und Kniestrümpfe tragen,**

(10)   **wie es in Bayern Mode ist.**

(8)

(9)

(10)

I wonder/ask myself/if/whether/I'll look good in them.

It really doesn't matter/it really doesn't make anything out/,

because many students wear them.

(11)   **Ich frage mich, ob mir das gut steht.**

(12)   **Eigentlich macht's nichts aus,**

(13)   **denn viele Studenten tragen sie.**

(11)

(12)

(13)

VARIATIONS

He looks good if he wears a tie.

                    tie.

                    bowtie.

I will change my clothes when I go home later.

If it's too cold for me, I stay at home.

              I don't go to the movies.

              I don't go to the beer parlor.

              I don't go to the country.

If it's too warm for me, I go to the seashore.

          I go swimming.

Er sieht gut aus, wenn er eine Krawatte trägt.

                  einen Schlips

                  eine Fliege

Ich ziehe mich um, wenn ich später nach Hause gehe.

Wenn es mir zu kalt ist, bleibe ich zu Hause.

                gehe ich nicht ins Kino.

                gehe ich nicht in die Bierstube.

                gehe ich nicht aufs Land.

Wenn es mir zu warm ist, fahre ich an den Strand.

                gehe ich schwimmen.

What color is your dress?	**Welche Farbe ist Ihr Kleid?**
It's red.	**Es ist rot.**
pink.	**rosa.***
orange.	**orangefarbig.**
yellow.	**gelb.**
green.	**grün.**
blue.	**blau.**
grey.	**grau.**
black.	**schwarz.**
brown.	**braun.**
white.	**weiß.**
It's expensive.	**Es ist teuer.**
cheap.	**billig.**
It cost 500 marks.	**Es kostete 500 Mark.**
40 pfennigs.	**40 Pfennig.**
I paid 500 marks for it.	**Ich bezahlte 500 Mark dafür.**
I bought it.	**Ich habe es gekauft.**
They sell Lederhosen here.	**Hier verkauft man Lederhosen.**
I will be happy when it gets warm again.	**Ich werde mich freuen, wenn es wieder warm wird.**
I won't need my sweater when it gets warm again.	**Ich werde den Pullover nicht brauchen, wenn es wieder warm wird.**
I will take hikes/outings/when it gets warm again.	**Ich werde Ausflüge machen, wenn es wieder warm wird.**
Perhaps I will wear leather pants and knee-socks, as it is the custom in Bavaria when it gets warm.	**Ich werde vielleicht Lederhosen und Kniestrümpfe tragen, wie es in Bayern Mode ist, wenn es wieder warm wird.**

---

* NOTE:
   Rosa is an exceptional adjective in that it never has an ending.

Whenever I go out, I wear a suit.	**Wenn ich ausgehe, trage ich einen Anzug.**
a (woman's) suit.	**ein Kostüm.**
/pants/trousers.	**eine Hose.**
a jacket.	**eine Jacke.**
a sport jacket.	**eine Sportjacke.**
a shirt.	**ein Hemd.**
socks.	**Socken.**
a tie.	**eine Krawatte.**
a tie.	**einen Schlips.**
a bowtie.	**eine Fliege.**
a dress.	**ein Kleid.**
shoes.	**Schuhe.**
I wear a rain coat when it rains.	**Ich trage einen Regenmantel, wenn es regnet.**
rubbers	**Gummischuhe,**
a cap	**eine Mütze,**
a hat	**einen Hut,**
Whenever I went to the theater, I wore a skirt.	**Wenn ich ins Theater ging, trug ich einen Rock.**
a blouse.	**eine Bluse.**
stockings.	**Strümpfe.**
Whenever I went to the country, I always wore a dirndl and sandals.	**Wenn ich aufs Land fuhr, trug ich immer ein Dirndlkleid und Sandalen.**
I wore a sport jacket whenever I went to the country.	**Ich trug eine Sportjacke, wenn ich aufs Land ging.**

STRUCTURE

A. The Double Infinitive

Notice the verb structure in the Basic Sentence

Zwar habe ich einen Hut. . .kaufen müssen.

Instead of a form of **haben** followed by a perfect participle, we find it followed by two infinitives. The explanation for this is that a finite form of **haben** may never occur in a clause which has a single infinitive not preceded by **zu.** A clause containing a finite form of **haben** may also have two or more infinitives, or it may have none, but it may not have only one. This rule sometimes forces a German clause to have two (or more) infinitives, when we might expect one infinitive and a perfect participle. This happens most often in the case of the perfect tenses of **dürfen,**

können, mögen, müssen, sollen and **wollen.** (This also applies to the verb **lassen** = "*to let*," as we shall see later.) When two infinitives occur together in this way, the construction is called a **double infin-** **itive.** A double infinitive is always the last element of the clause in which it occurs, regardless of whether it is a subordinate or a main clause. Study carefully the examples below.

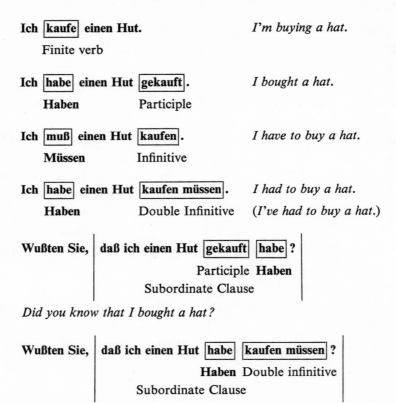

Ich kaufe einen Hut.   *I'm buying a hat.*
    Finite verb

Ich habe einen Hut gekauft .   *I bought a hat.*
    Haben   Participle

Ich muß einen Hut kaufen .   *I have to buy a hat.*
    Müssen   Infinitive

Ich habe einen Hut kaufen müssen .   *I had to buy a hat.*
    Haben   Double Infinitive   (*I've had to buy a hat.*)

Wußten Sie, | daß ich einen Hut gekauft habe ?
                           Participle **Haben**
                     Subordinate Clause

Did you know that I bought a hat?

Wußten Sie, | daß ich einen Hut habe kaufen müssen ?
                           Haben Double infinitive
                     Subordinate Clause

Did you know that I had to buy a hat?

B. German Money

The basic German monetary units are the **Mark** and the **Pfennig** (1 Mark = 100 Pfennigs). As with most German units of measurement, **Mark** and **Pfennig** are used only in their singular form, even if a plural meaning is intended.

Ich bezahlte 500 Mark dafür.   *I paid 500 marks for it.*

C. Review of Complex Sentences

Before going on with the pattern practices in this lesson, re-study carefully the structure of German complex sentences, as explained in Lesson XII.

PATTERN PRACTICES

I. *Answer the following questions in the affirmative:*

Ziehst du einen Anzug an, wenn du ausgehst?

Ziehen Sie ein Kostüm an, wenn Sie ausgehen?

Zieht er eine Hose an, wenn er ausgeht?

Zieht ihr Socken an, wenn ihr ausgeht?

Zieht er eine Jacke an, wenn er ausgeht?

Zieht man ein Hemd an, wenn man ausgeht?

Trägst du eine Krawatte, wenn du ausgehst?

Trägt er einen Schlips, wenn er ausgeht?

Trägt er eine Fliege, wenn er ausgeht?

Zieht sie ein Kleid an, wenn sie ausgeht?

Ja, ich ziehe einen Anzug an, wenn ich ausgehe.

  ein Kostüm an, wenn ich ausgehe.

er zieht eine Hose an, wenn er ausgeht.

wir ziehen Socken an, wenn wir ausgehen.

er zieht eine Jacke an, wenn er ausgeht.

man zieht ein Hemd an, wenn man ausgeht.

ich trage eine Krawatte, wenn ich ausgehe.

er trägt einen Schlips, wenn er ausgeht.

er trägt eine Fliege, wenn er ausgeht.

sie zieht ein Kleid an, wenn sie ausgeht.

II. *Answer in the negative:*

Gehen Sie ins Kino, wenn es regnet?

Wirst du dich freuen, wenn es wieder warm wird?

Wird er Ausflüge machen, wenn das Wetter wieder schön ist?

Trug sie immer ein Dirndlkleid und Sandalen, wenn sie aufs Land fuhr?

Tragen Sie eine Sportjacke, wenn Sie auf der Universität sind?

Bliebt ihr zu Hause, wenn es kalt war?

Ziehst du dich um, wenn du nach Hause gehst?

Sieht er gut aus, wenn er eine Fliege trägt?

Trug sie eine Bluse, wenn sie ins Theater ging?

Nein, ich gehe nicht ins Kino, wenn es regnet.

ich werde mich nicht freuen, wenn es wieder warm wird.

er wird keine Ausflüge machen, wenn das Wetter wieder schön ist.

sie trug nie ein Dirndlkleid und Sandalen, wenn sie aufs Land fuhr.

ich trage keine Sportjacke, wenn ich auf der Universität bin.

wir blieben nicht zu Hause, wenn es kalt war.

ich ziehe mich nicht um, wenn ich nach Hause gehe.

er sieht nicht gut aus, wenn er eine Fliege trägt.

sie trug keine Bluse, wenn sie ins Theater ging.

Ist es leicht, Deutsch zu lernen, wenn man nicht in Deutschland geboren ist?	es ist nicht leicht, Deutsch zu lernen, wenn man nicht in Deutschland geboren ist.

III. *Answer the questions in II, putting the* **wenn-***clause first:*

    Example: Gehen Sie ins Kino, wenn es regnet?   Nein, wenn es regnet, gehe ich nicht ins Kino.

IV. *Answer the question in I, putting the* **wenn-***clause first instead of the result clause.*

V. *Complete the statements, using the suggested subject:*

Wenn ich mich über das Wetter freue,	(er)	dann freut er sich auch über das Wetter.
Wenn er aufs Land fährt,	(ich)	fahre ich auch aufs Land.
Wenn wir ins Theater gehen,	(sie)	gehen sie auch ins Theater.
Wenn du Ausflüge machst,	(sie)	macht sie auch Ausflüge.
Wenn sie Wintermäntel tragen,	(wir)	tragen wir auch Wintermäntel.
Wenn sie einen Pullover braucht,	(du)	
Wenn ich ein rotes Kleid trage,	(sie)	
Wenn ihr nicht in die Bierstube geht,	(ich)	
Wenn wir in eine Vorlesung gehen,	(sie)	
Wenn ich mich übe,	(er)	

VI. *Reverse the clauses in the preceding practice:*

Er freut sich über das Wetter,	(ich)	wenn ich mich über das Wetter freue.
Ich fahre aufs Land,	(er)	wenn er aufs Land fährt.
Sie gehen ins Theater,	(wir)	wenn wir ins Theater gehen.
Sie macht Ausflüge,	(du)	wenn du Ausflüge machst.
Wir tragen Wintermäntel,	(sie)	wenn sie Wintermäntel tragen.
Du brauchst einen Pullover,	(sie)	
Sie trägt ein rotes Kleid,	(ich)	
Ich gehe nicht in die Bierstube,	(ihr)	
Sie geht in eine Vorlesung,	(wir)	
Er übt sich,	(ich)	

VII. *Supply the* **wenn-***clause for the result clause given, using the suggested subject and adjective:*

Sie trägt ein rotes Kleid,	(gelb, ich)	wenn ich ein gelbes trage.
Er trägt eine schwarze Sportjacke,	(braun, du)	wenn du eine braune trägst.
Wir tragen graue Socken,	(weiß, sie)	wenn sie weiße tragen.
Ich trage eine grüne Mütze,	(blau, er)	wenn er eine blaue trägt.
Sie tragen rote Hemden,	(orangefarbig, wir)	wenn wir orangefarbige tragen.
Sie trägt ein rosa Kleid,	(grau, ich)	wenn ich ein graues trage.
Ihr tragt teure Krawatten,	(billig, sie)	wenn sie billige tragen.

VIII. *Answer the question using the article of clothing suggested:*

Was tragen Sie, wenn es kalt ist?	(ein Wintermantel)	Ich trage einen Wintermantel, wenn es kalt ist.
Was trägst du, wenn es draußen kühl ist?	(ein Hut)	Ich trage einen Hut, wenn es draußen kühl ist.
Was braucht man, wenn man nicht frieren will?	(eine Hose)	Man braucht Hosen, wenn man nicht frieren will.
Was trugst du auf dem Lande?	(Lederhosen und Kniestrümpfe)	Ich trug Lederhosen und Kniestrümpfe auf dem Lande.
Was tragt ihr, wenn es regnet?	(Gummischuhe)	
Was soll sie tragen, wenn sie in die Stadt geht?	(ein Rock)	
Was trägt er auf dem Lande?	(eine Sportjacke)	
Was tragen Sie, wenn Sie ins Theater gehen?	(eine Krawatte)	
Was tragen Sie nicht, wenn das Wetter warm ist?	(kein Pullover)	

IX. *Answer the questions in the negative, using the color suggested:*

Trägt sie ein rotes Kleid?	(gelb)	Nein, sie trägt ein gelbes.
Trägt er eine schwarze Sportjacke?	(braun)	er trägt eine braune.
Tragen Sie graue Socken?	(weiß)	wir tragen weiße.
Tragen Sie eine grüne Mütze?	(blau)	ich trage eine blaue.
Tragt ihr rote Hemden?	(orangefarbig)	wir tragen orangefarbige.
Trägt sie ein rosa Kleid?	(grün)	sie trägt ein grünes.
Tragt ihr schwarze Schuhe?	(braun)	wir tragen braune.
Tragen Sie eine braune Fliege?	(schwarz)	ich trage eine schwarze.
Tragen Sie einen schwarzen Regenmantel?	(grau)	ich trage einen grauen.

X. *Restate each of the following sentences in the past tense:*

Wenn ich auf das Land fahre,
   trage ich immer ein Dirndlkleid und Sandalen.

Wenn es regnet,
   trage ich immer einen Regenmantel und Gummischuhe.

Wenn er auf dem Lande ist,
   trägt er immer eine Sportjacke.

Wenn er einen Schlips trägt,
   sieht er gut aus.

Wenn sie später nach Hause geht,
   zieht sie sich um.

Wenn es uns zu kalt ist,
   bleiben wir zu Hause.

Wenn es ihnen zu warm ist,
   fahren sie an den Strand.

Wenn der Winter besonders kalt ist,
   braucht man diese Kleidungsstücke.

Wenn ich ins Theater gehe,
   trage ich immer Strümpfe.

Wenn ich auf das Land fuhr,
   trug ich immer ein Dirndlkleid und Sandalen.

Wenn es regnete,
   trug ich immer einen Regenmantel und Gummischuhe.

Wenn er auf dem Lande war,
   trug er immer eine Sportjacke.

Wenn er einen Schlips trug,
   sah er gut aus.

XI. *Restate each of the following in the present perfect tense:*

Ich muß einen Hut kaufen.
Er kann viel arbeiten.
Man darf hier rauchen.

Er läßt uns fleißig üben.
Wir müssen Physik studieren.
Er will Arzt werden.

Er läßt uns immer wieder wiederholen.
Wir können gute Weine trinken.
Sie will es uns nicht erklären.

Ich habe einen Hut kaufen müssen.
Er hat viel arbeiten können.
Man hat hier rauchen dürfen.

Er hat uns fleißig üben lassen.
Wir haben Physik studieren müssen.
Er hat Arzt werden wollen.

Er hat uns immer wieder wiederholen lassen.
Wir haben gute Weine trinken können.
Sie hat es uns nicht erklären wollen.

VOCABULARY

der Anzug, -s, ⸚e suit
der Ausflug, -s, ⸚e outing
  Ausflüge machen to go on outings
aus-machen:
  es macht nichts aus it doesn't matter
aus-sehen, a, e, (ie) look, appear
bezahlen pay
billig cheap
blau blue
die Bluse, -n blouse
brauchen need
braun brown
das Dirndlkleid, -s, -er dirndl
eigentlich real, actual
die Farbe, -n color
die Fliege, -n bowtie
gelb yellow
glücklicherweise fortunately
grau gray
grün green
der Gummischuh, -s, -e overshoe, rubber
der Handschuh, -s, -e glove
das Hemd, -es, -en shirt
die Hose, -n pants, trousers
der Hut, -es, ⸚e hat
die Jacke, -n jacket
kaufen buy
das Kleid, -es, -er dress
das Kleidungsstück, -s, -e article (piece) of clothing
der Kniestrumpf, -s, ⸚e knee-sock
kosten cost
das Kostüm, -s, -e (woman's) suit
die Krawatte, -n tie
die Lederhose, -n, "*Lederhosen*," short leather pants

der Mantel, -s, ⸚ coat
die Mark mark (German monetary unit)
mit-bringen, brachte mit, mitgebracht bring along
die Mode, -n custom; fashion
  es ist Mode it's the custom
die Mütze, -n cap
orangefarbig orange
das Paar, -es, -e pair
der Pfennig, -s, -e pfennig (German monetary unit)
der Pullover pullover, sweater
der Regenmantel, -s, ⸚ rain coat
der Rock, -es, ⸚e skirt
rosa pink (undeclined adj.)
rot red
die Sandale, -n sandal
der Schal, -s, -s scarf
der Schlips, -es, -e tie
der Schuh, -(e)s, -e shoe
schwarz black
die Socke, -n sock
die Sportjacke, -n sport jacket
stehen:
  das steht mir gut that suits me, I look good in that
der Strand, -es beach
  an den Strand to the seashore
der Strumpf, -es, ⸚e stocking
teuer expensive
tragen, u, a, (ä) wear
unbedingt positive, absolute
verkaufen sell
vielleicht perhaps, maybe
weiß white
der Wintermantel, -s, ⸚ winter coat
zwar to be sure, of course

Lesson XVI

BASIC SENTENCES

Yesterday I met/became acquainted with/a couple of Johannes' friends,

(1) **Gestern habe ich ein paar von Johannes' Freunden kennengelernt,**

and we had a very interesting conversation.

(2) **und wir hatten eine sehr interessante Unterhaltung.**

They really thought
(that) I was a German.

(3) {**Sie glaubten tatsächlich,**
daß ich Deutscher wäre.

Just imagine that! (4) **Stellen Sie sich das nur vor!**

I didn't know myself
that my German is that/so/good. (5) {**Ich habe selber nicht gewußt,**
daß mein Deutsch so gut ist.

You should have been there! (6) **Sie hätten da sein sollen.**

(4)

(5)

(6)

(7)

(8)

They asked me
whether I had learned their language in the U.S.A.,
and whether I could also speak other languages.

(7)

(8)

Sie fragten mich,
ob ich ihre Sprache in den USA gelernt hätte,
und ob ich auch noch andere Sprachen könnte.

Would you like to know
how I answered?   (9)

I said I had learned German in America   (10)
and improved it in Germany/and had learned much besides in   (11)
   Germany/.

{ Möchten Sie wissen,
{ was ich darauf geantwortet habe?   (9)

Ich sagte, ich hätte Deutsch in Amerika gelernt,   (10)
und hätte in Deutschland viel dazu gelernt.   (11)

(9)   (10)   (11)

Whether my German is really as good as my English
is another question.   (12)

Whatever you say/let one say what one wants/,   (13)
I'm proud (of it)
that I can finally chat with Germans.   (14)

{ **Ob mein Deutsch wirklich so gut wie mein Englisch ist,**
{ **das ist eine andere Frage.**   (12)

Man sage, was man will,   (13)
{ **ich bin stolz darauf,**
{ **daß ich mich endlich mit Deutschen unterhalten kann.**   (14)

(12)

(13)

(14)

VARIATIONS

Let him come as soon as he can.	**Er komme, sobald er kann.**
Let him be what he wants to.	**Er sei, was er will.**
Let her write what she can.	**Sie schreibe, was sie kann.**
If I were only in Heidelberg!	**Wäre ich nur in Heidelberg!**
If you were	**Wärest du**
If he were	**Wäre er**
If we were	**Wären wir**
If you were	**Wäret ihr**
If they were	**Wären sie**
If you would only write me a letter!	**Schriebest du mir nur einen Brief!**
If he only had time!	**Hätte er nur Zeit!**
If we could only read that!	**Könnten wir das nur lesen!**

If he were only allowed to swim there!	Dürfte er dort nur schwimmen!
If he'd only tell the truth!	Sagte er nur die Wahrheit!
If you'd only work with me!	Arbeitetest du nur mit mir!
I'd like to know that!	Ich möchte das wissen!
Would you like to meet him?	Möchtest du ihn kennenlernen?
He'd like to go/travel/to Germany.	Er möchte nach Deutschland fahren.
We'd like to buy cigarettes.	Wir möchten Zigaretten kaufen.
Would you like to eat something more, children?	Möchtet ihr noch etwas essen, Kinder?
Would you like to take a walk with me?	Möchten Sie mit mir spazierengehen?
Is Fritz at home?	Ist Fritz zu Hause?
Was Dr. Schulz at home?	War Dr. Schulz zu Hause?
He'd like to know if/whether/Dr. Schulz was at home.	Er möchte wissen, ob Dr. Schulz zu Hause war.
They said that Dr. Schulz was (had been) at home.	Sie sagten, daß Dr. Schulz zu Hause gewesen wäre.
Will Mrs. Müller be at home tomorrow?	Wird Frau Müller morgen zu Hause sein?

He believed that she would be home tomorrow.
    hoped
	Er glaubte, daß sie morgen zu Hause sein würde.
	    hoffte,

He believes that she will be home tomorrow.
    hopes
	Er glaubt, daß sie morgen zu Hause sein wird.
	    hofft,

He said Fritz had been in Berlin, but I knew that already.	Er sagt, Fritz wäre in Berlin gewesen, aber das wußte ich schon.
He thought Fritz had been in Berlin, but I'm not sure of that.	Er glaubte, Fritz sei in Berlin gewesen, aber ich bin nicht davon überzeugt.
He knew Fritz had been in Berlin.	Er wußte, Fritz war in Berlin gewesen.
You ought to see that/just once/!	Sie sollten das nur einmal sehen!
You should have seen that!	Sie hätten das nur einmal sehen sollen!
He should be here now!	Er sollte jetzt hier sein!
He should have been here by now!	Er hätte schon hier sein sollen!
We had seen them yesterday.	Wir hatten sie gestern gesehen.
We could have seen/been able to see/them yesterday.	Wir hätten sie gestern sehen können.

He couldn't have seen them.	**Er hätte sie nicht sehen können.**
Is he sick?	**Ist er krank?**
No, but he looks as though he were sick.	**Nein, aber er sieht aus, als ob er krank wäre.**
Was she sick?	**War sie krank?**
No, but she looked as though she had been sick.	**Nein, aber sie sah aus, als ob sie krank gewesen wäre.**
You look as though you'd been sick.	**Sie sehen aus, als ob Sie krank gewesen wären.**
Yes, I really have been sick.	**Ja, ich bin wirklich krank gewesen.**
Would you tell me something?	**Würden Sie mir etwas sagen?**
I wouldn't tell him anything.	**Ich würde ihm nichts sagen.**
I wouldn't have told him anything.	**Ich hätte ihm nichts gesagt.**

STRUCTURE

A. The Subjunctive Mood

Compare the following two English sentences:

(1) *He can be here today.*

(2) *If he could only be here today!*

Sentence (1) is a direct statement of fact, while (2) is a wish that is not likely to be fulfilled. We express this difference by our choice of verb forms: "*can be*" in (1) and "*could be*" in (2). In these sentences, "*can*" is said to be in the INDICATIVE MOOD, "*could*" in the SUBJUNCTIVE MOOD. The definiteness of "*can*" may be contrasted with the indefiniteness of "*could*" by comparing the expressions

Can do! and *Could be!*

German uses the subjunctive mood much more frequently than English does. For a variety of reasons which we will explain shortly, German subjunctive verb forms are made in two ways, which we will call SUBJUNCTIVE I and SUBJUNCTIVE II. One set of personal endings is used for both subjunctives, but the stems differ. The subjunctive endings are:

TABLE XVI A

Pronoun	Subjunctive ending
ich, er, sie, es	-e
du	-est
wir, Sie, sie	-en
ihr	-et

B. Subjunctives of Weak Verbs

Subjunctive I is formed by adding the subjunctive endings to the infinitive stem.

Subjunctive II is identical with the simple past (indicative) tense.

The subjunctives of two typical weak verbs, **sagen** and **arbeiten,** are shown in the following table:

TABLE XVI B

Pronoun	Present Indicative	Subjunctive I	Subjunctive II and Past Indicative
ich	sag-e arbeit-e		sag-te arbeit-ete
du	sag-st | sag-est arbeit-est		sag-test arbeit-etest
er, sie, es	sag-t | sag-e arbeit-et | arbeit-e		sag-te arbeit-ete
wir, Sie, sie	sag-en arbeit-en		sag-ten arbeit-eten
ihr	sag-t | sag-et arbeit-et		sag-tet arbeit-etet

C. Subjunctives of Strong Verbs

Subjunctive I is based on the infinitive stem, as with weak verbs. Note that, by contrast with the present indicative forms, the Subjunctive I has no vowel change.

Subjunctive II is formed with the past tense stem, with the stem vowel umlauted, if possible.

The Subjunctives of two strong verbs, **tragen** and **gehen,** are shown in the following table.

TABLE XVI C

Pronoun	Present Indicative	Subjunctive I	Past Indicative	Subjunctive II
ich	trag-e geh-e		trug-Ø ging-Ø	trüg-e ging-e
du	träg-st geh-st	trag-est geh-est	trug-st ging-st	trüg-est ging-est
er, sie, es	träg-t geh-t	trag-e geh-e	trug-Ø ging-Ø	trüg-e ging-e
wir, Sie, sie	trag-en geh-en		trug-en ging-en	trüg-en
ihr	trag-t geh-t	trag-et geh-et	trug-t ging-t	trüg-et ging-et

D. Subjunctives of Past-Present Verbs

Subjunctive I is formed with the infinitive stem.

Subjunctive II is the same as the past indicative, but the stem vowels are umlauted, excepting **sollen** and **wollen**.

In the following table only the form used with **ich, er, sie,** and **es** is given; the other forms have the same personal endings as other verbs.

TABLE XVI D

Name Form	Present Indicative	Subjunctive I	Past Indicative	Subjunctive II
dürf-en	darf-Ø	dürf-e	durf-te	dürf-te
könn-en	kann-Ø	könn-e	konn-te	könn-te
mög-en	mag-Ø	mög-e	moch-te	möch-te
müss-en	muß-Ø	müss-e	muß-te	müß-te
soll-en	soll-Ø	soll-e	soll-te	
wiss-en	weiß-Ø	wiss-e	wuß-te	wüß-te
woll-en	will-Ø	woll-e	woll-te	

E. Subjunctive of sein

Note the Ø-endings in Subjunctive I.

TABLE XVI E

Pronoun	Present Indicative	Subjunctive I	Past Indicative	Subjunctive II
ich	bin	sei-Ø	war-Ø	wär-e
du	bist	sei-est	war-st	wär-est
er, sie, es	ist	sei-Ø	war-Ø	wär-e
wir, Sie, sie	sind	sei-en	war-en	wär-en
ihr	seid	sei-et	war-t	wär-et

F. Subjunctive of haben

TABLE XVI F

Pronoun	Present Indicative	Subjunctive I	Past Indicative	Subjunctive II
ich	hab-e		hat-te	hät-te
du	hast	hab-est	hat-test	hät-test
er, sie, es	hat	hab-e	hat-te	hät-te
wir, Sie, sie	hab-en		hat-ten	hät-ten
ihr	hab-t	hab-et	hat-tet	hät-tet

G. Subjunctive of werden

TABLE XVI G

Pronoun	Present Indicative	Subjunctive I	Past Indicative	Subjunctive II
ich	werd-e		wurd-e	würd-e
du	wir-st	werd-est	wurd-est	würd-est
er, sie, es	wird	werd-e	wurd-e	würd-e
wir, Sie, sie	werd-en		wurd-en	würd-en
ihr	werd-et		wurd-et	würd-et

H. Difference between Subjunctive I and II

Generally speaking, Subjunctive I is used mostly in formal writing or speech, while Subjunctive II is used in a more informal style as well. However, this will vary from speaker to speaker and from region to region, so it is best to be familiar with both kinds.

I. Uses of the Subjunctive

Use of a subjunctive verb form is usually not caused by sentence structure or by preceding words. With the exception of certain instances noted below, a German speaker uses a subjunctive whenever he feels uncertain about the statement he is making, or at least when he wants to give this impression for the sake of politeness.

More specifically, the subjunctive is always used for:

(1) Wishes which cannot be fulfilled, and which hence imply negative statements. In this case Subjunctive II is usually used. Such statements are not considered as complete sentences, but rather as "if-clauses" which are subordinate. In these expressions the finite verb is usually the first element, followed by the subject. This word order will be discussed further in Lesson XVII.

Wäre er nur in Heidelberg!

If he were only in Heidelberg!   (Implies: *He's not in Heidelberg.*)

Hätte er nur Zeit!

If he only had time!   (Implies: *He doesn't have time.*)

(2) Wishes and prayers which may be fulfilled and formal commands addressed to a third person. These expressions usually employ Subjunctive I forms. The subject comes first, followed by the finite verb. The context must determine whether such statements are wishes or commands.

Dein Reich komme!	*Thy kingdom come!*	**Sie komme herein!**	*Let her (have her) come in!*
Er werde ein guter Mann!	*May he become a good man!*	**Er schreibe mir einen Brief!**	*Have him write me a letter!*

(3) Commands to **Sie** or **wir** are also Subjunctive I forms, although except for the verb **sein** the Subjunctive I form corresponds with the name form.

Kommen Sie mit mir!	*Come with me!*	**Seien Sie stolz darauf!**	*Be proud of it!*
Gehen wir ins Kino!	*Let's go to the movies!*	**Seien wir wieder Freunde!**	*Let's be friends again!*

(4) To show uncertainty for the sake of politeness. Here Subjunctive II is usually used.

Ich möchte Zigaretten kaufen.   *I'd like to buy (some) cigarettes.*

Contrast this with:

Ich will Zigaretten kaufen.   *I want to buy (some) cigarettes.*

(5) To report statements, thoughts, wishes or hopes, when the speaker is not sure of their validity, or when he would not take responsibility for them. Either Subjunctive I or Subjunctive II may be used, although some Germans use an indicative. For example, see the dialog at the end of this section.

(6) A subjunctive is *always* used in a subordinate clause beginning with **als ob** ("*as if*"). See the dialog below.

(7) In conditional (*if...*, *then...*) sentences where there is an element of uncertainty. This will be taken up in Lesson XVII.
Study carefully the following dialog, and then compare it with the English translation which follows it.

Fritz: Ist dein Bruder krank? Er sieht so müde aus.

Max: Nein, er sagt nur, daß er krank **sei.** Ich glaube das aber gar nicht.

F: So? Er sieht so aus, als ob er eine lange Reise **gemacht hätte.**

M: So sieht er nur aus. **Möchtest** du wissen, warum er so müde ist? Ich **sagte** es dir nicht, wenn du nicht so ein guter Freund **wärest.** Mein Bruder ist nun gestern abend zu einer Party gegangen und hat stundenlang mit einer schönen Amerikanerin getanzt. Erst um vier Uhr ist er nach Hause gekommen. **Hättest** du ihn nur **sehen können!**

F: Ist das alles? Gott **sei** dank! Ich **hätte** schon **geglaubt,** er **sei** krank. Nun sag ihm, Max, er **sollte** das nächste Mal früher nach Hause **kommen.**

Fritz: *Is your brother sick? He looks so tired.*

Max: *No, he only says he's sick. But I don't believe that at all.*

F: *Really? He looks as if he'd made a long trip.*

M: *He just looks that way. Would you like to know why he's so tired? I wouldn't tell you, if you weren't such a good friend. Well, my brother went to a party last night and danced for hours with a pretty American girl. He didn't get home until four o'clock. If you only could've seen him!*

F: *Is that all? Thank goodness! I really would have thought he was sick. Well, tell him, Max, that he ought to come home earlier next time.*

J. The Subjunctive Past

Simple Subjunctive I and II are used to indicate present and future time. To express the idea of past time we use a perfect tense, formed from the appropriate subjunctive (I or II) form of **sein** or **haben,** plus a perfect participle. Study the examples below, as well as those in the Basic Sentences and Variations, and in the above conversation.

Wäre er nur hier!	*If he were only here!*
Wäre er nur hier gewesen!	*If he had only been here!*

In indirect discourse the reference may be not to present or future vs. past but to "same time as, or later time than, the time of the report," vs. "time previous to that of the report."

Er sagte, er ginge nach Hause.	*He said he was going home.*
Er sagte, er sei nach Hause gegangen.	*He said he had gone home.*
Sie sagte, sie schriebe mir einen Brief.	*She said she was writing me a letter.*
Sie sagte, sie habe mir einen Brief. geschrieben.	*She said she'd written me a letter.*

PATTERN PRACTICES

I. *Change the following statements into third person commands, using the subjunctive:*

Er kommt herein.	Er komme herein.
Sie schreibt ihrem Vater einen Brief.	Sie schreibe ihrem Vater einen Brief.
Er macht jetzt seine Aufgabe.	Er mache jetzt seine Aufgabe.
Sie fragt ihre Mutter nach ihm.	Sie frage ihre Mutter nach ihm.
Er ist stolz darauf, daß er Deutsch kann.	Er sei stolz darauf, daß er Deutsch kann.
Sie sagt, was sie tun will.	Sie sage, was sie tun will.
Er stellt sich das vor.	Er stelle sich das vor.

II. *Change the following wishes into negative statements of fact:*

Wäre er nur hier!	Er ist nicht hier.
Wäre ich nur in Heidelberg!	Ich bin nicht in Heidelberg.
Schriebe er mir nur einen Brief!	Er schreibt mir keinen Brief.
Hätte er nur Zeit!	Er hat keine Zeit.
Könnten wir das nur lesen!	Wir können das nicht lesen.
Arbeitetest du nur mit mir!	Du arbeitest nicht mit mir.
Wollte er die Reise nur machen!	Er will die Reise nicht machen.
Hätte er meinen Freund nur kennengelernt!	Er hat meinen Freund nicht kennengelernt.
Hätten wir eine interessante Vorlesung nur besuchen können!	Wir haben keine interessante Vorlesung besuchen können.
Hättet ihr nur da sein können!	Ihr hattet nicht da sein können.

III. *Reproduce the original wishes from the preceding negative statements:*

Example:

Er ist nicht hier.   Wäre er nur hier!

IV. *Change the following negative statements into wishes:*

Er war nicht hier.	Wäre er nur hier gewesen!
Ich war nicht in Berlin.	Wäre ich nur in Berlin gewesen!
Er schrieb mir keine Briefe!	Hätte er mir nur Briefe geschrieben!
Herr Müller hatte keine Zeit dafür.	Hätte Herr Müller nur Zeit dafür gehabt!
Wir konnten das nicht sehen.	Hätten wir das nur sehen können!
Er arbeitete nicht mit meinem Vater.	Hätte er nur mit meinem Vater gearbeitet!
Ihr wolltet die Reise nach Neuyork nicht machen.	Hättet ihr die Reise nach Neuyork nur machen wollen!

V. *Change the following statements of fact into observations, using the phrase* **als ob** *and the subjunctive:*

Er ist müde.	Er sieht aus, als ob er müde wäre.
Er ist reich.	reich wäre.
Sie ist krank gewesen.	Sie sah aus, als ob sie krank gewesen wäre.
Er hat eine lange Reise gemacht.	Er sah aus, als ob er eine lange Reise gemacht hätte.

VI. *Translate Pattern Practice V into English.*

VII. *Express your answers to the following questions as wishes, using the subjunctive of* **mögen**.

Lesen Sie ein Buch?		Nein, ich möchte aber ein Buch lesen.
Gehen Sie heute in die Stadt?		heute in die Stadt gehen.
Oper?		in die Oper gehen.
Kennt er Johannes Familie?	er	sie aber kennenlernen.
Lernt sie Deutsch?	sie	aber Deutsch lernen.
Ißt er jetzt zu Abend?	er	jetzt zu Abend essen.
Hört er sich jetzt die Schallplatten an?		sich aber jetzt die Schallplatten anhören.

VIII. *Report the following quotations, beginning with the phrase* **Er sagte:**

„Ich komme bald." Er sagte, er komme bald.

„Ich gehe schwimmen." gehe schwimmen.

„Ich habe nie Zeit." habe nie Zeit.

„Ich studiere an der Universität." studiere an der Universität.

„Ich rufe sie jeden Tag an." rufe sie jeden Tag an.

„Ich sage immer die Wahrheit." er sage immer die Wahrheit.

„Ich weiß die Anwort." er wisse die Antwort.

IX. *Restate each of your responses in Practice VIII, beginning with the phrase* **Er sagte, daß . . . :**

Example: Er sagte, er komme bald. Er sagte, daß er bald komme.

X. *Make indirect quotations of each of the following, as in Practice VIII:*

„Bald danach ging ich nach Hause." Er sagte, er wäre bald danach nach Hause gegangen.

„Ich habe Deutsch in Amerika gelernt." hätte Deutsch in Amerika gelernt.

„Ich habe nie Zeit gehabt, spazierenzugehen." hätte nie Zeit gehabt, spazierenzugehen.

„Wir hatten in Deutschland viel Deutsch hinzugelernt." Sie sagten, sie hätten in Deutschland viel Deutsch hinzugelernt.

„Ich habe mir das ansehen sollen." Er sagte, er hätte sich das ansehen sollen.

„Dr. Schulz war gestern zu Hause gewesen." Dr. Schulz wäre gestern zu Hause gewesen.

„Es war leicht für mich, mir das vorzustellen." es wäre leicht für ihn gewesen, sich das vorzustellen.

XI. *Translate into English each of your answers to Practice X.*

XII. *Make indirect quotations of the following, using the suggested introductory phrase:*

„Ich war gestern krank."	(Er sagte)	Er sagte, er wäre gestern krank gewesen.
„Fritz ist heute nicht zu Hause."	(Er weiß)	Er weiß, Fritz ist heute nicht zu Hause.
	(Er hofft)	hofft,
	(Er glaubt)	glaubt,
	(Er sagt)	sagt,
„Fritz war gestern nicht zu Hause."	(Er wußte)	wußte, war gestern
	(Er glaubte)	glaubte, wäre nicht zu Hause gewesen.
	(Er sagte)	sagte,
	(Er hoffte)	hoffte,

XIII. *Restate each of your answers to Practice XII, beginning the second clause with* **daß**:

Example:

> Er sagte, er wäre gestern krank gewesen.   Er sagte, daß er gestern krank gewesen wäre.

XIV. *Restate the Basic Sentences of Lesson XV as indirect quotations. Begin each sentence with* „**Peter sagte,**...", „**Er glaubte,** ...", *or some other introductory phrase, as appropriate.*

XV. *Do the same with the Basic Sentences of other lessons, as your instructor suggests.*

VOCABULARY

als ob as though
die Frage, -n question
glauben believe
hoffen hope
krank sick
selber oneself (myself, *etc.*)
so so
sobald as soon as
stolz (auf) proud (of)
  stolz darauf sein, daß __ be proud that __

tatsächlich real, actual
überzeugt (von) convinced (of), sure (of)
die Unterhaltung, -en conversation
sich vor-stellen imagine
die Wahrheit, -en truth
  die Wahrheit sagen tell the truth
zu-lernen:
  dazu (hinzu) lernen add to (improve) one's knowledge

Lesson XVII

BASIC SENTENCES

How stupid I am!	(1)	**Wie dumm ich bin!**
Everything's/gone/wrong.	(2)	**Alles ist schief gegangen.**
Would you like to hear about it/something about it/?	(3)	**Möchtest du etwas darüber hören?**
If I had only gotten up on time,	(4)	**Wenn ich nur rechtzeitig aufgestanden wäre,**
maybe nothing would have happened.	(5)	**wäre vielleicht nichts geschehen.**

But I did get up late/too late/.	(6)	**Doch bin ich eben zu spät aufgestanden.**
I had to get along without breakfast.	(7)	**Ich habe ohne Frühstück auskommen müssen.**
When I got to class, I discovered	(8)	**Als ich zur Vorlesung kam, bemerkte ich,**
that I'd left my books at home.	(9)	**daß ich meine Bücher zu Hause gelassen hatte.**

(6)

(7)

(8)

(9)

After classes/the lectures/, I wanted (to go) downtown.   (10)   **Nach den Vorlesungen wollte ich in die Stadt.**

I took the wrong streetcar,   (11)   **Ich bin mit der falschen Straßenbahn gefahren,**

and instead of (going to) the center I went to the station.   (12)   **und statt ins Zentrum bin ich zum Bahnhof gefahren.**

On the way home, I lost my wallet, with all (of) my money.   (13)   **Auf dem Wege nach Hause habe ich mein Portemonnaie mit meinem ganzen Geld verloren.**

(10)

(11)

(12)

(13)

And finally, I dropped my watch and it broke.	(14)	**Zum Schluß ließ ich meine Uhr fallen, und sie zerbrach.**
It doesn't run/go/any more.	(15)	**Sie geht nicht mehr.**
I'd like to forget all that happened.	(16)	**Ich möchte alles vergessen, was geschehen ist.**
If I had stayed at home, none of this would have happened.	(17)	**Wäre ich zu Hause geblieben, würde das alles nicht geschehen sein.**

(14)   (15)   (16)   (17)

VARIATIONS

What's the matter/What's going on here/?	**Was ist hier los?**
What's the matter with it?	**Was ist damit los?**
What's happened to you?	**Was ist dir passiert?**
Unfortunately my alarm clock didn't ring.	**Leider hat mein Wecker nicht geklingelt.**
Fortunately, the telephone rang.	**Glücklicherweise hat das Telefon geklingelt.**
I didn't have time to eat breakfast.	**Ich habe keine Zeit gehabt, um zu frühstücken.**

I took the wrong train.	Ich bin mit dem falschen Zug gefahren.
bus.	Autobus
right key.	habe den richtigen Schlüssel genommen.
I was/arrived/an hour late.	Ich bin eine Stunde zu spät angekommen.
I was late/I delayed myself/.	Ich habe mich verspätet.
I forgot (about) my appointment.	Ich habe meine Verabredung vergessen.
I was in a hurry.	Ich hatte es eilig.
I lost my key.	Ich habe meinen Schlüssel verloren.
I didn't notice him.	Ich habe ihn nicht bemerkt.
I wasn't being careful.	Ich war nicht vorsichtig.
I don't care.	Es macht mir nichts aus.
I waited for a streetcar for half an hour.	Ich habe eine halbe Stunde auf die Straßenbahn gewartet.
I stayed at my aunt's.	Ich blieb bei meiner Tante.
You're lucky.	Sie haben Glück.
You're out of luck, aren't you?	Sie haben Pech, nicht wahr?
I hurt myself/did myself hurt/.	Ich habe mir weh getan.
I tore my coat.	Ich habe mir den Mantel zerrissen.
I ruined my pants.	Ich habe mir die Hosen zerrissen.
I spilled coffee on my tie.	Ich habe auf meine Krawatte Kaffee verschüttet.
My pen doesn't work.	Meine Feder schreibt nicht.
I threw it away.	Ich habe sie weggeworfen.
I fixed it myself.	Ich habe sie selbst in Ordnung gebracht.
There's something wrong with it.	Damit ist etwas nicht in Ordnung.
Watch out!	Vorsicht! (Paß' auf!)
Did you do that by mistake/out of misunderstanding/?	Haben Sie das aus Versehen getan?
Well, I didn't do it on purpose.	Ich hab' es eben nicht mit Absicht getan.
I got on the bus.	Ich bin in den Autobus gestiegen.
off	Ich bin aus dem Autobus gestiegen.
I got into my car.	Ich bin in mein Auto gestiegen.
out of	Ich bin aus meinem Auto gestiegen.
How did you manage to get home?	Wie sind Sie nach Hause gekommen?
to see him?	Wie haben Sie ihn nur gesehen?

If you had gotten on the bus,
  you would have arrived on time.

If you had waited for the streetcar,
  you wouldn't have come late.

If you were not in a hurry,
  (then) I would show it to you.

If you could only manage it!
             see

Wenn Sie in den Bus gestiegen wären,
  würden Sie rechtzeitig dort angekommen sein.

Hätten Sie auf die Straßenbahn gewartet,
  würden Sie sich nicht verspätet haben.

Wenn du es nicht eilig hättest,
  so zeigte ich es dir.

Wenn Sie es nur machen könnten!
             sehen

STRUCTURE

A. "If-Result" Sentences

By "If-and-Result sentence" we mean a sentence containing two clauses of which one tells cause and the other effect.

Wenn die Sonne morgen scheint, wird es wieder warm.
If the sun shines tomorrow, it'll get warm again.

In this sentence, the event described in the second (main) clause is caused by the event described in the first (subordinate) clause. This relationship holds true for all conditional sentences, and we can call the subordinate clause the "IF-CLAUSE" and the main clause the "RESULT-CLAUSE."

B. "If-Clauses"

"If-clauses" can be stated in two ways:

(1) by beginning with **wenn** and ending with the finite verb:

        Wenn die Sonne morgen scheint, . . .   *If the sun shines tomorrow, . . .*

(2) by beginning with the finite verb:

        Scheint die Sonne morgen, . . .   *If the sun shines tomorrow, . . .*

C. "Result-Clauses"

"Result-clauses" may be preceded by **so** or **dann,** which correspond to English "*then*." This usually is done when the "if-clause" begins with a verb.

Scheint die Sonne morgen, so wird es wieder warm.

D. Order of Clauses in Conditional Sentences

Usually either clause may come first. However, an "if-clause" beginning with a verb *must* come first.

Wenn die Sonne morgen scheint, wird es wieder warm.   But: **Scheint die Sonne morgen, so wird es wieder warm.**

Es wird wieder warm, wenn die Sonne morgen scheint.

E. Unreal Conditions

If the "if-clause" hypothesizes something which is not true or which is open to considerable doubt, it logically follows that the "result-clause" will also be uncertain. Under these circumstances the result-clause in English usually contains *would*, while the if-clause contains a past tense; in German, the whole sentence is stated in the subjunctive, following the principles outlined in Lesson XVI. Very often the verb in the result clause of such a sentence will be formed from a subjunctive of **werden** plus an infinitive, although this is optional. Study carefully the following examples:

Indicative   **Wenn Sie mit dem Bus fahren, kommen Sie rechtzeitig dort an.**

If you travel by bus, you'll get there on time.

Subjunctive   **Wenn Sie mit dem Bus führen, kämen Sie rechtzeitig dort an.**

If you traveled (or were to travel) by bus, you would get there on time.

Wenn Sie mit dem Bus gefahren wären, wären Sie rechtzeitig dort angekommen.

If you had traveled by bus, you would have gotten there on time.

Indicative   **Arbeitet er fleißig, so bekommt er gute Noten.**

If he works hard, he gets good grades.

Subjunctive   **Arbeitete er fleißig, so würde er gute Noten bekommen.**

Arbeitete er fleißig, so bekäme er gute Noten.

If he would work hard, he would get good grades.

Hätte er fleißig gearbeitet, so würde er gute Noten bekommen haben.

If he had worked hard, he would have gotten good grades.

Indicative   **Ich zeige es dir, wenn du es nicht eilig hast.**

I'll show it to you, if you're not in a hurry.

Subjunctive   **Ich zeigte es dir, wenn du es nicht eilig hättest.**

Ich würde es dir zeigen, wenn du es nicht eilig hättest.

I would show it to you, if you weren't in a hurry.

Wenn du es nicht so eilig gehabt hättest, hätte ich es dir gezeigt.

Hättest du es nicht so eilig gehabt, so würde ich es dir gezeigt haben.

If you hadn't been in such a hurry, I would have shown it to you.

PATTERN PRACTICES

I. *Complete each sentence by adding the result clause, using* **ich** *as subject and keeping the same verb as an infinitive with a form of* **werden:**

Wenn er es sähe,	dann würde ich es auch sehen.
Wenn er es schriebe,	schreiben.
Wenn er aus dem Autobus stiege,	auch aus dem Autobus steigen.
Wenn er zu Hause bliebe,	zu Hause bleiben.
Wenn er dort rechtzeitig ankäme,	rechtzeitig ankommen.
Wenn er sich nicht verspätete,	mich auch nicht verspäten.
Wenn er es nicht eilig hätte,	es auch nicht eilig haben.
Wenn er ohne Frühstück auskommen müßte,	auch ohne Frühstück auskommen müssen.
Wenn er seine Bücher zu Hause ließe,	auch meine Bücher zu Hause lassen.
Wenn er ihn nicht bemerkte,	ihn auch nicht bemerken.

II. *Turn the preceding sentences around, completing them by adding the* **wenn-***clause:*

Ich würde es sehen,	wenn er es sähe.
Ich würde es schreiben,	schriebe.
Ich würde aus dem Autobus steigen,	aus dem Autobus stiege.
Ich würde zu Hause bleiben,	zu Hause bliebe.
Ich würde rechtzeitig ankommen,	rechtzeitig ankäme.
Ich würde mich nicht verspäten,	sich nicht verspätete.
Ich würde es nicht eilig haben,	es nicht eilig hätte,
Ich würde ohne Frühstück auskommen müssen,	ohne Frühstück auskommen müßte.
Ich würde meine Bücher zu Hause lassen,	seine Bücher zu Hause ließe.
Ich würde ihn nicht bemerken,	ihn nicht bemerkte.

III. *Complete the sentence, using* **wir** *as subject and using the conditional:*

Wenn er es gesehen hätte,	so hätten wir es auch gesehen.
Wenn er es geschrieben hätte,	geschrieben.
Wenn er aus dem Autobus gestiegen wäre,	wären auch aus dem Autobus gestiegen.
Wenn er zu Hause geblieben wäre,	auch zu Hause geblieben.
Wenn er rechtzeitig dort angekommen wäre,	rechtzeitig angekommen.
Wenn er sich nicht verspätet hätte,	hätten uns auch nicht verspätet.
Wenn er es nicht eilig gehabt hätte,	es auch nicht eilig gehabt.
Wenn er seine Bücher zu Hause gelassen hätte,	unsere Bücher auch zu Hause gelassen.
Wenn er ihn nicht bemerkt hätte,	ihn auch nicht bemerkt.

IV. *Reverse III as in II:*

Wir würden es gesehen haben,	wenn er es gesehen hätte.
geschrieben haben,	geschrieben hätte.
aus dem Autobus gestiegen sein,	aus dem Autobus gestiegen wäre.
zu Hause geblieben sein,	zu Hause geblieben wäre.
rechtzeitig dort angekommen sein,	rechtzeitig dort angekommen wäre.
uns nicht verspätet haben,	sich nicht verspätet hätte.
es nicht eilig gehabt haben,	es nicht eilig gehabt hätte.
unsere Bücher zu Hause gelassen haben,	seine Bücher zu Hause gelassen hätte.
ihn nicht bemerkt haben,	ihn nicht bemerkt hätte.

V. *Complete the statements, using the suggested pronoun subjects:*

Wenn er es sähe,	(ihr)	dann würdet ihr es auch sehen.
Wenn du es schriebest,	(er)	würde er es auch schreiben.
aus dem Autobus stiegest,	(ich)	würde ich auch aus dem Autobus steigen.
zu Hause bliebest,	(wir)	würden wir auch zu Hause bleiben.
rechtzeitig dort ankämest,	(er)	würde er auch rechtzeitig dort ankommen.
dich nicht verspätetest,	(ich)	
ich es nicht eilig hätte,	(du)	
ohne Frühstück auskommen müßte,	(er)	
er seine Bücher zu Hause ließe,	(ihr)	
ich ihn nicht bemerkte,	(Sie)	

VI. *Change the following* **wenn**-*clauses, placing the finite verb first:*

Wenn ich ihn gesehen hätte, so wäre nichts schief gegangen.	Hätte ich ihn gesehen, so wäre nichts schief gegangen.
Wenn ich es gekauft hätte, so wäre nichts schief gegangen.	Hätte ich es gekauft, so wäre nichts schief gegangen.
Wenn ich gegangen wäre, so wäre nichts schief gegangen.	Wäre ich gegangen, so wäre nichts schief gegangen.
Wenn du es verständest, so ginge nichts schief.	Verständest du es, so ginge nichts schief.

Wenn sie das schriebe, so ginge nichts schief.

Wenn er das gewollt hätte, so wäre nichts schief gegangen.

Wenn er es sähe, so ginge nichts schief.

Wenn wir zu Hause geblieben wären, so wäre nichts schief gegangen.

Wenn ich das gewußt hätte, so wäre nichts schief gegangen.

VII. *Restate each of the following sentences so that the result-clause does not contain any form of* **werden:**

Wenn er es sähe,	Wenn er es sähe,
dann würde ich es auch sehen.	dann sähe ich es auch.
Wenn er es schriebe,	Wenn er es schriebe,
dann würdest du es auch schreiben.	dann schriebest du es auch.
Wenn er aus dem Autobus stiege,	Wenn er aus dem Autobus stiege,
dann würde sie auch aus dem Autobus steigen.	dann stiege sie auch aus dem Autobus.
Wenn er zu Hause bliebe,	Wenn er zu Hause bliebe,
dann würden sie auch zu Hause bleiben.	dann blieben sie auch zu Hause.
Wenn er rechtzeitig dort ankäme,	Wenn er rechtzeitig dort ankäme,
dann würde ich auch rechtzeitig dort ankommen.	dann käme ich auch rechtzeitig dort an.
Wenn er sich nicht verspätete,	Wenn er sich nicht verspätete,
dann würden wir uns auch nicht verspäten.	dann verspäteten wir uns auch nicht.
Wenn er es nicht eilig hätte,	Wenn er es nicht eilig hätte,
dann würdet ihr es auch nicht eilig haben.	dann hättet ihr es auch nicht eilig.
Wenn er ohne Frühstück auskommen müßte,	Wenn er ohne Frühstück auskommen müßte,
dann würde ich auch ohne Frühstück	dann müßte ich auch ohne Frühstück
auskommen müssen.	auskommen.
Wenn er seine Bücher zu Hause ließe,	Wenn er seine Bücher zu Hause ließe,
dann würde sie ihre Bücher auch zu Hause lassen.	dann ließe sie ihre Bücher auch zu Hause.
Wenn er ihn nicht bemerkte,	Wenn er ihn nicht bemerkte,
dann würde ich ihn auch nicht bemerken.	dann bemerkte ich ihn auch nicht.

VIII. *Restate the following sentences, as in Practice VII:*

Wenn er es gesehen hätte,
    dann würde ich es auch gesehen haben.

Wenn er es geschrieben hätte,
    dann würdest du es auch geschrieben haben.

Wenn er aus dem Autobus gestiegen wäre,
    dann würde ich auch aus dem Autobus gestiegen sein.

Wenn er zu Hause geblieben wäre,
    dann würden sie auch zu Hause geblieben sein.

Wenn er rechtzeitig dort angekommen wäre,
    dann würde ich auch rechtzeitig dort angekommen sein.

Wenn er sich nicht verspätet hätte,
    dann würden wir uns auch nicht verspätet haben.

Wenn er es nicht eilig gehabt hätte,
    dann würdet ihr es auch nicht eilig gehabt haben.

Wenn er seine Bücher zu Hause gelassen hätte,
    dann würde sie ihre Bücher auch zu Hause gelassen haben.

Wenn er ihn nicht bemerkt hätte,
    dann würden wir ihn auch nicht bemerkt haben.

Wenn er es gesehen hätte,
    dann hätte ich es auch gesehen.

Wenn er es geschrieben hätte,
    dann hättest du es auch geschrieben.

Wenn er aus dem Autobus gestiegen wäre,
    dann wäre ich auch aus dem Autobus gestiegen.

Wenn er zu Hause geblieben wäre,
    dann wären sie auch zu Hause geblieben.

VOCABULARY

die Absicht, -en intention
  mit Absicht on purpose
auf-passen pay attention
  Paß' auf! Watch out!
aus-kommen, a, ist o ohne get along without
das Auto, -s, -s auto, car
der Autobus, -ses, -se bus
bemerken notice
dumm stupid
eben barely, just
eilig:
  es eilig haben be in a hurry
fallen:
  fallen lassen drop, let fall

falsch wrong
das Geld, -es money
geschehen, a, ist e, (ie) happen
das Glück, -es good luck
  Glück haben be lucky
klingeln ring
lassen, ie, a, (ä) leave
leider unfortunately
los:
  los sein (mit) be wrong (with), be the matter (with)
Was ist los? What's the matter?
nehmen, a, genommen, (nimmt) take
die Ordnung, -en order
  in Ordnung bringen fix

(die Ordnung, -en)
  in Ordnung sein be in order, be working
  nicht in Ordnung sein have something wrong, be out of order
passieren, ist passiert happen (to)
Pech:
  Pech haben be out of luck, have bad luck
das Portemonnaie, -s, -s wallet
rechtzeitig on time, at the right time
schenken give, grant
schief:
  schief gehen go wrong
der Schluß, -(ss)es, Schlüsse end
  zum Schluß finally
der Schlüssel, -s, — key
statt (*gen.*) instead of
steigen:
  in (aus) — steigen get into (out of) —
die Straßenbahn, -en streetcar

das Telefon, -s, -e telephone
die Uhr, -en watch, clock
verlieren, o, o lose
verschütten spill
Versehen:
  aus Versehen by mistake, out of misunderstanding
sich verspäten be late
Vorsicht! Watch out!
vorsichtig careful
der Wecker, -s, — alarm clock
der Weg, -(e)s, -e way
  auf dem Wege nach Hause on the way home
weg-werfen, a, o, (i) throw away
weh:
  weh tun (*dat.*) hurt
das Zentrum, -s, Zentren center
zerbrechen, a, o, (i) break
zerreißen, zerriß, zerrissen tear

Lesson XVIII

BASIC SENTENCES

—Oooh! I feel awful!	(1)	**—Ach, es geht mir schlecht!**
—What's the matter with you?	(2)	**—Was ist mit dir los?**
Are you sick?	(3)	**Bist du krank?**
–I'm just about dying.	(4)	**—Ich liege fast im Sterben.**

(1)

(2)

(3)

(4)

—What hurts? (5)

—Oh!—

Only my head, my eyes, my ears,
my teeth, my throat, my hands,
and my legs.

—Do you have a fever? } (7–8)
Let's have a look!

—Was tut dir weh?

—Ach—

Nur der Kopf, die Augen, die Ohren,
die Zähne, der Hals, die Hände
und die Beine.

{ —Hast du Fieber?
Sehen wir mal nach!

(5)

(6)

(7-8)

No, your temperature is perfectly/completely/normal. (9)	Nein, die Temperatur ist ganz normal.
—I know exactly what the trouble is. (10)	—Ich weiß genau, was los ist.
It's nothing serious/no serious thing/. (11)	Es ist keine ernste Sache.
I have a bad cold/caught myself a heavy cold/, that's all. (12)	Ich habe mich stark erkältet, das ist alles.

If I hadn't gone out in the rain without rubbers yesterday,	(13)	**Wenn ich nicht gestern ohne Gummischuhe in den Regen hinausgegangen wäre,**
I wouldn't have caught it/caught cold/.	(14)	**hätte ich mich nicht erkältet.**
—Well, stay home today	(15)	**—Also, bleib heute zu Hause,**
and in bed,/and in bed of course/,	(16)	**und zwar im Bett,**
and you'll be better in a while/soon/.	(17)	**und bald wird es dir besser gehen.**
—I hope so/Hopefully/.	(18)	**—Hoffentlich.**

(13)

(14)

(15)

(16)

(17)

(18)

VARIATIONS

I	feel	good, fine.	**Ich fühle mich**	**wohl.**
		better.		**besser.**
		wonderful.	**Es geht mir**	**wunderbar.**
		bad.		**schlecht.**
		awful/frightfully bad/.		**furchtbar schlecht.**
		worse.		**schlechter.**
I	feel	cold /It is to me too cold/.	**Es ist mir**	**zu kalt.**
		hot.		**zu heiß.**
		cool.		**zu kühl.**
		warm.		**zu warm.**

I am	sick.		Ich bin	krank.	
	tired.			müde.	
	exhausted.			erschöpft.	
	healthy.			gesund.	
	weak.			schwach.	
	strong.			stark.	
	refreshed.			erfrischt.	
You look	pale.		Du siehst	blaß	aus.
	bad.			schlecht	
	well.			gut	
My	head	hurts (aches).	Der Kopf	tut mir weh.	
	nose		Die Nase		
	eyes		Die Augen	tun	
	ears		Die Ohren	tun	
His	mouth		Der Mund	tut ihm	
	back		Der Rücken		
	chest		Die Brust		
	stomach		Der Magen		
	leg		Das Bein		
	foot		Der Fuß		
	arm		Der Arm		
Her	hand		Die Hand	tut ihr weh.	
	finger		Der Finger		
	toes		Die Zehen	tun	
	shoulder		Die Schulter	tut	
	neck		Der Nacken		
	throat		Der Hals		

I don't feel like taking   medicine.

Ich habe keine Lust, Medizin einzunehmen.

a pill.

eine Pille einzunehmen.

I feel like   a walk.

Ich habe Lust, spazierenzugehen.

a bath.

zu baden.

a shower.

unter die Brause zu gehen.

I hope (that) you'll feel better soon.	**Ich hoffe, daß es dir bald besser geht.**
you didn't catch a cold.	**du dich nicht erkältet hast.**
I have a bad cold.	**Ich habe mich stark erkältet.**
slight	**leicht**
It's nothing serious /It's not a serious matter/.	**Es ist keine ernste Sache.**
dangerous.	**gefährliche**

STRUCTURE

A. The Definite Article in Obvious Ownership

When referring to parts of the body, articles of clothing or anything else for which ownership is obvious, German uses the definite article rather than a possessive adjective. Of course, when ownership is *not* obvious, a possessive adjective or genitive noun will be used. Note the following contrasts:

Ich wasche mir die Hände.	**Ich wasche seine Hände.**
I'm washing my hands.	*I'm washing his hands.*
Er trägt heute den Wintermantel.	**Er trägt heute meinen Wintermantel.**
He's wearing his overcoat today.	*He's wearing my overcoat today.*

B. Some Sensation Expressions

(1) Pain—Instead of using a verb equivalent to English "to hurt" German uses the expression **tun. . .weh**. The object of **tun** in this case is always dative.

Der Kopf tut mir weh.	*My head hurts (me).*
Die Brust tut ihm weh.	*His chest hurts (him).*
Die Finger tun uns weh.	*Our fingers hurt (us).*

Compare these examples with the last set in Section A, and notice the use of the definite article for body parts.

(2) Other specific physical sensations, especially heat and cold, are expressed as follows:

Es ist mir kalt.	*I'm cold/It is cold for me/.*
Es war ihm heiß.	*He was hot/It was hot for him/.*

(3) Non-specific sensations of physical or emotional states are expressed with the reflexive verb **sich fühlen** or, less frequently, **sein**.

Ich fühle mich wohl.	**Er fühlt sich krank.**	**Wir sind müde.**
I feel fine.	*He feels sick.*	*We're tired.*

C. Mal in First-Person Plural Suggestions—*Let's*...

The suggestion in the first-person plural often contains the adverb **mal,** a shortened form of **einmal** (*"once"*), which simply serves to make the command less formal.

Gehen wir mal ins Kino!	**Arbeiten wir mal zusammen!**
Let's go to the movies!	*Let's work together!*

PATTERN PRACTICES

I. Answer the following questions with the adverbs suggested:

Wie fühlen Sie sich?	(gut)	Es geht mir gut.
Wie fühlt er sich?	(wunderbar)	Es geht ihm wunderbar.
Wie fühlst du dich?	(schlecht)	Es geht mir schlecht.
Wie fühltet ihr euch gestern?	(besser)	Es ging uns gestern besser.
Wie haben sie sich letzte Woche gefühlt?	(schlechter)	Es ist ihnen letzte Woche schlechter gegangen.
Wie fühlte sie sich nach dem Gewitter?	(furchtbar schlecht)	Es ging ihr nach dem Gewitter furchtbar schlecht.
Wie fühltest du dich während des Winters?	(gut)	Es ging mir während des Winters gut.

II. Answer the following by stating the opposite:

Ist es Ihnen kalt?		Gar nicht! Es	ist mir heiß.	
War	kühl?		war	warm.
Fühlen Sie sich krank?		Ich fühle	mich	gesund.
Fühlten	besser?		fühlte	schlechter.
	gut?			schlecht.
Ist es Ihnen schlecht gegangen?		Es ist mir gut	gegangen.	
ihm gut		ihm schlecht		
euch		uns		

III. Answer the following questions with the words given in parentheses:

Was tut dir weh?	(der Kopf)	Der Kopf tut mir weh.	
	(die Nase)	Die Nase	
	(die Augen)		

Was tut ihr weh?   (die Ohren)

                               (der Mund)

                               (der Rücken)

Was tut euch weh?   (die Brust)

                               (der Magen)

                               (das Bein)

Was tut ihm weh?   (der Fuß)

                               (der Arm)

                               (die Hand)

IV. *Answer the following questions, using first person plural suggestions and the nouns in parentheses:*

Was sollen wir machen?	(ins Theater)	Gehen wir mal ins Theater!
Was möchten Sie sich anhören?	(die Oper)	Hören wir uns mal die Oper an!
Wohin sollen wir fahren?	(nach Oberammergau)	
Was möchten Sie lesen?	(die Zeitschrift)	
Wo sollen wir essen?	(im Ratskeller)	
Wo sollen wir spazieren gehen?	(im Wald)	
Was wollt ihr euch heute abend anschauen?	(Fernsehen)	

V. *Answer the following questions with conditional statements, beginning with the phrase,* **"Ja, aber wäre ich nicht da geblieben, … ":**

Hast du dich erkältet?

                                      Ja, aber wäre ich nicht da geblieben,
                                           dann hätte ich mich nicht erkältet.

Hast du den Film gesehen?

                                      Ja, aber wäre ich nicht da geblieben,
                                           dann hätte ich den Film nicht gesehen.

Hast du das rote Kleid gekauft?

                                      Ja, aber wäre ich nicht da geblieben,
                                           dann hätte ich das rote Kleid nicht gekauft.

Hast du seine Mutter kennengelernt?

                                      Ja, aber wäre ich nicht da geblieben,
                                           dann hätte ich seine Mutter nicht kennengelernt.

Hast du die Vorlesung besucht?

                                      Ja, aber wäre ich nicht da geblieben,
                                           dann hätte ich die Vorlesung nicht besucht.

Hast du die Reise machen können?

                                      Ja, aber wäre ich nicht da geblieben,
                                           dann hätte ich die Reise nicht machen können.

VI. *Review all pattern practices in Lessons XIV–XVI.*

VOCABULARY

der Arm, -es, -e arm
das Bein, -es, -e leg
besser better
blaß pale
Brause:
  unter die Brause gehen take a shower
die Brust, ⁓e chest
ein-nehmen, a, eingenommen, (nimmt) take (medicine)
sich erkälten catch a cold
ernst serious
erschöpft exhausted
das Fieber, -s fever
der Finger, -s, __ finger
sich fühlen feel
furchtbar awful, frightful
gefährlich dangerous
genau exact
gesund healthy
der Hals, -es, ⁓e throat
hinaus-gehen, ging hinaus, ist hinausgegangen go out
hoffentlich hopeful(ly); I hope so
der Kopf, -es, ⁓e head

leicht slight
Lust:
  Lust haben, etwas zu tun feel like doing something
  keine Lust haben not to feel like
der Mund, -es, -e (and ⁓er) mouth
nach-sehen, a, e (sieht) take a look
  Sehen wir mal nach! Let's have a look!
der Nacken, -s, __ neck
die Nase, -n nose
normal normal
das Ohr, -es, -en ear
die Pille, -n pill
der Rücken, -s, __ back
die Sache, -n thing, matter
die Schulter, -n shoulder
schwach weak
stark strong; heavy, bad (cold, rain, etc.)
sterben, a, ist o, (i) to die
Sterben:
  im Sterben liegen be dying, be on one's deathbed
wohl fine, well
die Zehe, -n toe

Lesson XIX

BASIC SENTENCES

Yesterday (the) Müllers invited me to dinner, and I	(1)
met/became acquainted with/the whole family.	(2)
I liked them all very much/won them dearly/right away,	(3)
but Mr. Müller made the greatest impression on me.	(4)

(1) **Gestern haben Müllers mich zum Abendessen eingeladen,**

(2)   **und ich habe die ganze Familie kennengelernt.**

(3) **Ich habe sie alle sofort sehr lieb gewonnen,**

(4)   **aber Herr Müller hat mich am meisten beeindruckt.**

He seems like/I find (that) he is/a fine person, (5)

very intelligent and cheerful. (6)

He looks very much like Johannes, (7)

and could well be his older brother. (8)

He's not as tall as Johannes, (9)

is a bit heavier/weighs somewhat more/, (10)

and is bald. (11)

But he has the same light blue eyes and blond hair as (12)

his son.

He's about sixty-five, (13)

but he's as strong and healthy as a forty-year-old man. (14)

(5) Ich finde, er ist ein famoser Mensch,

(6) sehr intelligent und lustig.

(7) Er sieht Johannes sehr ähnlich,

(8) und könnte wohl sein älterer Bruder sein.

(9) Er ist nicht so groß wie Johannes,

(10) wiegt etwas mehr

(11) und ist kahlköpfig.

(12) Aber er hat die gleichen hellblauen Augen und blondes Haar wie sein Sohn.

(13) Er ist ungefähr fünfundsechzig,

(14) aber er ist ebenso rüstig wie ein vierzigjähriger Mann.

(5)

(6)

(7)

(8)

(9)

(10)

(11)

(12)

(13)

(14)

VARIATIONS

I'll describe him to you.	Ich beschreibe ihn dir.	She has dark hair.	Sie hat dunkles Haar.
He's handsome.	Er ist hübsch.	black	schwarzes
tall (big).	groß.	brown	braunes
short (little).	klein.	red	rotes
strong.	stark.	grey	graues
weak.	schwach.	white	weißes
healthy.	gesund.		
young.	jung.	He's bald.	Er ist kahlköpfig.
old.	alt.		
stout.	dick.	He has blue eyes.	Er hat blaue Augen.
thin.	dünn.	brown	braune
slim.	schlank.		
intelligent.	intelligent.	Is he as tall as Johannes?	Ist er so groß wie Johannes?
clever.	klug.	old	alt
dumb.	dumm.	clever	klug
cheerful.	lustig.		

		Johannes is taller than he.	Johannes ist größer als er.
		shorter	kleiner
Johannes is stronger than he.	Johannes ist stärker als er.		
weaker	schwächer		
healthier	gesünder		
younger	jünger		
older	älter		
I'm stouter than Richard.	Ich bin dicker als Richard.		
thinner	dünner		
slimmer	schlanker		
more intelligent	intelligenter		
cleverer	klüger		
dumber	dummer		
more cheerful	lustiger		

She's not as pretty as her sister.	Sie ist nicht so hübsch wie ihre Schwester.
old	alt
slim	schlank
He has a straight nose.	Er hat eine gerade Nase.
crooked	krumme
pointed	spitze
He wears glasses.	Er trägt eine Brille.
He has more money than his friend.	Er hat mehr Geld als sein Freund.
less	weniger
He has broad shoulders.	Er hat breite Schultern.
He is six feet/two meters/tall.	Er ist zwei Meter groß.
He smokes cigarettes.	Er raucht Zigaretten.
cigars.	Zigarren.
a pipe.	eine Pfeife.
The more, the merrier!	Je mehr, desto lustiger!
hotter, better!	heißer, besser!
I'm feeling better and better.	Es geht mir immer besser!
worse worse.	schlechter.

STRUCTURE

A. Comparative Forms of Adjectives and Adverbs

English adjective and adverb forms such as "*nicer*," "*bigger*," "*greener*," "*faster*," "*slower*" and "*better*" are called COMPARATIVES.

Grass is greener than hay.   *Horses run faster than dogs* (*run*).

Many English comparatives are formed by adding -*er* to the base form; some comparatives, however, are formed by using the adverb "*more*" with the base form and a few, such as "*good, better*," are irregular.

German comparatives are formed by adding **-er** to the base. In some comparatives, the vowel of the stem is umlauted; these forms, as well as a few irregular ones, must be learned as vocabulary.

In the case of attributive adjectives, the adjective endings are added to the base plus **-er**.

ein gut-er Mann	**ein klein-es Kind**	**eine groß-e Bank**
a good man	*a small child*	*a big bank*
ein besser-er Man	**ein kleiner-es Kind**	**eine größer-e Bank**
a better man	*a smaller child*	*a bigger bank*

B. Als in Comparisons—*than*

In comparisons, German uses **als** where English uses "*than*."

Er läuft schneller als Johannes.	*He runs faster than Johannes.*
Fritz hat mehr Freunde als ich.	*Fritz has more friends than I.*
Maria ist größer als ihre Schwester.	*Maria is taller than her sister.*

C. So... wie... in Comparisions—*as... as...*

English comparisons may be made by inserting the positive (base) form of the adjective or adverb into the frame "*as...as...*" German has a similar construction, but the frame is **so...wie...**

Ist Heidelberg so groß wie Darmstadt?	*Is Heidelberg as big as Darmstadt?*
Einer ist so gut wie der andere.	*One is as good as the other.*
Er hat so viel Geld wie ich.	*He's got as much money as I (have).*
Ilse ist nicht so schön wie Martha.	*Ilse isn't as pretty as Martha.*
Er kann nicht so schell laufen wie ich.	*He can't run as fast as I (can).*

An English variation of "*as...as...*" is "*just as...as....*" The German equivalent of this is **ebenso...wie...**

Einer ist ebenso gut wie der andere.	*One is just as good as the other.*
Ilse ist ebenso schön wie Martha.	*Ilse is just as pretty as Martha.*

D. Comparisons with Infinitives and Perfect Participles

Although infinitives and participles usually come at the end of their sentence or clause, Germans often prefer to let a comparison come last, even if an infinitive or participle is present.

Ich kann schnell boxed(**lesen**) **.**	*I can read fast.*
Ich kann schneller boxed(**lesen**) **als Johannes.**	*I can read faster than Johannes.*
Er hat viele Freunde boxed(**gehabt**) **.**	*He had many friends.*
Er hat mehr Freunde boxed(**gehabt**) **als ich.**	*He had more friends than I (had).*

E. Immer in Comparisons

The German equivalents of such English expressions as "*hotter and hotter,*" "*faster and faster,*" etc., are formed by using the adverb **immer** with the comparative form of the adjective or adverb.

immer besser	*better and better*	**immer interessanter**	*more and more interesting*	**immer langsamer**	*slower and slower*
immer kälter	*colder and colder*	**immer schöner**	*more and more beautiful*		

This construction is also used where English uses a form of "*keep*" plus an "*-ing*" verb form plus a comparative.

Er arbeitet immer schwerer.   *He keeps working harder.*
He works harder and harder.

Das Wetter wurde immer schlechter.   *The weather kept getting worse.*
The weather got worse and worse.

F. Je..., desto... in Comparisons—*the...-er, the...-er*

The German equivalent for English comparative relationship expressions using the frame "*the ..., the...*" is **je..., desto...**

Je heißer, desto besser.   *The hotter, the better.*   **Je mehr, desto lustiger.**   *The more, the merrier.*

In this usage, **je** is considered as a subordinating conjunction, and **desto** as a coordinating conjunction. Note the word order in the following German examples.

Je mehr er arbeitete, desto schneller arbeitete ich.
The more he worked, the faster I worked.
Je länger er im Bett blieb, desto besser fühlte er sich.
The longer he stayed in bed, the better he felt.
Je älter er wird, desto schwächer wird er.
The older he gets, the weaker he gets.

G. Attributive Adjectives without Nouns

When a German noun is obvious, it may be omitted or "understood." If an attributive adjective is present, the adjective has the same ending that it would have if the noun were actually there.

Er trägt ein braunes Hemd, aber ich trage ein weißes.   **Er hat eine schöne Freundin, aber ich habe eine schönere.**
He's wearing a brown shirt, but I'm wearing a white one.   *He has a pretty girl friend, but I've got a prettier one.*

PATTERN PRACTICES

I. *Answer in the negative, using the comparative form of the adjective given:*

Ist er so groß	wie Johannes?	Nein, er ist größer	als Johannes.
klug		klüger	
klein		kleiner	
stark		stärker	
intelligent		intelligenter	
alt		älter	
jung		jünger	
gesund		gesünder	
rüstig		rüstiger	
stolz		stolzer	

II. *Answer in the negative, using the comparative form of* **viel (e)** :

Hat er so viele Freunde	gehabt	wie ich?	Nein, er hat mehr Freunde	gehabt	als Sie.
viel Geld			Geld		
viele gute Noten	bekommen		gute Noten	bekommen	
viel Wein	getrunken		Wein	getrunken	
Kaffee			Kaffee		
viel ____	gegessen		____	gegessen	
viele Zigaretten	geraucht		Zigaretten	geraucht	
viel ____	geraucht		____	geraucht	
viele Länder	besucht		Länder	besucht	
Geschichten	erzählt		Geschichten	erzählt	

III. *Answer in the affirmative, using* **immer** *and the comparative of the suggested adjective, retaining the same tense:*

Ist es heute heiß?	Ja, und es wird immer heißer.
War gestern	wurde
Ist gewesen?	ist geworden.
Ist es heute kühl?	wird kühler.
War gestern	wurde
Ist gewesen?	ist geworden.

Ist	es heute	warm?		Ja, und es wird	immer wärmer.
War	gestern				
Ist		gewesen?			
Ist	heute	kalt?			
War	gestern				
Ist		gewesen?			

IV. *Answer the following questions, using* **noch** *and the comparative form of the adverb:*

Kann er ebenso	gut	wie Johannes schreiben?	Er kann noch besser	als Johannes schreiben.
	schön	singen?	schöner	singen.
	viel	essen?	mehr	essen.
	schnell	laufen?	schneller	laufen.
Deutsch ebenso fließend		sprechen?	Deutsch noch fließender	sprechen.
ebenso schwer		arbeiten?	noch schwerer	arbeiten.
	fleißig		fleißiger	
	oft	reisen?	öfter	reisen.

V. *Complete the following statements, using* **desto** *and the comparative form of the adverb:*

Je schneller	er arbeitete,	desto schneller	mußte ich arbeiten.
schwerer		schwerer	
fleißiger		fleißiger	
langsamer		langsamer	
besser		besser	
mehr		mehr	
weniger		weniger	
länger		länger	

VI. *Translate Practice V into English.*

VII. *Complete the following statements, using the comparative form of the adjective but omitting the noun:*

Er liest ein gutes Buch,	aber ich lese ein besseres.
Er kennt ein schönes Mädchen,	kenne ein schöneres.
Sie bekommt gute Noten,	bekomme bessere.
schlechte Noten,	schlechtere.
Er wohnt in einem großen Haus,	wohne in einem größeren.
kleinen	kleineren.
einer interessanten Stadt,	einer interessanteren.

VIII. *Complete, using the comparative but omitting the noun:*

Das ist ein billiger Schlips,	aber hier ist ein billigerer.
sind lange Socken,	sind längere.
ist ein teures Kleid,	ist ein teureres.
eine breite Straße,	
sind moderne Gebäude,	
ist eine kurze Geschichte,	
ein strenges Klima,	
ein hoher Berg,	

IX. *As in VIII:*

Du hast	einen kleinen Wagen,	aber ich habe einen kleineren.
Du bist	krank,	bin kränker.
Sie hat	blondes Haar,	habe blonderes.
Er ist	schwach,	bin schwächer.
Er hat	eine krumme Nase,	habe eine krummere.
Sie haben	dunkles Haar,	habe dunkleres.
Er hat	ihn gern,	habe ihn lieber.
Sie ist	lustig,	
Sie sind	fleißig,	
Sie wachen spät auf,		
Du bist	blaß,	

X. *Prepare a two-minute oral report, describing someone you know. Include such items as physical features, age, occupation, etc., and explain why you like or dislike him or her.*

VOCABULARY

ähnlich:
    ähnlich sehen (*dat.*) look like, resemble
als than
beeindrucken make an impression on, impress
beschreiben, ie, ie describe
blond blond
die Brille, -n pair of (eye)glasses
dick stout
dünn thin
famos fine, "swell"
gerade straight
gleich same; similar, alike; equal
hell:
    hellblau (*etc.*) light blue (*etc.*)
immer:
    immer besser (*etc.*) better and better (*etc.*)
intelligent intelligent
je..., desto... the..., the...

kahlköpfig bald
klug, ¨er, ¨st* clever, intelligent
krumm crooked
lieb:
    lieb gewinnen, a, o get to like
meist:
    am meisten the most
das *or* **der Meter, -s** meter
die Pfeife, -n pipe
schlank slim
spitz pointed, sharp
ungefähr about, approximately
vierzigjährig:
    ein vierzigjähriger (*etc.*) **Mann** a 30-year old (*etc.*) man
weniger less
wiegen, o, o weigh
die Zigarre, -n cigar

---

* From here on, we list the comparative and superlative forms for any adjective whose stem-vowel becomes umlauted, or for which these forms are otherwise unexpected.

Lesson XX

BASIC SENTENCES

And the others in the family?	(1)	**Und die anderen in der Familie?**
They're very likable, too—	(2)	**Sie sind auch sehr liebenswürdig—**
—polite, lively and gay.	(3)	**höflich, lebhaft und lustig.**

Mrs. Müller is a short, plump woman	(4)	Frau Müller ist eine kleine, dicke Frau
with a full, friendly face—	(5)	mit einem vollen, freundlichen Gesicht—
a typical mother.	(6)	eine typische Mutter.
Of all the members of the family she's the most silent.	(7)	Von allen Mitgliedern der Familie ist sie am schweigsamsten.

She hardly says anything.	(8)	**Sie sagt nicht viel.**
Except for Mr. Müller, I liked Johannes' sister most of all.	(9)	**Außer Herrn Müller** **hatte ich Johannes' Schwester am liebsten.**
She isn't exactly the prettiest girl that I've ever seen.	(10)	**Sie ist nicht gerade das schönste Mädchen,** **das ich je gesehen habe.**
But, just like her father, she has (a good sense of) humor,	(11)	**Aber, ganz wie ihr Vater,** **hat sie Humor**
and she is very intelligent.	(12)	**und ist sehr intelligent.**
To be sure, all (the) Müllers are clever people;	(13)	**Zwar sind alle Müllers kluge Menschen;**
but that's scarcely surprising,	(14)	**aber das ist kaum überraschend,**
since the father is one of the most intelligent people I know.	(15)	**da der Vater einer der intelligentesten Menschen ist, die ich kenne.**
So you can always be sure of spending a pleasant evening in their home.	(16)	**Darum kann man immer einen angenehmen Abend bei ihnen verbringen.**

(8)

(9)

(10)

(11)

(12)

(13)

(14)

(15)

(16)

VARIATIONS

What kind of a girl is Else?	**Was für ein Mädchen ist Else?**
I think she's very friendly.	**Mir scheint sie sehr freundlich.**
She seems very friendly, to me.	
She's more friendly than Gertrud.	**Sie ist freundlicher als Gertrud.**
She's the friendliest girl I know.	**Sie ist das freundlichste Mädchen, das ich kenne.**
What kind of a person is Robert?	**Was für ein Mensch ist Robert?**
I think he's very nice.	**Ich finde ihn sehr nett.**
He's much nicer than Max.	**Er ist viel netter als Max.**
He's the nicest person I've ever met.	**Er ist der netteste Mensch, den ich je kennengelernt habe.**
Is Hans as tall as you? No, he's taller.	**Ist Hans so groß wie du? Nein, er ist größer.**
He's the tallest boy in the school.	**Er ist der größte Junge in der Schule.**
I like Hans very much.	**Ich habe Hans sehr gern.**
I like him better than Karl.	**Ich habe ihn lieber als Karl.**
I like him best of all.	**Ich habe ihn am liebsten.**
Do you know Mr. Springer?	**Kennen Sie Herrn Springer?**
I know him well.	**Ich kenne ihn gut.**
Hanna knows him better.	**Hanna kennt ihn besser.**
His sister knows him best.	**Seine Schwester kennt ihn am besten.**
How can I get to New York the fastest?	**Wie komme ich am schnellsten nach Neuyork?**
A bus wouldn't be fast enough.	**Ein Bus wäre nicht schnell genug.**
The train is faster.	**Der Zug ist schneller.**
By plane is the fastest.	**Mit dem Flugzeug geht's am schnellsten.**
How old is she?	**Wie alt ist sie?**
She's older than her sister.	**Sie ist älter als ihre Schwester.**
She's the oldest girl in the family.	**Sie ist das älteste Mädchen in der Familie.**
He's very young.	**Er ist sehr jung.**
He's younger than Josef.	**Er ist jünger als Josef.**
He's the youngest son in the family.	**Er ist der jüngste Sohn der Familie.**
Well, what do you think of Hans?	**Was halten Sie denn von Hans?**

I think he's very unfriendly.	Mir scheint er sehr unfreundlich.
clever.	klug.
polite.	höflich.
impolite.	unhöflich.
well-brought-up./well-mannered.	gut erzogen.
badly brought-up./bad-mannered.	schlecht erzogen.
industrious.	fleißig.
lazy.	faul.
patient.	geduldig.
impatient.	ungeduldig.
educated.	gebildet.
sad.	traurig.
happy.	glücklich.
calm, quiet.	ruhig.
talkative.	redselig.

He laughs a lot.	Er lacht viel.
smiles	lächelt
complains	klagt
She cries	Sie weint

STRUCTURE

A. Superlative Forms of Adjectives

English adjectives which have an -est ending, or which are preceded by "most," are called *superlatives*. The superlatives of German adjectives are formed by adding the ending -st- to the stem (-est- if the stem ends in -d or -t) and then adding the regular adjective endings. The stem of the superlative is the same as the stem of the comparative.

TABLE XX A

Positive	Comparative	Superlative
ein alt-er Mann	ein ält-er-er Mann	unser ält-est-er Mann
der jung-e Bruder	der jüng-er-e Bruder	der jüng-st-e Bruder
eine neu-e Kirche	eine neu-er-e Kirche	ihre neu-st-e Kirche
die groß-e Bank	die größ-er-e Bank	die größ-te Bank
mein gut-es Kind	mein besser-es Kind	mein best-es Kind
das interessant-e Buch	das interessant-er-e Buch	das interessant-est-e Buch
Ihre alt-en Freunde	Ihre ält-er-en Freunde	Ihre ält-est-en Freunde
gut-e Noten	besser-e Noten	die best-en Noten

B. Superlative Forms of Adverbs

Superlatives of German adverbs are always preceded by **am (an+dem).** The superlative adverb has the same stem as the comparative form plus the superlative ending **-st** (or **-est** if the stem ends in **-d** or **-t**) plus **-en.** While adverbs do not otherwise have declensional endings, the **am** which always precedes the superlative forces an **-en.**

Meine Schwester kennt mich am besten.
My sister knows me best.

Johannes kann am schnellsten laufen.
Johannes can run the fastest.

Note that predicate adjectives may also have the **am-**superlative.

C. Participial Adjectives

The perfect participle of almost any German verb can be used as an adjective. If such a participial adjective occurs before the noun it modifies (attributive position), it has the usual adjective endings. Such adjectives are often accompanied by an adverb.

Herr Müller ist ein gebildeter Mann.
Mr. Müller is an educated man.
Der gut erzogene Mann, den Sie gestern kennengelernt haben, ist Deutscher.
The well-mannered man whom you met yesterday is a German.

D. Gerundives

German gerundives are special verb forms used as adjectives. (They are also used occasionally as adverbs.) They are different from perfect participles in that they are never used to form verb tenses. Most German gerundives are formed by adding **-d** to the name form of the verb. In attributive position gerundives take the usual adjective endings. The English equivalents of German gerundives are usually adjectives ending in "*-ing*."

War seine Antwort nicht überraschend?

Wasn't his answer surprising?

Ja, das war tatsächlich eine überraschende Antwort.

Yes, that really was a surprising answer.

Attributive gerundives are often used in place of relative clauses. Most of the time, the English equivalent of such a construction will be a relative clause.

Mein Professor ist	ein Mann, der immer langsam spricht.
Mein Professor ist	ein immer langsam sprechender Mann.
My professor is	*a man who always speaks slowly.*

More complicated constructions using gerundives and participial adjectives will be taken up in Lesson XXI.

PATTERN PRACTICES

I. *Answer the following questions, giving the adjective in the superlative degree:*

Ist sie älter als ihre Schwestern?	Ja, sie ist die älteste Schwester von allen.
Ist er jünger als seine Brüder?	er ist der jüngste Bruder von allen.
Bist du höflicher als deine Brüder?	ich bin der höflichste Bruder von allen.
Sind Sie fleißiger als Ihre Schwestern?	ich bin die fleißigste Schwester von allen.
Sind sie größer als die anderen Kinder?	sie sind die größten Kinder von allen.
Bin ich höflicher als meine Schwestern?	du bist die höflichste Schwester von allen.
Ist sie eine bessere Freundin als Hanna?	sie ist die beste Freundin von allen.
Ist er ein lustigerer Junge als Peter?	er ist der lustigste Junge von allen.
Ist er geduldiger als die anderen Lehrer?	er ist der geduldigste Lehrer von allen.

II. *Answer the following questions affirmatively with the adjective in the superlative degree:*

Ist Robert ein gemütlicher Mensch?   Ja, er ist der gemütlichste Mensch,
den ich je kennengelernt habe.

Ist Robert ein schweigsamer Mensch?   Ja, er ist der schweigsamste Mensch,
den ich je kennengelernt habe.

Ist Robert ein kluger Mensch?   Ja, er ist der klügste Mensch,
den ich je kennengelernt habe.

Ist Else ein höfliches Mädchen?
Ist Else ein freundliches Mädchen?
Ist Frau Schmidt eine ruhige Frau?
Ist Frau Schmidt eine redselige Frau?
Ist Frau Schmidt eine schöne Frau?

III. *Complete the sentence using the comparative and then the superlative:*

Er ist nett,	und sie ist netter,	aber du bist am nettsten.
glücklich,	glücklicher,	glücklichsten.
klug,	klüger,	klügsten.
dick,	dicker,	dicksten.
stark,	stärker,	stärksten.
groß,	größer,	größten.
redselig,		
gut,		
gesund,		
ruhig,		
schwach,		
traurig,		

IV. *Answer in the affirmative, using the superlative adverb:*

Läuft er nicht schnell? — Ja, er läuft am schnellsten.

Schreibt er nicht gut? — er schreibt am besten.

Singt sie nicht schön? — sie singt am schönsten.

Spricht sie nicht schlecht? — sie spricht am schlechtesten.

Haben Sie ihn nicht gern? — ich habe ihn am liebsten.

Spielt er nicht gut? — er spielt am besten.

Komme ich mit dem Flugzeug nicht schnell nach Neuyork? — Sie kommen am schnellsten mit dem Flugzeug dahin.

Kennst du ihn nicht gut? — ich kenne ihn am besten.

V. *Use the following predicative adjectives as attributive adjectives:*

War der Film aufregend? — Ja, es war ein aufregender Film.

War die Antwort überraschend? — es war eine überraschende Antwort.

War das Mädchen reizend? — es war ein reizendes Mädchen.

War der junge Mann gut erzogen? — er war ein gut erzogener junger Mann.

War die Stadt wieder aufgebaut? — es war eine wieder aufgebaute Stadt.

War der Geschäftsmann bekannt? — er war ein bekannter Geschäftsmann.

War seine Frau gut angezogen? — sie war eine gut angezogene Frau.

VI. *Answer in the negative, using the verbs on the left as adjectives:*

Sitzt der Anzug gut? — Nein, es ist ein schlecht sitzender Anzug.

Schläft das Kind ruhig? — es ist ein unruhig schlafendes Kind.

Fliegt das Flugzeug schnell? — es ist ein langsam fliegendes Flugzeug.

Geht diese Uhr gut? — es ist eine schlecht gehende Uhr.

Spricht der Junge schnell?

Sieht die Frau schlecht aus?

Arbeitet der Mann gut?

Sieht die Dame schön aus?

VII. *Translate Practice VI into English.*

VOCABULARY

angezogen:
   gut angezogen well-dressed
bilden shape; train, educate
   gebildet (well-) educated
darum so, therefore
erziehen bring up (a child)
   gut (schlecht) erzogen well (badly) brought up; well (ill) mannered
faul lazy
freundlich friendly
geduldig patient
gerade:
   nicht gerade das schönste not exactly the prettiest
das Gesicht, -s, -er face
glücklich happy
halten, ie, a (ä) von hold an opinion of
   Was halten Sie von __? What do you think of __?
höflich polite
der Humor, -s:
   Humor haben have a sense of humor

je ever
kaum hardly
klagen complain
lächeln smile
lebhaft lively
liebenswürdig likable
das Mitglied, -s, -er member
nett nice
redselig talkative
ruhig quiet, calm
scheinen, ie, ie seem
   mir scheint I think, it seems to me
schweigsam silent, taciturn
traurig sad
typisch typical
überraschen surprise
überraschend surprising
voll full
weinen cry (= weep)

Lesson XXI

BASIC SENTENCES

Recently Johannes told me his family's history.   (1)   **Neulich hat mir Johannes die Geschichte seiner Familie erzählt.**

His grandfather owned a small book shop in Munich   (2)   **Sein Großvater besaß in München eine kleine Buchhandlung,**

which was going along very well.   (3)   **die sehr gut ging.**

(1)

(2)

(3)

(4)

(5)

(6)

Johannes' father, whose name is Heinrich, (4)	**Johannes' Vater, der Heinrich heißt,**
was old enough in 1914 (5)	**war im Jahre 1914 alt genug,**
to enter the Kaiser's service. (6)	**um in des Kaisers Dienste einzutreten.**
After the end of the First World War (7)	**Nach dem Ende des ersten Weltkrieges**
he went back to his home town. (7a)	**kehrte er in seine Heimatstadt zurück.**

(7)

(7-a)

(8)

(9)

(10)

Soon after that/thereafter/,			**Bald danach,**
when the grandfather died/had died/of pneumonia,	}	(8)	**als der Großvater an Lungenentzündung gestorben war,**
the father inherited the business.		(9)	**erbte der Vater das Geschäft.**
At first he was successful.		(10)	**Zunächst hatte er Erfolg.**

But, because of the steadily worsening times/the always worse   (11)   **Aber wegen der immer schlechter werdenden Zeiten**
    becoming times/,

he decided ⎫   ⎧**entschloß er sich,**
           ⎬   (12)   ⎨
to sell the book store. ⎭   ⎩**die Buchhandlung zu verkaufen.**

Then he moved to Heidelberg,   (13)   **Dann zog er nach Heidelberg,**

where, with (the) help of some relatives,   (14)   **wo er mit Hilfe von einigen Verwandten**

he opened a new book store.   (15)   **eine neue Buchhandlung eröffnete.**

(11)

(12)

(13)

(14)

(15)

VARIATIONS

As a child he lived in Munich.

He left (departed).

He left his village   to become a soldier.

      hometown   sailor.

      farm   flier.

In 1913 he was old enough to fight.

In 1914 he served in the army.

In 1943 I enlisted in the navy.

               air force.

Als Kind wohnte er in München.

Er fuhr ab.

  ging fort.

Er verließ sein Dorf,   um Soldat zu werden.

      seine Heimatstadt,   Matrose

      seinen Hof,   Flieger

In Jahre 1913 war er alt genug, um zu kämpfen.

1914 diente er im Heer.

Im Jahre 1943 meldete ich mich freiwillig zur Marine.

               Luftwaffe.

Before the war things were good/we had good times/.	Vor dem Kriege hatten wir gute Zeiten.
My father's business flourished.	Meines Vaters Geschäft blühte.
When the war broke out, (the) times became worse.	Als der Krieg ausbrach, wurden die Zeiten schlechter.
After had broken out,	Nachdem ausgebrochen war,
As soon as broke out,	Sobald ausbrach,
During the war the business was in poor condition.	Während des Krieges machte das Geschäft nicht gut.
nearly went bankrupt.	beinahe Bankrott.
Then the business improved greatly.	Dann ging das Geschäft viel besser.
At the time of the Armistice my father was very poor.	Zur Zeit des Waffenstillstands war mein Vater sehr arm.
After our enemies had been defeated, the soldiers returned home.	Nachdem die Feinde besiegt worden waren, kehrten die Soldaten nach Hause zurück.
In times of peace, my father was rather well-to-do/lived in rather good circumstances/.	In Friedenszeiten lebte mein Vater in ziemlich guten Verhältnissen.
Are you moving?	Ziehen Sie um?
I'm moving away.	⎰ Ich ziehe fort. ⎱ weg.
I'm moving to Berlin.	Ich ziehe nach Berlin.
I'm moving (into) a new house.	Ich beziehe ein neues Haus.
Well, how long did the war last?	Wie lange dauerte denn der Krieg?
It lasted five and a half years.	Er dauerte fünfeinhalb Jahre.
Who won?	Wer hat gesiegt?
The Americans, British, French and Russians.	Die Amerikaner, Engländer, Franzosen und Russen.
Who lost/Who were the vanquished/?	Wer waren die Besiegten?
The Germans, Italians and Japanese.	Die Deutschen, Italiener und Japaner.
Fortunately, we won.	Glücklicherweise haben wir gewonnen.
Unfortunately, we lost.	Unglücklicherweise haben wir verloren.
There is a man who is dying.	Dort ist ein Mann, der stirbt.
There is a dying man.	Dort ist ein sterbender Mann.
There is a man who is waiting patiently.	⎰ Da ist ein Mann, der geduldig wartet. ⎱ Da ist ein geduldig wartender Mann.

That's a business that's flourishing.

{**Das ist ein Geschäft, das blüht.**
{**Das ist ein blühendes Geschäft.**

That is a party which is taking place this evening.

{**Das ist eine Party, die heute abend stattfindet.**
{**Das ist eine heute abend stattfindende Party.**

Is that the man who is moving to Berlin?

{**Ist das der Mann, der nach Berlin zieht?**
{**Ist das der nach Berlin ziehende Mann?**

I know the man who is moving to Berlin.

{**Ich kenne den Mann, der nach Berlin zieht.**
{**Ich kenne den nach Berlin ziehenden Mann.**

STRUCTURE

The Long Attribute

We have already seen how participial adjectives and gerundives can be used with simple adverbial modifiers when used in attributive position. If complex adverbs, such as prepositional phrases, are used along with such adjectives, the result is called a *long attribute*. Long attributes are much more common in written German than in the spoken language. In scholarly writing they may be of great length and complexity. Since English has no construction of this kind, the English equivalent of a German long attribute is usually a relative clause.

Es ist | **das über Heidelberg geschriebene Buch.** |

It's | *the book that was written about Heidelberg.* |

Peter ist | **ein in Heidelberg studierender Amerikaner.** |

Peter is | *an American who is studying in Heidelberg.* |

Herr Müller erbte das Geschäft von | **seinem an Lungenentzündung gestorbenen Vater.** |

Mr. Müller inherited the business from | *his father, who had died of pneumonia.* |

PATTERN PRACTICES

I. *Combine each of the following pairs of sentences, using the conjunction* **als**:

Die Zeiten wurden schlechter. Der Krieg brach aus.	Die Zeiten wurden schlechter, als der Krieg ausbrach.
Er diente im Heer. Der Krieg brach aus.	Er diente im Heer, als der Krieg ausbrach.
Er mußte im Heer dienen. Der Krieg brach aus.	Er mußte im Heer dienen, als der Krieg ausbrach.
Ich zog nach Berlin. Die Zeiten wurden besser.	Ich zog nach Berlin, als die Zeiten besser wurden.
Mein Vater wurde sehr arm. Das Geschäft machte beinahe Bankrott.	Mein Vater wurde sehr arm, als das Geschäft beinahe Bankrott machte.
Er verließ sein Dorf. Er trat in des Kaisers Dienste ein.	Er verließ sein Dorf, als er in des Kaisers Dienste eintrat.
Der Sohn erbte das Geschäft. Der Vater starb an Lungenentzündung.	Der Sohn erbte das Geschäft, als der Vater an Lungenentzündung starb.
Er eröffnete eine neue Gaststätte. Seine Familie zog nach Heidelberg.	Er eröffnete eine neue Gaststätte, als seine Familie nach Heidelberg zog.

II. *Restate each of the answers to I, placing the* **als-** *clause first:*

Example:

Die Zeiten wurden schlechter, als der Krieg ausbrach.	Als der Krieg ausbrach, wurden die Zeiten schlechter.

III. *Combine each of the following pairs of sentences, using the suggested conjunction:*

Wir kehrten in unsere Heimatstadt zurück. Die Feinde waren besiegt worden.	(nachdem)	Wir kehrten in unsere Heimatstadt zurück, nachdem die Feinde besiegt worden waren.
	(weil)	Wir kehrten in unsere Heimatstadt zurück, weil die Feinde besiegt worden waren.
	(denn)	Wir kehrten in unsere Heimatstadt zurück, denn die Feinde waren besiegt worden.
	(da)	Wir kehrten in unsere Heimatstadt zurück, da die Feinde besiegt worden waren.

Ich habe seine Schwester sehr lieb.	(weil)	Ich habe seine Schwester sehr lieb, weil sie intelligenter ist als ich.
Sie ist intelligenter als ich.	(obgleich)	Ich habe seine Schwester sehr lieb, obgleich sie intelligenter ist als ich.
	(und)	Ich habe seine Schwester sehr lieb, und sie ist intelligenter als ich.
	(aber)	Ich habe seine Schwester sehr lieb, aber sie ist intelligenter als ich.

IV. *Translate into English the answers to Exercises I–III.*

V. *Combine the following pairs of sentences, by making a relative clause of the second:*

Ich kannte einen Amerikaner. Er war Ingenieur.	Ich kannte einen Amerikaner, der Ingenieur war.
Mein Vater hatte ein Geschäft. Es machte Bankrott.	Mein Vater hatte ein Geschäft, das Bankrott machte.
Ich las ein Buch über einen Krieg. Er fand im neunzehnten Jahrhundert statt.	Ich las ein Buch über einen Krieg, der im neunzehnten Jahrhundert stattfand.
Johannes' Vater ist in des Kaisers Dienste eingetreten. Er heißt Heinrich.	Johannes' Vater, der Heinrich heißt, ist in des Kaisers Dienste eingetreten.
Ich habe Johannes' Mutter sehr lieb. Sie ist eine typisch deutsche Frau.	Ich habe Johannes' Mutter, die eine typisch deutsche Frau ist, sehr lieb.
Das ist ein lustiges Lied. Wir haben es oft gesungen.	Das ist ein lustiges Lied, das wir oft gesungen haben.

VI. *Restate each of the following sentences, using a relative clause instead of the long attribute:*

Das ist ein viel gelesenes Buch.	Das ist ein Buch, das man viel liest.
Ich kenne einen an der Universität studierenden jungen Mann.	Ich kenne einen jungen Mann, der an der Universität studiert.
Wegen der immer schlechter werdenden Zeiten verließ er sein Dorf.	Wegen der Zeiten, die immer schlechter wurden, verließ er sein Dorf.

Das ist ein nur selten gesungenes Lied.

Hier ist das gestern verkaufte Auto.

Hier ist der gestern gekaufte Sessel.

Das ist eine heute abend stattfindende Party.

Hier ist die von der Mutter mitgebrachte Milch.

VII. *Translate into English each of the original sentences in VI.*

VIII. *Answer each of the following questions, using the long attribute construction:*

Ist der Arzt in Heidelberg bekannt?	Er ist ein in Heidelberg bekannter Arzt.
Besuchen viele Leute das Schloß?	Ja, es ist ein von vielen Leuten besuchtes Schloß.
Kaufen viele Leute dieses Buch?	Ja, es ist ein vou vielen Leuten gekauftes Buch.
Ist seine Theorie sehr überraschend?	
Ist die Gaststätte tatsächlich berühmt geworden?	
Verkaufte er das Auto gestern?	

VOCABULARY

ab-gehen, ging ab, ist abgegangen leave, depart, go away
ab-fahren, u, ist a, (ä) leave, depart, go away
arm poor
aus-brechen, a, ist o, (i) break out
Bankrott bankrupt
  Bankrott machen go bankrupt
besiegen conquer, defeat
besitzen, besaß, besessen own
beziehen, bezog, bezogen move into, occupy
blühen flourish
die Buchhandlung, -en bookstore
dienen (*dat.*) serve
der Dienst, -es, -e service
ein-treten, a, ist e, (tritt) enter, go in
sich entschließen, o, o decide
erben inherit
der Erfolg, -s, -e success
  Erfolg haben be successful
eröffnen open, establish, set up
der Feind, -es, -e enemy
der Flieger, -s, — flier
fort-ziehen, zog fort, ist fortgezogen move away (change residences)
freiwillig: voluntary
  sich freiwillig melden (zu) volunteer (for), enlist (in)
die Friedenszeit:
  in Friedenszeiten in times of peace, in peacetime
gewinnen, a, o win
halb:
  fünfeinhalb (*etc.*) five and a half (*etc.*)
das Heer, -es, -e army

die Heimatstadt, ⸚e home town
die Hilfe help
  mit Hilfe (*gen.*) with the help of
der Kaiser, -s Kaiser, emperor
kämpfen fight
der Krieg, -es, -e war
die Luftwaffe, -n air force
die Lungenentzündung pneumonia
der Matrose, -n, -n sailor
sich melden zu join, sign up with
nachdem after (*conj.*)
die Marine navy
der Russe, -n, -n Russian (person)
siegen (no object) win, be victorious
der Soldat, -en, -en soldier
sterben:
  an __ sterben die of __
statt-finden, a, u take place
um-ziehen, zog um, ist umgezogen move (change residence)
das Verhältnis, -(ss)es, -(ss)e circumstance
  in guten Verhältnissen leben be well-to-do, well off
verlassen, ie, a, (ä) leave behind, abandon
der Waffenstillstand, -s Armistice
der Weltkrieg, -s, -e world war
Zeit:
  zur Zeit +*gen.* at the time of
ziehen, zog, ist gezogen nach move (change residence) to
zunächst at first
zurück-kehren return, go back

Lesson XXII

BASIC SENTENCES

Soon after his arrival in Heidelberg

Johannes' father became acquainted with a pretty and lively girl.

He fell in love with her,

and she returned his love.

(1) **Bald nach seiner Ankunft in Heidelberg**

(2) **lernte Johannes' Vater ein schönes und lebhaftes Mädchen kennen.**

(3) **Er verliebte sich in sie,**

(4) **und sie erwiderte seine Liebe.**

(5)

(6)

(7)

Since his business venture was successful/was going well/, they were able to celebrate their engagement in 1927, and in 1928 they (were) married.	(5) (6) (7)	**Da sein Geschäft gut ging,** **konnten sie 1927 ihre Verlobung feiern,** **und im Jahre 1928 heirateten sie.**

My friend was the fourth of five children,
who were born to the (married) couple.

(8–9)

He came into the world on October 26, 1940.

(10)

During the war Europe suffered greatly,

(11)

but since (the) end of the war
everything has improved/goes upward again/.

(12)

Mein Freund war das vierte von fünf Kindern,
die dem Ehepaar geboren wurden.

Er kam am 26. Oktober 1940 zur Welt.

Während des Krieges litt Europa sehr,

aber seit Kriegsende
geht alles wieder aufwärts.

(12)

(8-9)

(11)

(10)

Since the family fortunately had no money worries,   (13)

and since Johannes had worked diligently at the "Gymnasium"   (14)
/ (German high school),

he was able to enroll in the university without any trouble   (15)
/without anything further/.

Here is where I met him/made his acquaintance/.   (16)

Da die Familie glücklicherweise keine Geldsorgen hatte,

und da Johannes auf dem Gymnasium fleißig gearbeitet hatte,

konnte er sich ohne weiteres an der Universität einschreiben lassen.

Hier habe ich seine Bekanntschaft gemacht.

(13)

(14)

(15)

(16)

VARIATIONS

He arrived on the	1st of	January.		Er kam am	1. Januar	(ersten Januar)	an.
	2nd	February.			2. Februar	(zweiten Februar)	
	3rd	March.			3. März	(dritten März)	
	10th	April.			10. April	(zehnten April)	
	19th	May.			19. Mai	(neunzehnten Mai)	
	20th	June.			20. Juni	(zwanzigsten Juni)	
	21st	July.			21. Juli	(einundzwanzigsten Juli)	
	22nd	August.			22. August	(zweiundzwanzigsten August)	

/date on letterhead:/

September	6, 1964		6. September	1964	*or*	6. 9. 64
October	7, 1964		7. Oktober	1964		7. 10. 64
November	8, 1964		8. November	1964		8. 11. 64
December	11, 1964		11. Dezember	1964		11. 12. 64

In 1927 he did that.   1927 hat er das gemacht.

He did that in 1927.   Er hat das im Jahre 1927 gemacht.

In 1066 William conquered England.   1066 hat Wilhelm England erobert.

William conquered England in 1066.   Wilhelm hat England im Jahre 1066 erobert.

I own an apartment.   Ich besitze eine Wohnung.

The apartment belongs to me.   Die Wohnung gehört mir.

We moved from Munich to Heidelberg.   Wir sind von München nach Heidelberg gezogen.

You get a position.   Man bekommt eine Stellung.

You change positions.   Man wechselt die Stellung.

You give a position up.   Man gibt die Stellung auf.

You accept a position.   Man nimmt eine Stellung an.

One decides to do something.   Man entschließt sich, etwas zu tun.

I introduced him to my girl friend.   Ich habe ihn meiner Freundin vorgestellt.

He fell in love with a young woman.   Er hat sich in eine junge Dame verliebt.

Hans married Hilde.   Hans hat Hilde geheiratet.

They have gotten married.   Sie haben geheiratet.

Ingeborg is expecting a baby.	Ingeborg erwartet ein Kind.
having	bekommt
Germany lost the Second World War.	Den Zweiten Weltkrieg hat Deutschland verloren.
The United States won the Second World War.	Den Zweiten Weltkrieg haben die Vereinigten Staaten gewonnen.
During wartime everything was very difficult.	Während des Krieges war alles sehr schwer.
peacetime much better.	Im Frieden ———— viel besser.
Many soldiers were killed.	Viele Soldaten kamen um.
He was in the army during the Hitler era.	Er war während der Hitlerzeit im Heer.
navy	in der Kriegsmarine.
air force	in der Luftwaffe.
He was a soldier.	Er war Soldat.
sailor.	Matrose.
flyer.	Flieger.
officer.	Offizier.
He died of a sickness.	Er ist an einer Krankheit gestorben.
He lived a long time.	Er hat lange gelebt.
He is a soldier.	Er ist Soldat.
We fought against the soldiers.	Wir haben gegen die Soldaten gekämpft.
You travel to Germany.	Man fährt nach Deutschland.
You fly to Germany.	Man fliegt nach Deutschland.
You travel to Germany by ship.	Man fährt mit dem Schiff nach Deutschland.
You travel around in Germany.	Man reist in Deutschland herum.
You remain in Germany.	Man bleibt in Deutschland.
You return to the United States.	Man kehrt nach den Vereinigten Staaten zurück.
Tomorrow we go abroad.	Morgen fahren wir ins Ausland.
Tomorrow we'll have the opportunity to go abroad.	Morgen haben wir Gelegenheit, ins Ausland zu fahren.
Cigarettes are sold here.	{ Hier verkauft man Zigaretten.
	{ Hier werden Zigaretten verkauft.
Cigarettes were sold here.	{ Hier verkaufte man Zigaretten.
	{ Hier wurden Zigaretten verkauft.

Books will be sold here.

{ Hier wird man Bücher verkaufen.
{ Hier werden Bücher verkauft werden.

Books have been sold here.

{ Hier hat man Bücher verkauft.
{ Hier sind Bücher verkauft worden.

Shoes had been sold here.

{ Hier hatte man Schuhe verkauft.
{ Hier waren Schuhe verkauft worden.

German is spoken in Germany.

In Deutschland wird Deutsch gesprochen.

German is spoken by my friends.

Von meinen Freunden wird Deutsch gesprochen.

             him.

Von ihm ———————

The engagement was celebrated yesterday.

{ Die Verlobung wurde gestern gefeiert.

     wedding

{ Die Hochzeit

STRUCTURE

A. Ordinal Numbers

English numbers such as "*first, second*," etc. are called ORDINALS. German ordinal numbers have adjective endings, unlike the cardinal numbers (**eins, zwei,** etc.) which do not have endings. The stem of a German ordinal number is usually formed by adding **-t-** to the cardinal number, or **-st-** if the cardinal number ends in **-g, -d, -t.** The German ordinals corresponding to English "*first*," "*third*," and "*seventh*" are irregular and must be learned as vocabulary.

TABLE XXII A

Cardinal	Ordinal	Cardinal	Ordinal
eins	erst-	dreizehn	dreizehnt-
zwei	zweit-	achtzehn	achtzehnt-
drei	dritt-	zweiundzwanzig	zweiundzwanzigst-
vier	viert-	fünfunddreißig	fünfunddreißigst-
fünf	fünft-	achtundvierzig	achtundvierzigst-
sechs	sechst-	sechsundachtzig	sechsundachtzigst-
sieben	siebt-	hundert	hundertst-
acht	acht-	tausend	tausendst-
neun	neunt-	zwölfhundert	zwölfhundertst-
zehn	zehnt-	hundertvierundzwanzig	hundertvierundzwanzigst-

As in English, the longer ordinals are rarely written out. In English we write the Arabic numeral, followed by "*-th, -st, -nd, -rd.*" Germans write only the Arabic number followed by a period (.), regardless of the ending of the ordinal.

TABLE XXII B

Ordinal	Abbreviation
erst-	1.
dritt-	3.
einundzwanzigst-	21.

B. Dates

German dates are given in the order day—month—year (as opposed to English month—day—year). German dates are preceded by the definite article, and usually they are in the accusative case, unless they are preceded by the preposition **am** (=Eng. "*on*"), or unless they stand as predicate nominatives. Notice that if the year is given, it is not preceded by a comma, as in English.

Den 11. Januar zog ich fort.
I moved away January 11th.

Er kommt am 14. Juli an.
He's arriving on July 14th.

Heute ist der 5. März 1963. (Predicate nominative)
Today is March 5, 1963.

C. Years as Dates

When giving a year alone as a date, Germans either use the number of the year by itself, or precede it with **im Jahre.** In German the word **in** can never precede the number of a year, as "*in*" does in English.

$$\left.\begin{array}{l} \textbf{1945} \\ \textbf{im Jahre 1945} \end{array}\right\} = \textit{in 1945}$$

Der Erste Weltkrieg endete 1918.

Der Erste Weltkrieg endete im Jahre 1918.
World War I ended in 1918.

D. The Passive

English sentences which have verb constructions made from a form of "*be*" plus a perfect participle are called *passive sentences*. Typical English passive sentences are:

> *Shoes are sold here.*   *German is spoken in Germany.*

Verbs used in passive sentences are said to be in the PASSIVE VOICE. The German passive voice is made from a form of **werden** plus a perfect participle.

> **Schuhe werden hier verkauft.**   **Deutsch wird in Deutschland gesprochen.**
> *Shoes are sold here.*   *German is spoken in Germany.*

In the perfect tenses **worden,** a special participle of **werden,** is used. (The usual participle of **werden** is **geworden.**)

Present   **Deutsch** **wird** **in Deutschland** **gesprochen** .

           German *is* *spoken* *in Germany.*

Future   **Deutsch wird in Deutschland** **gesprochen** **werden** .

           German will *be* *spoken* *in Germany.*

Past   **Deutsch** **wurde** **in Deutschland** **gesprochen** .

           German *was* *spoken* *in Germany.*

Present Perfect   **Deutsch ist in Deutschland** **gesprochen** **worden** .

           German has *been* *spoken* *in Germany.*

Pluperfect   **Deutsch war in Deutschland** **gesprochen** **worden** .

           German had *been* *spoken* *in Germany.*

Notice that the tense of **werden** is the same as the tense of "*be*."

E. Man as Equivalent for the Passive

In English we often avoid using a passive in order to be less formal. To do this we use the pronoun "*they*" in an impersonal sense. Thus,

They sell cigarettes here.

means the same as, but is less formal than,

Cigarettes are sold here.

German has a similar way of forming an informal equivalent for the passive. Here German uses the impersonal pronoun **man.**

| *Formal* | **Zigaretten werden hier verkauft.** | *Informal* | **Man verkauft hier Zigaretten.** |
| | *Cigarettes are sold here.* | | *They sell cigarettes here.* |

F. Special Use of the Passive

In German the passive is used (usually only formally) to express an activity when no actual subject is expressed. The impersonal pronoun **es** is used, unless some other sentence element comes first.

> **Es wurde bei der gestrigen Party gesungen.**
> **Bei der gestrigen Party wurde gesungen.**
> *There was singing at yesterday's party.*

Note that in the second German sentence no subject is expressed.

PATTERN PRACTICES

I. *Restate each of the following sentences as passives:*

Man sieht ihn oft in Heidelberg.	Er wird oft in Heidelberg gesehen.
Hilde	Hilde
sie	Sie werden
mich	Ich werde
Man verkauft hier Strümpfe.	Hier werden Strümpfe verkauft.
Zigaretten.	Zigaretten
Lederhosen.	Lederhosen
Zeitungen.	Zeitungen

II. *Restate each of the following as a past event, using the past tense:*

Bei der Party heute werden Lieder gesungen.   Bei der Party gestern wurden Lieder gesungen.

                            Karten gespielt.   Karten gespielt.

        wird   getanzt.   wurde   getanzt.

                          geplaudert.   geplaudert.

Ein Kind wird ihr   heute geboren.   Ein Kind wurde ihr   gestern geboren.

             ihnen   ihnen

Ihre Verlobung wird heute gefeiert.   Ihre Verlobung wurde gestern gefeiert.

   Hochzeit   Hochzeit

III. *Restate each of your answers to II as questions, beginning with the phrase* **"Wissen Sie . . ."**:

Bei der Party gestern   wurden Lieder gesungen.   Wissen Sie, daß bei der Party gestern Lieder gesungen wurden?

                        Karten gespielt.   Wissen Sie, daß bei der Party gestern Karten gespielt wurden?

              wurde   getanzt.   Wissen Sie, daß bei der Party gestern getanzt wurde?

                        geplaudert.

Ein Kind wurde ihr   gestern geboren.

                 ihnen

Ihre Verlobung wurde gestern gefeiert.

   Hochzeit

IV. *Answer in the affirmative, using the present perfect of the passive:*

Wurde der Krieg von den USA gewonnen?   Ja, der Krieg ist von den USA gewonnen worden.

       er am zwanzigsten Oktober geboren?   er ist am zwanzigsten Oktober geboren worden.

Wurde ihre Verlobung im letzten Jahre gefeiert?   ihre Verlobung ist im letzten Jahre gefeiert worden.

              am Sonntag gefeiert?   am Sonntag gefeiert worden.

Wurden sie letzten Sommer vorgestellt?   sie sind letzten Sommer vorgestellt worden.

Wurde Johannes' Aufgabe von seiner Schwester   Johannes' Aufgabe ist von seiner Schwester

    gemacht?   gemacht worden.

Wurden Sie letzten Freitag von ihm gesehen?   ich bin letzten Freitag von ihm gesehen worden.

Wurde die Stellung aufgegeben?   die Stellung ist aufgegeben worden.

               angenommen?   angenommen worden.

V. *Translate into English each of your answers in Practice IV.*

VI. *Restate each of your answers in IV, using the pluperfect of the passive:*

    Example:

    Der Krieg ist von den USA gewonnen worden.   Der Krieg war von den USA gewonnen worden.

VII. *Lesen und erklären Sie den folgenden modernen deutschen Witz!*

    Karl: Man sagt, der große Kommunist ist neulich gestorben.   Hans: Ja — worden.

VIII. *In 500 German words, write your autobiography.*

VOCABULARY

die Ankunft, ⸚e arrival
aufwärts upwards, forward
  aufwärts gehen improve
das Ausland, -(e)s, ins Ausland (to) abroad
an-nehmen, a, angenommen, (nimmt an) accept
auf-geben, a, e (i) give up, relinquish
die Bekanntschaft, -en acquaintance
bekommen, a, o get, obtain
  ein Kind bekommen have a baby
dritt- third
das Ehepaar, -s, -e (married) couple
ein-schreiben:
  sich einschreiben lassen enroll
erobern conquer
erwarten expect
erwidern return, render in kind
feiern celebrate
der Friede, -ns (no *pl.*) peace
gehören (*dat.*) belong (to)
die Geldsorge, -n worry over money
die Gelegenheit, -en opportunity
  Gelegenheit haben have a chance (opportunity)
das Gymnasium, -s, Gymnasien "Gymnasium" (German high school)
heiraten marry, get married

herum-reisen (in) travel around (in)
die Hitlerzeit the Hitler era
die Hochzeit, -en wedding
die Krankheit, -en sickness
das Kriegsende, -s end of a war
  seit Kriegsende since the end of the war
die Kriegsmarine, -n navy
leben live
leiden, litt, gelitten suffer
die Liebe love
der Offizier, -s, -e officer
töten kill
um-kommen, kam um, ist o die
sich verlieben (in+ *acc.*) fall in love (with)
die Verlobung, -en engagement
von by
vor-stellen introduce, present (to)
wechseln change (get another), exchange
weiter:
  ohne weiteres without any further trouble
die Welt, -en world
  zur Welt kommen be born, come into the world
die Wohnung, -en apartment

Lesson XXIII

BASIC SENTENCES

(1)

(2)

(3)

(4)

Johannes—Hello! Is this seven-one-nine-four?	(1)	**Johannes—Hallo! Ist dies sieben-eins-neun-vier?**
Fritz —Yes! Storm speaking.	(2)	**Fritz —Ja! Hier Storm.**
J. —Hi, Storm! This is Müller.	(3)	**J. —Tag, Storm. Hier Müller.**
I called to invite you to dinner at our place.	(4)	**Ich habe angerufen, um Sie zum Abendessen bei uns einzuladen.**

Do you have anything/something/special planned for (5)   **Haben Sie heute abend etwas Besonderes vor?**
tonight?

I'd like to introduce our American guest to you.   (6)   **Ich möchte Ihnen unseren amerikanischen Gast vorstellen.**

F.   —I'd like to/Very gladly/.   (7)   F.   **—Sehr gerne!**

It's nice of you to invite me.   (8)   **Es ist nett von Ihnen, mich einzuladen.**

(5)

(6)

(7)

(8)

I have nothing special planned;	(9)	**Ich habe nichts Besonderes vor;**
but I wouldn't want to cause/make/you any inconvenience.	(10)	**ich möchte Ihnen aber keine Umstände machen.**
J. —Don't be silly.	(11)	**J. —Aber nein, keineswegs.**
How would it be if I pick you up about five o'clock?	(12)	**Wie wäre es, wenn ich Sie gegen fünf Uhr abholte?**

F.	—Let's say about six instead/rather/.	(13)	
	You see, I have a report to write,	(14)	
	which I have to turn in by Monday.	(15)	
J.	—Okay. It's a deal/done/. I'll come by about six.	(16)	
	Until then, so long.	(17)	
F.	—Thanks for the call.	(18)	
J.	—Good-bye/Until hearing again/.	(19)	

F.	—Sagen wir lieber gegen sechs.
	Ich habe nämlich ein Referat zu schreiben,
	das ich bis Montag einreichen muß.
J.	—Also gut! Abgemacht! Ich komme gegen sechs vorbei.
	Bis dahin, tschüß.
F.	—Danke für den Anruf!
J.	—Auf Wiederhören.

(13)

(14)

(15)

(16)

(17)

(18)

(19)

VARIATIONS

I'm calling him up.	**Ich rufe ihn an.**
I called him up.	**Ich habe ihn angerufen.**
It was nice of him to call me up.	**Es war nett von ihm, mich anzurufen.**
They're inviting us.	**Sie laden uns ein.**
They had invited us.	**Sie hatten uns eingeladen.**
It was nice of them to invite us.	**Es war nett von ihnen, uns einzuladen.**
I introduced him to my mother.	**Ich stellte ihn meiner Mutter vor.**
I wanted to introduce him to my mother.	**Ich wollte ihn meiner Mutter vorstellen.**
How would it be, if I introduced you to him?	**Wie wäre es, wenn ich Sie ihm vorstelle?**
It was nice of you to introduce me to him.	**Es war nett von Ihnen, mich ihm vorzustellen.**
Please hand in your report.	**Bitte, reichen Sie Ihr Referat ein!**
I've already handed it in.	**Ich hab' es schon eingereicht.**
I remembered to hand it in on time.	**Ich habe daran gedacht, es rechtzeitig einzureichen.**
Would you pick me up?	**Würden Sie mich abholen?**
I'll be glad to pick you up.	**Es wird mich freuen, Sie abzuholen.**

I'm sorry that I didn't pick you up yesterday.	**Es tut mir leid, daß ich Sie gestern nicht abgeholt habe.**
Are you planning something for tonight?	**Hast du heute abend etwas vor?**
No, I wasn't planning anything.	**Nein, ich habe nichts vor.**
No, I hadn't planned anything.	**Nein, ich hatte nichts vor.**
Can you imagine that?	**Können Sie sich das vorstellen?**
No, I can't imagine such a thing.	**Nein, so etwas kann ich mir nicht vorstellen.**
It was easy for me to imagine something like that.	**Ich konnte mir so etwas gut vorstellen.**
It would be hard for me to imagine that.	**Ich könnte mir so etwas nur schwer vorstellen.**
Don't be silly.	**Machen Sie keine Witze!**
Don't worry.	**Machen Sie sich keine Sorgen!**
Don't go to any trouble.	**Machen Sie keine Umstände!**
Do you want to make a date with me?	**Wollen Sie sich mit mir verabreden?**
It's a deal!	**Abgemacht!**
Don't make such a bad face!	**Machen Sie nicht so ein böses Gesicht!**
Let's get ready.	**Wir wollen uns fertig machen.**

I bought something special.   **Ich habe etwas Besonderes gekauft.**

new.	**Neues**
extraordinary.	**Außerordentliches**
pretty.	**Schönes**
wonderful.	**Wunderbares**

I haven't bought anything different.   **Ich habe nichts Anderes gekauft.**

big.	**Großes**
heavy.	**Schweres**
light.	**Leichtes**

I had planned to write a paper.   **Ich hatte vor, ein Referat zu schreiben.**

letter.	**einen Brief**
book.	**ein Buch**
chapter.	**ein Kapitel**
essay.	**einen Aufsatz**
report.	**einen Bericht**
article.	**einen Artikel**

Excuse me. Do you have a phone?	**Verzeihung! Haben Sie Telefon?**
Yes, but it's a private one.	**Ja, aber es ist ein Privattelefon.**
Please go to the public phone booth	**Bitte, gehen Sie zur öffentlichen Fernsprechstelle,**
and dial/choose/the number.	**und wählen Sie die Nummer!**
This number isn't in the phone book.	**Diese Nummer steht nicht im Telefonbuch.**
Then I'd call Information.	**Dann würde ich die Auskunft anrufen.**
The line is busy/occupied/.	**Die Leitung ist besetzt.**
Whom did you call?	**Wen haben Sie angerufen?**
I called Johannes.	**Ich habe Johannes angerufen.**
Whom did you see?	**Wen hast du gesehen?**
I saw my mother.	**Ich habe meine Mutter gesehen.**
Whom did you help?	**Wem haben Sie geholfen?**
I helped my friend.	**Ich habe meinem Freund geholfen.**
From whom did you hear that?	**Von wem haben Sie das gehört?**
I heard that from Wilhelm.	**Von Wilhelm habe ich das gehört.**

STRUCTURE

A. Review of Stressed Adverbs

The sentences which follow form a review of the position of stressed adverbs in relation to their verbs. As a help in pronunciation and to keep the stressed adverbs prominent, we will artificially indicate them with capital letters, although this is not done in actual written German.

EIN-laden: *invite*

Wir laden unsere Freunde EIN.	*We're inviting our friends.*
Fritz wird uns EINladen.	*Fritz is going to invite us.*
Sie wollten ihn nicht EINladen.	*They didn't want to invite him.*
Es war nett von ihnen, sie EINzuladen.	*It was nice of them to invite her.*
Er hat mich nie EINgeladen.	*He's never invited me.*
Er lud mich jeden Tag EIN.	*He invited me every day.*
Hätte ich ihn nur EINgeladen!	*If I'd only invited him!*

AN-kommen: *arrive*

Er kommt übermorgen AN.	*He's arriving day after tomorrow.*
Sie sind gestern in Berlin ANgekommen.	*They arrived in Berlin yesterday.*
Sie wird um acht Uhr ANkommen.	*She'll arrive at eight o'clock.*
Man muß immer rechtzeitig dort ANkommen.	*You always have to get there on time.*
Ich wußte nicht, daß er immer so spät ANkommt.	*I didn't know that he always arrives so late.*
Bis heute war er immer früh ANgekommen.	*Until today he'd always arrived on time.*

B. Wer, Wen, Wem, Wessen—*who? whom? whose?*

Just as English has an object form of "*who*," German has accusative, dative, and genitive forms of **wer**, which are **wen, wem,** and **wessen** respectively, and which correspond to similar forms of the relative pronoun **der.** While some speakers of English rarely use "*whom*" except formally, Germans do use the proper form of **wer.**

Wer war das?	*Who was that?*	**Mit wem haben Sie gesprochen?**	*Whom did you talk to?*
Wen haben Sie gesehen?	*Whom did you see?*	**Wessen Handschuh ist dies?**	*Whose glove is this?*

In adjective clauses, relative pronouns, and not forms of **wer,** are used.

     Herr Schmidt ist der Mann, der hier wohnt.   *Mr. Schmidt is the man who lives here.*

PATTERN PRACTICES

I. *Restate the following sentences in the past tense:*

Ich rufe ihn an.	Ich rief ihn an.
Sie laden uns ein.	Sie luden uns ein.
Ich stelle ihn meiner Mutter vor.	Ich stellte ihn meiner Mutter vor.
Er reicht sein Referat ein.	Er reichte sein Referat ein.
Wir holen sie ab.	Wir holten sie ab.
Was hast du Dienstag vor?	Was hattest du Dienstag vor?
Wir stellen uns das vor.	Wir stellten uns das vor.
Sie sehen sich die Schaufenster an.	Sie sahen sich die Schaufenster an.
Sie zieht das blaue Kleid an.	Sie zog das blaue Kleid an.
Ihr steigt den Berg hinauf.	Ihr stiegt den Berg hinauf.

II. *Restate each of your responses in Practice I in the present perfect:*

> Ich habe ihn angerufen.
>
> Sie haben uns eingeladen.
>
> Ich habe ihn meiner Mutter vorgestellt.
>
> Er hat sein Referat eingereicht.
>
> Wir haben sie abgeholt.

III. *Change the sentences in Practice II to the past perfect:*

> *Example:*
>
> Ich habe ihn angerufen.   Ich hatte ihn angerufen.

IV. *Introduce an infinitive phrase into the following sentences, beginning with the phrase,* **"Es war nett von Ihnen, . . .":**

Ich habe ihn angerufen.	Es war nett von Ihnen, ihn anzurufen.
Wir haben Sie eingeladen.	mich einzuladen.
Ich habe ihn meiner Mutter vorgestellt.	ihn Ihrer Mutter vorzustellen.
Ich habe sein Referat eingereicht.	sein Referat einzureichen.
Wir haben sie abgeholt.	sie abzuholen.
Ich bin früh angekommen.	früh anzukommen.

V. *Express the following as suggestions, beginning with the phrase,* **"Wie wäre es, . . .":**

Sie ruft ihn an.	Wie wäre es, wenn sie ihn anriefe?
Er lädt ihn ein.	er ihn einlüde?
Sie stellt ihn ihrer Mutter vor.	sie ihn ihrer Mutter vorstellte?
Er reicht sein Referat ein.	
Wir holen sie ab.	
Ich sehe mir das berühmte Bild an.	
Sie zieht das neue Kleid an.	
Wir steigen den Berg hinauf.	

VI. *Change the following sentences to* **daß** *clauses, beginning with the phrase,* "**Wissen Sie, . . .**":

Er kam um sieben Uhr an.   Wissen Sie, daß er um sieben Uhr ankam?

Sie haben sich die Bücher angesehen.   sie sich die Bücher angesehen haben?

Wir fahren morgen ab.

Er hat uns seiner Mutter vorgestellt.

Ich habe vor, nach München zu fahren.

Er war um sechs Uhr vorbeigekommen.

Sie reichte ihr Referat ein.

VII. *Answer the following questions in the negative, using the word* **nichts** *with the adjective:*

Haben Sie etwas Besonderes   gekauft?   Nein, ich habe nichts Besonderes   gekauft.

Haben Sie   Neues   gesehen?   ich habe   Neues   gesehen.

Hat   er   Außerordentliches getan?   er hat   Außerordentliches getan.

Habt ihr   Interessantes   gefunden?

Hat   sie   Anderes   gesagt?

Hast du heute etwas Schweres   getan?
                    Leichtes

Haben sie etwas Schönes im Tiergarten gesehen?

VIII. *Follow the statement on the left with a question about identity, using* **wen** *or* **wem** *and the suggested preposition if there is one:*

Ich hörte das gestern.   (von)   Von wem hörten Sie das?

Ich rief ihn Dienstag an.   Wen riefen Sie Dienstag an?

Er wohnte bei einer Familie in München.   (bei)   Bei wem wohnte er in München?

Sie unterhielten sich eine ganze Stunde über die Mädchen.   (über)   Über wen unterhielten sie sich eine ganze Stunde?

Ich habe der Dame geholfen.

Ich habe das für meine Freundin gemacht.   (für)

Wir sprachen über einen Rechtsanwalt.   (über)

Sie ist mit dem Jungen in die Stadt gegangen.   (mit)

Wir warten auf einen Freund.   (auf)

VOCABULARY

ab-holen   "pick up," come by for, call for
ab-machen   arrange
abmachen:
   Abgemacht!   It's a deal!
Also gut!   Okay!
der Anruf, -s, -e   call ('phone)
an-rufen, ie, u   to call up (on the 'phone)
der Artikel, -s, __   article
der Aufsatz, -es, ∺e   essay
die Auskunft, ∺e   piece of information
außerordentlich   unusual, extraordinary
der Bericht, -s, -e   report
besetzt   occupied, taken; busy ('phone)
besonder   special
bis:
   bis Montag (*etc.*)   by Monday (*etc.*)
   bis dahin   till then
böse   bad
ein-reichen   hand in
etwas:
   etwas Neues (*etc.*)   something new (*etc.*)
die Fernsprechstelle, -n   'phone booth
fertig:
   fertig machen   to make ready
Hallo!   Hello! (on the 'phone)
das Kapitel, -s, __   chapter
keineswegs   in no way; not at all

leid:
   Es tut mir leid.   I am sorry.
die Leitung, -en   line, connection ('phone)
lieber   instead, rather
nett   nice
   es ist nett von Ihnen   it's nice of you
nichts:
   nichts Neues (*etc.*)   nothing new (*etc.*)
die Nummer, -n   number
öffentlich   public
privat   private
das Referat, -s, -e   paper, report
so etwas   something like that
die Sorge, -en   trouble, anxiety
   sich Sorgen machen   worry
das Telefonbuch, -es, ∺er   'phone-book
Tschüß!   So long!
der Umstand, -s, ∺e   formality, ceremony
   Umstände machen (*dat.*)   cause inconvenience, make trouble (for);
     go to some trouble
vorbei-kommen, a, ist o   come past
vor-haben, hatte vor, vorgehabt   have on the agenda, have plans
wählen   to choose; dial (a 'phone number)
wer, wen, wem, wessen   who, whom, whose
wiederhören:
   Auf Wiederhören   good-bye (over the 'phone)
der Witz, -es, -e   joke
   Witze machen   make jokes, be silly, "kid"

Lesson XXIV

BASIC SENTENCES

Yesterday's dinner was very pleasant.	(1)	**Das Abendessen gestern war recht gemütlich.**
Mrs. Müller is an excellent cook,	(2)	**Frau Müller ist eine ausgezeichnete Köchin,**
and the food tasted first-rate.	(3)	**und das Essen schmeckte prima.**
The Germans like to begin with a hot soup.	(4)	**Die Deutschen fangen gerne mit einer heißen Suppe an.**

(1)

(2)

(3)

(4)

We had a thick meat and vegetable soup	(5)	**Wir bekamen eine dicke Fleisch-und Gemüsesuppe,**
which is called *Kraftbrühe mit Einlage*/which one names strength-broth with thickening/.	(6)	**die man Kraftbrühe mit Einlage nennt.**
The main course consisted of roast beef, potatoes with (a) sauce, and green salad.	(7)	**Das Hauptgericht bestand aus Rinderbraten, Kartoffeln mit Soße und grünem Salat.**
With the meal we ate bread and butter;	(7a)	**Dazu aßen wir Brot und Butter;**
and we drank beer,	(8–9)	**und wir tranken Bier,**
which was too warm for my taste.		**das für meinen Geschmack zu warm war.**

(5)

(7)

(7-a)

"KRAFTBRÜHE MIT EINLAGE"

(6)

(8-9)

Many Germans like to drink beer with their meals.

Naturally there was dessert, too.

Mrs. Müller served us a splendid apple strudel with whipped cream.

With/the/dessert we drank a cup of strong coffee.

At the end I was so full

that I could hardly get up from the table.

(10) **Viele Deutsche trinken gerne Bier zu ihren Mahlzeiten.**

(11) **Natürlich gab es auch Nachtisch.**

(12) **Frau Müller servierte uns einen herrlichen Apfelstrudel mit Schlagsahne.**

(13) **Mit dem Nachtisch tranken wir eine Tasse starken Kaffee.**

(14) **Am Ende war ich so satt,**

(15) **daß ich kaum vom Tisch aufstehen konnte.**

(10) (11) (12) (13) (14) (15)

VARIATIONS

What brand of tobacco do you smoke?	**Welche Tabakmarke rauchen Sie?**
No smoking!	**Rauchen verboten!**
The food is tasty/tastes good/.	**Das Essen schmeckt gut.**
smells good.	**riecht gut.**
The Germans usually don't eat rolls with potatoes at the same meal.	**Gewöhnlich essen die Deutschen nicht Brötchen und Kartoffeln zur gleichen Mahlzeit.**
For supper they often eat "open sandwiches."	**Zu Abend essen sie oft belegte Brote.**
An "open sandwich" is a piece of bread with cheese or meat on it.	**Ein belegtes Brot ist ein Stück Brot mit Käse oder Fleisch darauf.**
At noon they often eat ham or sausage with eggs, vegetables and a salad.	**Zu Mittag essen sie oft Schinken oder Wurst mit Eiern, Gemüse und Salat.**
Afterwards they often have fruit.	**Hinterher essen sie oft Obst.**
The wife does/washes/the dishes.	**Die Frau spült das Geschirr.**
dries	**trocknet ab.**
The Germans like to eat fish very much.	**Die Deutschen essen sehr gerne Fisch.**
In the afternoon the German woman drinks a cup of coffee with a friend (an acquaintance).	**Nachmittags trinkt die Deutsche eine Tasse Kaffee mit einer Bekannten.**
They don't drink tea as often as coffee.	**Sie trinken nicht so viel Tee wie Kaffee.**
In a restaurant the German orders a bottle of wine or a bottle of mineral water.	**In einer Gaststätte bestellt der Deutsche eine Flasche Wein oder eine Flasche Mineralwasser.**
In Bavaria, however, they like to drink beer most of all.	**Aber in Bayern trinkt man am liebsten Bier.**
There you can also find wonderful apple juice, especially in the country.	**Da findet man auch wunderbaren Apfelsaft, besonders auf dem Lande.**
And during the cherry season/harvest/you can order a wonderful cherry tart.	**Und zur Zeit der Kirschernte kann man eine wunderbare Kirschtorte bestellen.**
You find all sorts of candies in a candy store.	**In einem Süßwarengeschäft findet man allerlei Süßigkeiten.**
By the way, the Germans like to eat ice cream very much.	**Übrigens essen die Deutschen sehr gerne Eis.**
The Germans like to drink strong coffee.	**Die Deutschen trinken gern starken Kaffee.**
A German (male) likes to drink strong coffee.	**Ein Deutscher trinkt gern starken Kaffee.**

A German (female)	likes to drink strong coffee.	**Eine Deutsche trinkt gern starken Kaffee.**
The German (male)		**Der Deutsche**
The German (female)		**Die Deutsche**
Many Germans	like	**Viele Deutsche trinken**
We Germans	like	**Wir Deutsche(n) trinken**
All Germans		**Alle Deutschen**
Some Germans		**Einige Deutsche**

I saw the Germans during supper.

Ich habe die   Deutschen beim Abendessen gesehen.

	the German (male)	**den**	**Deutschen**
	the German (female)	**die**	**Deutsche**
	a few Germans	**einige**	**Deutsche**
	a German (male)	**einen**	**Deutschen**
	a German (female)	**eine**	**Deutsche**

We ate/took in/a snack with the Germans.

Wir haben einen Imbiß mit den   Deutschen eingenommen.

	the German (male).	**dem**	**Deutschen**
	the German (female).	**der**	**Deutschen**
	some/a few/Germans.	**einigen**	**Deutschen**
	a German (male).	**einem**	**Deutschen**
	a German (female).	**einer**	**Deutschen**

VOCABULARY

ab-trocknen dry (off)
der Apfelsaft, -(e)s apple juice
der Apfelstrudel, -s, __ apple strudel
ausgezeichnet excellent
der (die) Bekannte, -n, -n acquaintance (*m.*, *f.*)
belegt laid down;
  belegtes Brot open sandwich
bestehen, bestand, bestanden (aus) consist (of)
bestellen order (from someone)
  das Brot, -es, -e bread, loaf of bread
das Brötchen, -s, __ roll
die Butter butter

das Ei, -es, -er egg
das Eis, -(s)es ice cream
das Essen food
der Fisch, -es, -e fish
die Flasche, -n bottle
das Fleisch, -es meat
das Gemüse, -s vegetable
das Geschirr, -s dishes, crockery, table utensils
der Geschmack, -s taste
das Hauptgericht, -(e)s, -e main course
herrlich splendid
hinterher afterwards

der Imbiß, -(ss)es, -(ss)e   snack, "bite"

die Kartoffel, -n   potato

der Käse, -s   cheese

die Kirschernte, -n   the cherry harvest

die Kirschtorte, -n   cherry pie

die Köchin, -nen   cook (*f.*)

(die) Kraftbrühe mit Einlage   (strength) broth with thickening

die Mahlzeit, -en   meal

das Mineralwasser, -s   mineral water

der Nachtisch, -es, -e   dessert

das Obst, -es   fruit

prima   first-rate

recht   very, quite, really

riechen, o, o   smell

der Rinderbraten, -s   roast beef

der Salat, -(e)s, -e   salad

satt   full, satiated

der Schinken, -s, ___   ham

die Schlagsahne   whipped cream

schmecken   taste (give off a taste)

servieren   serve

die Soße, -n   sauce

spülen   wash

das Stück, -es, -e   piece

die Suppe, -n   soup

die Süßigkeit, -en   candy

das Süßwarengeschäft, -(e)s, -e   candy shop

die Tabakmarke, -n   brand of tobacco

die Tasse, -n   cup

der Tee, -s   tea

verbieten, o, o   forbid

die Wurst, ⁝e   sausage

zu:

    zur Mahlzeit   with a meal

Review Questions

1. Haben Sie einen älteren Bruder? Wie heißt er?
2. Können Sie mir sagen, wo der Bahnhof ist?
3. Wie alt werden Sie nächstes Jahr sein?
4. Wie ist Ihr Vorname?
5. Wo will Peter studieren?
6. Was kann man in Neuyork sehen?
7. Seit wann sind Sie hier auf der Universität?
8. Wie lange lernen Sie schon Deutsch?
9. Was machen Sie früh am Morgen?
10. Was macht Peter nach dem Abendessen?
11. Wie lange arbeiten Sie jeden Tag zu Hause?
12. Wohin geht Peter nach den Vorlesungen?
13. Worüber sprechen Sie am liebsten?
14. Um wieviel Uhr gingen Sie gestern zu Bett?
15. Zu welchen Jahreszeiten war Peter in Heidelberg?
16. Wie lange wohnte Peter in Heidelberg?
17. Wie war das Wetter in Heidelberg, als Peter da war?
18. Wie lange dauert Ihre Studienzeit?
19. Warum möchten Sie nach Deutschland fahren?
20. Was haben Sie bei der Party gemacht?
21. Wohin sind Sie nach der Party gegangen?
22. Wohin hatten Sie das Mädchen eingeladen?
23. Was lernten Sie in der Mittelschule?
24. Wofür interessieren Sie sich jetzt?
25. Was muß man machen, um gute Noten zu bekommen?
26. Was muß man machen, um gut Deutsch zu lernen?
27. Was studieren Sie auf der Universität?
28. Was für eine Stadt ist Heidelberg?
29. Wie alt ist Heidelberg?
30. Welche Kleidungsstücke sollte man tragen, wenn man ins Theater geht?
31. Was trägt man oft auf dem Lande in Deutschland?
32. Worüber haben sich Ihre Freunde bei der Party unterhalten?
33. Beschreiben Sie Ihre Familie!
34. Warum ist alles heute schief gegangen?
35. Erzählen Sie einen Witz auf Deutsch!
36. Sind Sie kürzlich krank gewesen? Was tat Ihnen weh?
37. Wie fühlen Sie sich jetzt?
38. Wo hat Herr Müller als Kind gewohnt?
39. Warum hat er seine Geburtsstadt verlassen?
40. Was haben die Müllers in der Nachkriegszeit gemacht?
41. Was für ein Geschäft hatte Johannes' Großvater?
42. Warum sind die Müllers nach Heidelberg umgezogen?
43. Wie ist es ihnen während der Hitlerzeit gegangen?
44. Was lehrt Johannes' Schwester?
45. Was mußte Johannes tun, um Physiker zu werden?
46. Beschreiben Sie einen Freund oder eine Freundin!
47. Was ist der Unterschied zwischen einem deutschen belegten Brot und einem amerikanischen Sandwich?
48. Warum ruft Johannes Fritz Storm an?
49. Wen rufen Sie am liebsten an?
50. Beschreiben Sie ein deutsches Abendessen!

Vocabulary

A

der Abend, -s, -e evening
  jeden Abend every evening
  am Abend in the evening
Abend! 'Evening!
das Abendbrot, -s, -e supper
abends in the evening
aber but
ab-fahren, u, ist a, (ä) leave, depart, go away
ab-gehen, ging ab, ist abgegangen leave, depart, go away
Abgemacht! It's a deal!
ab-holen "pick-up," come by for, call for
ab-machen arrange
die Absicht, -en intention
  mit Absicht on purpose
ab-trocknen dry
ach! oh!
ähnlich (dat.) like, similar (to)
  ähnlich sehen (dat.) look like, resemble
der Akzent, -s, -e accent
alle everyone
allerlei all sorts of
alles everything
allgemein:
  im allgemeinen in general
als as; when; than
als ob as though
also well...
also gut! Okay!
alt (̈er, ̈est) old
Amerika, -s America
der Amerikaner, -s, __ American
die Amerikanerin, -nen American (woman)
amerikanisch American (adj.)
an (acc., dat.) at; to; on
  am Mittag (etc.) at noon (etc.)
  am besten (etc.) best (etc.)
ander other

der Anfang, -s, ̈e beginning
  am Anfang at first; at the beginning
  von Anfang an from the beginning
an-fangen, i, a, (ä) begin
angenehm pleasant
angestellt employed
angezogen:
  gut angezogen well-dressed
sich an-hören listen to
an-kommen, a, ist o arrive
die Ankunft, ̈e arrival
an-nehmen, a, angenommen, (nimmt an) accept
der Anruf, -s, -e call ('phone)
an-rufen, ie, u to call up (on the 'phone)
sich an-schauen watch, look at
sich an-sehen, a, e, (ie) look at
die Antwort, -en the answer
antworten (dat.) answer (someone)
sich an-ziehen, zog an, angezogen get dressed
der Anzug, -s, ̈e suit
der Apfelsaft, -(e)s apple juice
der Apfelstrudel, -s, __ apple strudel
April April
die Arbeit, -en work
arbeiten work; study (be at work over one's books)
die Arithmetik arithmetic
arm poor
der Arm, -es, -e arm
der Artikel, -s, __ article
der Arzt, -es, ̈e doctor
auch also, too
  auch nicht not...either
  auch noch in addition, yet another
auf (acc., dat) on, upon; to; toward; at
  auf Deutsch in German
  auf Wiedersehen! Good-bye, so long!
auf-bauen construct, build
  wieder-auf-bauen rebuild, reconstruct
die Aufgabe, -n homework, assignment
auf-geben, a, e, (i) give up, relinquish

auf-hören   stop, cease
auf-machen   open
die Aufnahme, -n   photo
auf-passen   pay attention
   paß' auf!   watch out!
aufregend   exciting
der Aufsatz, -es, ¨e   essay
auf-stehen, stand auf, ist aufgestanden   get up, stand up
auf-wachen, ist aufgewacht   wake up
aufwärts   upwards, forward
   aufwärts gehen   improve
das Auge, -s, -n   eye
August   August
aus (*dat.*)   out of; from; made of
aus-brechen, a, ist o, (i)   break out
der Ausdruck, -s, ¨e   expression
der Ausflug, -s, ¨e   outing
   Ausflüge machen   go on outings
aus-gehen, ging aus, ist ausgegangen   go out
ausgezeichnet   excellent
aus-kommen, a, ist o:
   auskommen ohne   get along without
die Auskunft, ¨e   piece of information
das Ausland, -(e)s:
   ins Ausland   (to) abroad
aus-machen:
   es macht nichts aus   it doesn't matter
sich aus-ruhen   relax
aus-sehen, a, e, (ie)   appear, look
außer (*dat.*)   except; besides; out of
außerhalb (*gen.*)   outside
außerordentlich   unusual, extraordinary
die Aussprache, -n   pronunciation
auswendig lernen   learn by heart
sich aus-ziehen, zog aus, ausgezogen   get undressed
das Auto, -s, -s   auto, car
der Autobus, -ses, -se   bus

B
baden   bathe
der Bahnhof, -s, ¨e   railroad station

bald   soon
das Ballett, -s   ballet
die Bank, ¨e   bench
die Bank, -en   bank
bankrott   bankrupt
   Bankrott machen   go bankrupt
der Baum, -s, ¨e   tree
bedecken   cover
bedeuten   mean
beeindrucken   make an impression on, impress
beginnen, a, o   begin
behalten, ie, a, (ä)   retain, remember
bei (*dat.*)   for, at
   bei (*dat.*) **nebenan**   next to
   bei schlechtem Wetter   in (during) bad weather
die beiden   the two, the both
das Bein, -es, -e   leg
beinahe   almost
bekannt: known
   wohlbekannt   well-known
der (die) Bekannte, -n, -n   acquaintance (*m., f.*)
die Bekanntschaft, -en   acquaintance
bekommen, a, o   receive, get
   ein Kind bekommen   have a baby
belegen   take, register for
belegt   laid down
   belegtes Brot   open sandwich
bemerken   notice
bereit   ready
der Berg, -es, -e   mountain
der Bericht, -s, -e   report
berühmt   famous
beschreiben, ie, ie   describe
besetzt   occupied, taken; busy ('phone)
besiegen   conquer, defeat
besitzen, besaß, besessen   own
besonder   special
besonders   especially
besser   better
bestehen, bestand, bestanden (aus)   consist (of)

bestehen, bestand, bestanden   pass (a course)

bestellen   order (in a restaurant)

besuchen   visit, attend

das Bett, -s, -en   bed

bewölkt   cloudy

bezahlen   pay

beziehen, bezog, bezogen   move into, occupy

die Bibliothek, -en   library

das Bier, -s, -e   beer

die Bierstube, -n   beer-hall

das Bild, -s, -er   picture

billig   cheap

die Biologie   biology

bis (*acc.*)   up to, till, until
   bis Montag (*etc.*)   by Monday (*etc.*)
   bis dahin   till then
   bis zu (*dat.*)   until

ein bißchen   a little

bitte   please

bitte sehr   you're welcome

bitten, a, e   ask
   bitten + *acc.* + zu + *infin.*   ask someone to do something
   bitten + *acc.* + um   ask someone for something

blaß (blasser, blassest, or blässer, blässest)   pale

blau   blue

bleiben, ie, ist ie   stay

der Bleistift, -s, -e   pencil

blond   blond

bloß   just, merely

blühen   flourish

die Blume, -n   flower

die Bluse, -n   blouse

der Boden, -s, ⸚   ground; floor

böse   bad

brauchen   need; use

braun   brown

die Brause, -n   shower (bath)
   unter die Brause gehen   take a shower
   sich unter die Brause stellen   take a shower

breit   wide

der Brief, -s, -e   letter

die Brille, -n   pair of (eye) glasses

bringen, brachte, gebracht   bring

das Brot, -s, -e   bread, loaf of bread

das Brötchen, -s, __   roll

der Bruder, -s, ⸚   brother

die Brust, ⸚e   chest, bosom

die Buchhandlung, -en   bookstore

das Buch, -s, ⸚er   book

das Büro, -s, -s   office

bürsten   brush
   sich die Haare bürsten   brush one's hair

der Bus, -ses, -se   bus

die Butter   butter

C

das Café, -s, -s   coffee house

die Chemie   chemistry

D

da   since (= because), as, inasmuch as, there

da-:
   damit
   damit   with it
   danach   after it
   darauf   on it
   darüber   over, about it
   draußen   outside it
   drinnen   inside it

dagegen   on the other hand

daher   therefore

dahin   (to) there, to that place

die Dame, -n   lady

danke   thank you
   danke vielmals   thanks very much
   danke sehr   thank you very much, thanks a lot

dann   then

darum   so, therefore

das   that

daß   that (*conj.*)

dauern   last, endure

dein, deine   your

denn   because; for (because); since

denn   well,...

denken, dachte, gedacht (an)   think (about)

der, die, das   the (definite article); (stressed) that, those

der, die, das   who, which, that (relative pronouns)

deutsch   German (*adj.*)

(das) Deutsch   German (language)

der (die) Deutsche, -n, -n   German (person)

Deutschland, -s   Germany

die Deutschstunde, -n   German class

Dezember   December

der Dichter, -s, ___   poet

dick   stout

dienen (*dat.*)   serve

der Dienst, -es, -e   service

Dienstag   Tuesday

dies   this

dieser, diese, dieses   this

diesseits (*gen.*)   on this side (of)

die Differentialrechnung   differential calculus

das Dirndlkleid, -s, -er   dirndl

doch   still, yet, even so, nevertheless

Donnerstag   Thursday

das Dorf, -es, ⁻er   village

dort   there

dort drüben   over there

draußen, nach draußen   outside

drei   three

dreißigjährig:

   ein dreißigjähriger (*etc.*) **Mann**   a 30-year-old (*etc.*) man

dritt-   third

du   you (familiar singular)

dumm   stupid

dunkel   dark

dünn   thin

durch (*acc.*)   through

durch-fallen, ie, ist a, (ä)   fail, flunk

dürfen, durfte, gedurft, (darf)   be allowed to

der Durst, -es   thirst

   Durst haben   be thirsty

E

eben   barely, just

ebenso...wie...   just as...as...

die Ecke, -n   corner

   um die Ecke   around the corner

das Ehepaar, -s, -e   (married) couple

das Ei, -es, -er   egg

eigentlich   real, actual

eilig:

   es eilig haben   be in a hurry

ein, eine   a, an (indefinite article)

einer, eine, ein(e)s   one

einige   several, a few, some

ein-laden, u, a, (ladet *or* **lädt ein)**   invite

einmal (zweimal, *etc.***)**   once (twice, two times, *etc.*)

   nicht einmal   not even

ein-nehmen, a, eingenommen, (nimmt)   take (medicine, food)

ein-reichen   hand in

eins   one

eine Eins   a "one," an A (mark in school)

ein-schlafen, ie, ist a, (ä)   fall asleep

ein-schreiben:

   sich einschreiben lassen   enroll

einst   once, one day (long ago)

ein-treten, a, ist e, (i)   enter, go in

das Eis, -es   ice; ice cream

die Eltern   parents

das Ende, -s, -n   end

   zu Ende gehen   come to an end; end

   am Ende   at the end

endlich   final

eng   narrow

England, -s   England

der Engländer, -s ___   Englishman

englisch   English (*adj.*)

das Englisch   English (language)

entfernt:
    weit entfernt far away
sich entschließen, o, o decide
entzücken charm
er he, it
erben inherit
die Erdkunde geography
der Erfolg, -s, -e success
    Erfolg haben be successful
erfrischt refreshed
sich erinnern (an + *acc.***)** remember
sich erkälten catch a cold
erklären explain
ernst serious
erobern conquer
eröffnen open, establish, set up
erschöpft exhausted
erst first
    erst vor ein paar Jahren (*etc.*) just (only) a couple of years ago
erstaunlich amazing, astonishing
erwarten expect
erwidern return, render in kind
erzählen tell, relate, recount
erzogen:
    gut (schlecht) erzogen well(badly) brought-up; well-(ill-) mannered
es it
    es gibt (*acc.*) there is, there are
    es ist there is
    es sind there are
essen, aß, gegessen, (ißt) eat
    zu Mittag (zu Abend) essen eat lunch (dinner)
das Essen food
etwas something
    etwas Neues (*etc.*) something new (*etc.*)
euer, eure your

F
die Fabrik, -en factory
das Fach, -es, ̈er subject, field of study
fahren, u, ist a, (ä) go

fallen, ie, ist a, (ä) go down, fall
    fallen lassen drop
falsch wrong
die Familie, -n family
der Familienname, -n, -n family name
famos fine, "swell"
die Farbe, -n color
fast almost
    fast niemals almost never, hardly ever
    fast nie almost never, hardly ever
faul lazy
Februar February
die Feder, -n pen
der Fehler, -s, ⎯ error
feiern celebrate
der Feind, -es, -e enemy
das Feld, -es, -er field
das Fenster, -s, ⎯ window
das Fernsehen, -s television
    sich Fernsehen anschauen watch television
die Fernsehsendung, -en television program
die Fernsprechstelle, -n 'phone booth
fertig finished; ready
    fertig sein mit be finished with
    fertig machen make ready
das Fieber, -s fever
der Film, -s, -e movie
finden, a, u find
der Finger, -s, ⎯ finger
der Fisch, -es, -e fish
die Flasche, -n bottle
das Fleisch, -es meat
fleißig industrious
die Fliege, -n bow-tie
fliegen, o, ist o fly
der Flieger, -s, ⎯ flier
fließen, o, ist geflossen flow
fließend fluent
das Flugzeug, -s, -e airplane
    mit dem Flugzeug by airplane

der Fluß, -sses, ⸚sse   river
fort-ziehen, zog fort, ist fortgezogen   move away (change residence)
fragen (*acc., acc.*)   ask (somebody something)
die Frage, -n   question
 eine Frage stellen   ask a question
der Franzose, -n, -n   Frenchman
das Französisch   French (language)
die Frau, -en   woman; wife; Mrs.
das Fräulein, -s, __   young woman; Miss
Freitag   Friday
freiwillig: voluntary
 sich freiwillig melden   volunteer, enlist
die Fremdsprache, -n   foreign language
sich freuen   be glad
 sich freuen auf   look forward to
der Freund, -s, -e   friend
die Freundin, -nen   girl friend
freundlich   friendly
der Friede, -ns   peace
 im Frieden   during peace time
die Friedenszeit, -en   peacetime
frieren, o, ist o   freeze
früh   early
 gestern früh   yesterday morning
der Frühling, -s, -e   spring
das Frühstück, -s, -e   breakfast
frühstücken   eat breakfast
führen   lead
sich fühlen   feel
für (*acc.*)   for
furchtbar   awful, frightful
der Fuß, -es, ⸚e   foot
 zu Fuß gehen   walk
der Fußball, -s, ⸚e   football
das Fußballspiel, -s, -e   football game
der Fußweg, -s, -e   footpath

G
ganz: whole, complete
 den ganzen Morgen   all morning

gar kein   no...at all; not...any at all
gar nichts   nothing at all
die Gaststätte, -n   restaurant
das Gebäude, -s, __   building
geben, a, e, (i)   give
 es gibt (*acc.*)   there is, there are
gebildet   (well-) educated
das Gebirge, -s,   mountain range
geboren   born
geduldig   patient
gefährlich   dangerous
gefallen, ie, a, (ä) (*dat.*)   please
gegen (*acc.*)   at about; towards; against
die Gegend, -en   region
gegenüber (*dat.*)   opposite
gehen, ging, ist gegangen   go
 Es geht mir gut.   I'm fine.
 Wie geht es Ihnen?   How are you?
gehören (*dat.*)   belong (to)
gelb   yellow
das Geld, -es   money
die Geldsorge, -n   worry over money
die Gelegenheit, -en   opportunity
 Gelegenheit haben   have a chance (opportunity)
das Gemüse, -s   vegetable
gemütlich   comfortable, pleasant, nice
genau   exact
genug   enough
die Geologie   geology
die Geometrie   geometry
gerade   straight
 nicht gerade das schönste   not exactly the prettiest
geradeaus   straight ahead
gern (gerne)   gladly
 gern haben (*acc.*)   like
das Geschäft, -s, -e   shop
der Geschäftsmann, -es, Geschäftsleute   businessman
geschehen, a, ist e   happen
die Geschichte, -n   story; history
das Geschirr, -s   dishes, crockery, table utensils

der Geschmack, -s   taste
das Gesicht, -s, -er   face
gestern   yesterday
gesund, ¨er, ¨est   healthy
gewinnen, a, o   win
gewiß   certain
das Gewitter, -s, __   thunderstorm
gewöhnlich   usual
das Glas, -es, ¨er   glass
glauben   believe
gleich   just, right, directly
gleich   same; similar, alike, equal
das Glück, -es   good luck
  Glück haben   to be lucky
glücklich   happy
glücklicherweise   fortunately
die Grammatik   grammar
grau   gray
(das) Griechisch   Greek (language)
groß, ¨er, größt, __   big
  Ich habe großen Durst (Hunger).
  I'm very thirsty (hungry).
die Großeltern   grandparents
die Großmutter, ¨   grandmother
der Großvater, -s, ¨   grandfather
grün   green
der Gummischuh, -s, -e   overshoe, rubber
gut (besser, best)   good; well
  Guten Abend!   Good evening!
  Guten Morgen!   Good morning!
  Gute Nacht!   Good night!
  Guten Tag!   Hello! Good day!
das Gymnasium, -s, Gymnasien   "Gymnasium" (German high school)

H

das Haar, -s, -e   hair
haben, hatte, gehabt, (hat)   have
der Hafen, -s, ¨   harbor
halb:
  halb zwölf   eleven-thirty
  fünfeinhalb (etc.)   five and a half (etc.)

Hallo!   Hello! (on the 'phone)
der Hals, -es, ¨e   throat
halten, ie, a, (ä) (von)   hold an opinion (of)
  Was halten Sie von...?   What do you think of...?
die Hand, ¨e   hand
der Handschuh, -s, -e   glove
häßlich   ugly
das Hauptfach, -s, ¨er   major subject (course of study)
das Hauptgericht, -s, -e   main course (of a meal)
die Haupstraße, -n   Main Street
das Haus, -es, ¨er   house
  zu Hause   at home
  nach Hause   (to) home
die Hausarbeit   housework
(das) Hebräisch   Hebrew (language)
das Heer, -es, -e   army
das Heimatland, -s, ¨er   native country
die Heimatstadt, ¨e   hometown
heiraten   marry, get married
heiß   hot
heißen, ie, ei   to be called
  Ich heiße Müller.   My name is Müller.
helfen, a, o, (i) (dat.)   help
hell   light, bright
  hellblau (etc.)   light blue (etc.)
das Hemd, -es, -en   shirt
her-:
  heraus   out
  herein   in
der Herbst, -es, -e   autumn, fall
der Herr, -n, -en   gentleman; Mr.
herrlich   splendid
herum-reisen (in)   travel around (in)
heute   today
  heute morgen (etc.)   this morning (etc.)
hier   here
hierher   (to) here
die Hilfe   help
  mit Hilfe+gen.   with the help of
der Himmel, -s   sky

hin-:
    hinaus out
    hinein in
hinaus-gehen, ging hinaus, ist hinausgegangen go out
hinten, nach hinten back, behind
hinter (*acc., dat.*) behind
hinterher afterwards
die Hitlerzeit the Hitler era
hoch, hoher, hohe, hohes (höher, höchst) high
die Hochzeit, -en wedding
der Hof, -es, ⁼e farm
hoffen hope
hoffentlich hopeful(ly); I hope so
höflich polite
hören hear
die Hose, -n pants, trousers
das Hotel, -s, -s hotel
hübsch pretty
der Humor, -s:
    Humor haben have a sense of humor
der Hund, -s, -e dog
das Hündchen, -s, __ dog (affectionate), "pooch"
der Hunger, -s hunger
    Hunger haben be hungry
der Hut, -es, ⁼e hat

I
ich I
ihr you (familiar plural)
ihr, ihre her
Ihr, Ihre your
der Imbiß, -(ss)es, -(ss)e snack, "bite"
immer always
    immer besser (*etc.*) better and better (*etc.*)
    Immer eins nach dem anderen! One thing at a time!
    immer wieder wiederholen repeat over and over again
in (*acc., dat.*) in, into
    in einem Monat in a month
    im Januar (*etc.*)
        Frühling (*etc.*)

der Ingenieur, -s, -e engineer
das Ingenieurwesen, -s engineering
innerhalb (*gen.*) within, inside (of)
intelligent intelligent
interessant interesting
sich interessieren für be interested in
der Italiener, -s, __ Italian (person)
(das) Italienisch Italian (language)

J
ja yes; certainly
    ja schon already
die Jacke, -n jacket
das Jahr, -s, -e year
die Jahreszeit, -en season, time of year
Januar January
der Japaner, -s, __ Japanese
jawohl yes, of course
je ever
je..., desto... the..., the...
jeder everyone
jeder, jede, jedes each, every
    jeden Tag (Morgen, Mittag, Nachmittag, *etc.***)** every day (morning, *etc.*)
jemand anybody, someone
jenseits (*gen.*) on that (the other) side (of)
jetzt now
Juli July
jung (⁼er, ⁼st) young
der Junge, -n, -n boy
Juni June
die Jura (*pl.*) (study of) law

K
der Kaffee, -s coffee
kahlköpfig bald
der Kaiser, -s, __ Kaiser, emperor
kalt (⁼er, ⁼est) cold
kämmen comb
    sich die Haare kämmen comb one's hair

kämpfen fight
das Kapitel, -s, ___ chapter
die Karte, -n card
  Karten spielen play cards
die Kartoffel, -n potato
der Käse, -s, ___ cheese
die Katze, -n cat
kaufen buy
kaum hardly
kein, keine not a, not any, no
keineswegs in no way; not at all
der Keller, -s, ___ cellar
kennen, kannte, gekannt know
kennen-lernen get to know
das Kind, -s, -er child
das Kino, -s, -s movie theater
die Kirche, -n church
die Kirschernte, -n cherry harvest
die Kirschtorte, -n cherry pie
klagen complain
die Klasse, -n class
das Klavier, -s, -e piano
das Kleid, -es, -er dress
das Kleidungsstück, -s, -e article (piece) of clothing
klein small
das Klima, -s climate
klingeln ring
klug (¨er, ¨st) clever, intelligent
der Kniestrumpf, -s, ¨e knee-sock
die Köchin, -nen cook (*f.*)
kommen, kam, ist gekommen come
können, konnte, gekonnt, (kann) can
der Kopf, -es, ¨e head
kosten cost
das Kostüm, -s, -e (woman's) suit
die Kraftbrühe mit Einlage (strength-)broth with thickening
krank sick
das Krankenhaus, -es, ¨er hospital
die Krankenpflege nursing
die Krankenschwester, -n nurse

die Krankheit, -en sickness
die Krawatte, -n tie
der Krieg, -es, -e war
das Kriegsende, -s, -n end of war
  seit Kriegsende since the end of the war
die Kriegsmarine, -n navy
krumm crooked
kühl cool
die Kunst, ¨e art
kurz (¨er, ¨est) short
kürzlich recently, not long ago

L

das Laboratorium, -s, Laboratorien laboratory
lächeln smile
lachen laugh
der Laden, -s, ¨ store
das Land, -es, ¨er country
die Landstraße, -n road
lang (¨er, ¨st) long
  eine ganze Stunde lang for a whole hour
lange for a long time
  Wie lange? (For) how long?
langsam slow
lassen, ie, a, (ä) have (something done), have (someone do something); leave, let
das Latein Latin (language)
laufen, ie, ist au, (äu) run
leben live
lebhaft lively
die Lederhosen (*pl.*) "*Lederhosen*," short leather pants
legen lay, put
lehren teach
der Lehrer, -s, ___ teacher
die Lehrerin, -nen teacher (woman)
leicht easy; light; slight
leid:
  Es tut mir leid I am sorry
leiden, litt, gelitten suffer
leider unfortunately

die Leitung, -en   line, connection ('phone)
lernen   study, learn
lesen, a, e, (ie)   read
leuchten   glow
die Leute (*pl.*)   people
lieb:
    lieb gewinnen, a, o   get to like
die Liebe   love
lieben   love
liebenswürdig   likable
lieber   instead, rather
das Lied, -s, -er   song
liegen, a, e   lie (recline)
links   to the left
die Literatur, -en   literature
los:
    los sein (mit)   be wrong (with), be the matter (with)
    Was ist los?   What's the matter?
die Luft   air
die Luftwaffe, -n   air force
die Lungenentzündung   pneumonia
Lust:
    Lust haben, etwas zu tun   feel like doing something
    keine Lust haben   not to feel like
lustig   enjoyable

M
machen   do; make
das Mädchen, -s, ___   girl
der Magen, -s, ˸   stomach
Mai   May
die Mahlzeit, -en   meal
mal   once
man   you, one
manche   many
mancherlei   many kinds of
manchmal   sometimes
der Mann, -es, ˸er   man; husband
der Mantel, -s, ˸   coat
die Marine, -n   navy

die Mark   Mark (German monetary unit)
der Markt, -es, ˸e   market
März   March
die Mathematik (sing.)   mathematics
der Matrose, -n, -n   sailor
die Medizin, -en   medicine (the field; also "medicament")
mehr   more
    nicht mehr   not any more
mein, meine   my
meist:
    am meisten   the most
sich melden zu   join, sign up with
der Mensch, -en, -en   person
das *or* **der Meter, -s, ___**   meter
die Milch   milk
mild   mild
das Mineralwasser, -s   mineral water
die Minute, -n   minute
mit (*dat.*)   with
mit-bringen, brachte mit, mitgebracht   bring along
das Mitglied, -s, -er   member
der Mittag, -s, -e   noon
das Mittagessen, -s, ___   lunch
die Mittelschule, -n   high school
die Mitternacht, ˸e   midnight
Mittwoch   Wednesday
die Mode, -n   custom; fashion
    Es ist Mode.   It's the custom.
modern   modern
mögen, mochte, gemocht, (mag)   like to
möglich   possible
der Monat, -s, -e   month
der Mond, -s   moon
Montag   Monday
der Morgen, -s, ___   morning
Morgen!   'Morning!
morgen   tomorrow
    morgen früh   tomorrow morning
morgens   in the morning
müde   tired

Mühe:
    mit Mühe und Not with difficulty and hardship
der Mund, -es, -e (and ̈er) mouth
das Museum, -s, Museen museum
die Musik music
müssen, mußte, gemußt, (muß) have to, must
die Mutter, ̈ mother
die Mütze, -n cap

N
nach (*dat.*) after; behind; toward
    nach fünf Minuten in five minutes; five minutes later
    nach Amerika (Deutschland, etc.) to America (Germany, *etc.*)
    nach Hause (to) home
nachdem after (*conj.*)
der Nachmittag, -s, -e afternoon
nachmittags in the afternoon
nach-schlagen, u, a, (ä) look up (a word in a dictionary)
nach-sehen, a, e, (ie) take a look
    Sehen wir mal nach! Let's have a look!
nächst next
    nächste Woche, nächsten Monat, etc. next week, month, *etc.*
die Nacht, ̈e night
der Nachtisch, -es, -e dessert
das Nachtlokal, -s, -e nightclub
nachts at night
der Nacken, -s, ___ neck
die Nähe nearness; vicinity
    in der Nähe nearby
der Name, -ns, -n name
nämlich ...you see,...
die Nase, -n nose
naßkalt (̈er, ̈est) raw (wet-cold)
natürlich natural
die Naturwissenschaft, -en natural science
neben (*acc., dat.*) next to, near
nehmen, a, genommen, (nimmt) take
nein no
nett nice
    Es ist nett von Ihnen. It's nice of you.

neu new
neulich recently
nicht not
    nicht wahr? isn't it? doesn't it? aren't you? (*etc.*)
nichts nothing
    nichts Neues (etc.) nothing new (*etc.*)
nie never
niemals never
niemand no one, nobody
nirgends nowhere
nirgendwo, nirgendwo hin nowhere
noch else; still, yet; besides
    noch nicht not yet
der Norden, -s north
    im Norden in the north
    nach dem Norden (to the) north, northward
normal normal
die Note, -n grade, mark
November November
die Nummer, -n number
nun well
nur only

O
ob whether
oben, nach oben up (stairs)
die Oberschule, -n high school
das Obst, -(e)s fruit
obwohl although
oder or
öffentlich public
der Offizier, -s, -e officer
oft often
ohne (*acc.*) without
das Ohr, -(e)s, -en ear
Oktober October
der Omnibus, (der Bus), -ses, -se bus
    mit dem Omnibus (Bus) by bus
der Onkel, -s, ___ uncle
die Oper, -n opera

die Ordnung, -en   order
  in Ordnung bringen   fix
  in Ordnung sein   be in order, be working
  nicht in Ordnung sein   have something wrong, be out of order
orangefarbig   orange
der Osten, -s   east

P
das Paar, -es, -e   pair
ein paar (*nom. pl.*)   a couple of
die Pädagogik   education
der Park, -s, -s   park
die Party, -s   party
passieren, ist passiert (*dat.*)   happen (to)
Pech:
  Pech haben   be out of luck, have bad luck
die Pfeife, -n   pipe
der Pfennig, -s, -e   pfennig (German monetary unit)
die Philosophie, -n   philosophy
die Physik (*sing.*)   physics
der Physiker, -s, —   physicist
die Pille, -n   pill
der Platz, -es, ⁺e   square, plaza; seat, place
plaudern   chat
plötzlich   sudden(ly)
die Politik (*sing.*)   politics
das Portemonnaie, -s, -s   wallet
die Post, Postämter   post office
die Post   mail
prima   first-rate
privat   private
der Professor, -s, -en   professor
die Prüfung, -en   exam
die Psychologie   psychology
der Pullover, -s —   pullover, sweater
putzen   polish
  sich die Zähne putzen   brush one's teeth

R
das Radio, -s, -s   radio
sich rasieren   shave

raten, ie, a, (rät)   guess
das Rathaus, -es, ⁺er   city hall
der Ratskeller, -s, —   rathskeller
rauchen   smoke
das Recht, -s   law (the field)
recht   very, quite, really
rechts   to the right
der Rechtsanwalt, -s, ⁺e   lawyer
rechtzeitig   on time, at the right time
redselig   talkative
das Referat, -s, -e   paper, report
der Regen, -s   rain
der Regenmantel, -s, ⁺   rain coat
regnen   rain
rein   pure
reisen, reiste, ist gereist   travel
richtig   correct
riechen, o, o   smell
der Rinderbraten, -s   roast beef
der Rock, -(e)s, ⁺e   skirt
rosa   pink
rot   red
der Rücken, -s, —   back
rufen, ie, u   call
ruhig   quiet, calm
der Russe, -n, -n   Russian (person)
(das) Russisch   Russian (language)

S
die Sache, -n   thing, matter
sagen   say
der Salat, -s, -e   salad
Samstag   Saturday
die Sandale, -n   sandal
satt   full, satiated
der Satz, -es, ⁺e   sentence
der Schal, -s, -s   scarf
die Schallplatte, -n   phonograph record
das Schaufenster, -s, —   show window, shop window
scheinen, ie, ie   shine

scheinen, ie, ie   seem
   mir scheint   I think, it seems to me
schenken   give, grant
   Beachtung schenken (*dat.*)   pay attention (to)
schief:
   schief gehen   go wrong
das Schiff, -es, -e   ship
   mit dem Schiff   by ship
der Schinken, -s, __   ham
schlafen, ie, a, (ä)   sleep
schläfrig   sleepy
das Schlafzimmer, -s, __   bedroom
die Schlagsahne   whipped cream
schlank   slim
schlecht   poor, bad
der Schlips, -es, -e   tie
das Schloß, -(ss)es, ⸚(ss)er   castle
der Schluß, -(ss)es, ⸚sse   end
   zum Schluß   finally
der Schlüssel, -s, __   key
schmecken   taste (give off a taste)
der Schnee, -s   snow
schneien   snow
schnell   fast
schon   already
schön   pretty
das Schönheit, -en   beauty
schreiben, ie, ie   to write
der Schuh, -es, -e   shoe
die Schule, -n   school
die Schulter, -n   shoulder
schwach (⸚er, ⸚st)   weak
schwarz   black
schweigsam   silent, taciturn
schwer   hard
die Schwester, -n   sister
die Schwierigkeit, -en   difficulty
schwimmen, a, o   swim
   schwimmen gehen   go swimming

der See, -s, -n   lake
sehen, a, e, (ie)   see
die Sehenswürdigkeit, -en   sight (tourist attraction)
sehr   very
sein, war, ist gewesen, (ist)   be
sein, seine   his, its
seit (*dat.*)   since
   Er ist seit drei Wochen da.   He's been there for three weeks.
   seit wann...?   for how long...? since when...?
seitdem   since then
der Sekretär, -s, -e   secretary
die Sekretärin, -nen   secretary
selber   oneself (myself, *etc.*)
selbst   even
selten   seldom
September   September
servieren   serve
der Sessel, -s, __   easy chair
sich setzen   sit down
sie   she, it; they
Sie   you
siegen (no object)   win, be victorious
singen, a, u   sing
sitzen, saß, gesessen   sit
So?   Huh? H'm?
so   so
   so etwas   something like that
   so...wie...   as...as...
sobald   as soon as
die Socke, -n   sock
sofort   right away
der Sohn, -es, ⸚e   son
der Soldat, -en, -en   soldier
sollen, sollte, gesollt, (soll)   be supposed to
der Sommer, -s, __   summer
sondern   rather, but
Sonnabend   Saturday
die Sonne   sun
Sonntag   Sunday

sonst:

Was sonst? What else?

die Sorge, -n trouble, anxiety

sich Sorgen machen worry

die Soße, -n sauce

(das) Spanisch Spanish (language)

spät late

Wie spät ist es? What time is it? How late is it?

später later

spazieren gehen take a walk

spielen play

spitz pointed, sharp

die Sportjacke, -n sport jacket

die Sprache, -n language

sprechen, a, o, (i) speak

spülen wash

die Staatskunde (*sing.*) politics

die Stadt, ⸚e city

in der Stadt in the city, downtown

stark (⸚er, ⸚st) strong; bad, heavy (cold, rain, *etc.*)

statt (*gen.*) instead of

statt-finden, a, u take place

stehen, stand, ist gestanden:

das steht mir gut that suits me, I look good in that

stehen, stand, ist gestanden stand

steigen, ie, ist ie climb, go up

steigen in (aus) get into (out of)

stellen: put, place

eine Frage stellen ask a question

sich stellen go up (to), place oneself (at)

sich unter die Brause stellen take a shower

sterben, a, ist o, (i), (an) to die (of)

im Sterben liegen be dying, be on one's deathbed

der Stern, -s, -e star

stolz (auf) proud (of)

stolz darauf sein, daß... be proud that...

der Strand beach

an den Strand to the seashore

die Straße, -n street

die Straßenbahn, -en streetcar

streng severe

der Strumpf, -es, ⸚e stocking

das Stück, -es, -e piece

der Student, -en, -en student

die Studentin, -nen (female) student, co-ed

studieren study (be taking courses)

die Stunde, -n hour; class, period, lesson

der Süden, -s south

die Suppe, -n soup

die Süßigkeit, -en candy

das Süßwarengeschäft, -(e)s, -e candy store

T

die Tabakmarke, -n brand of tobacco

der Tag, -es, -e day

eines Tages some day

Tag! Hi!

tags in the daytime

tagsüber all day long

das Tal, -s, ⸚er valley

die Tante, -n aunt

tanzen dance

die Tasse, -n cup

tatsächlich real, actual

der Tee, -s tea

der *or* **das Teil, -s, -e** part, share

zum Teil in part, partly

das Telefon, -s, -e telephone

das Telefonbuch, -es, ⸚er phonebook

die Temperatur, -en temperature

teuer expensive

das Theater, -s, __ theater

das Tier, -es, -e animal

der Tiergarten, -s, ⸚ zoo, zoological garden

der Tisch, -es, -e table

die Tochter, ⸚ daughter

töten kill

tragen, u, a, (ä) wear

traurig sad

treffen, traf, getroffen, (trifft) meet

die **Trigonometrie** trigonometry
trinken, a, u drink
trotz (*gen.*) in spite of
trotzdem nevertheless, anyway
Tschüß! So long!
tun, tat, getan (tue, tust, tut, tun) do
die **Tür, -en** door
typisch typical

U

die **U-Bahn** (= Untergrundbahn), **-en** subway
  mit der U-Bahn by subway
(sich) üben practice
über (*acc., dat.*) about; over, across
überall, überall hin everywhere
über-sehen, a, e, (ie) see out over
überraschen surprise
  überraschend surprising
übersetzen translate
überzeugt (von) convinced (of), sure (of)
übrigens by the way, incidentally
die **Uhr, -en** watch, clock
  es ist sieben Uhr it's seven o'clock
  um sieben Uhr at seven o'clock
  um wieviel Uhr (at) what time
  Wieviel Uhr ist es? What time is it?
um (*acc.*) around, about
um...zu... in order to...
die **Umgebung, -en** surrounding region
der **Umstand, -s, ⸚e** formality, ceremony
  Umstände machen (*dat.*) cause inconvenience, make trouble (for),
    go to some trouble
um-ziehen, zog um, ist umgezogen move (change residences)
sich um-ziehen, zog um, umgezogen change clothes
unansehnlich unattractive (to look at)
unbedingt positive, absolute
und and
ungefähr about, approximately
die **Universität, -en** university
unser, unsere our

unten, nach unten down (stairs)
unter (*acc., dat.*) under, below; among
sich unterhalten, ie, a, (ä) have a conversation; have a good time
die **Unterhaltung, -en** conversation
die **Unterricht** instruction
unterrichten instruct, teach
der **Unterschied, -(e)s, -e** difference
die **USA** (*pl.*) the U.S.A.

V

der **Vater, -s, ⸚** father
die **Verabredung, -en** date, appointment
verbieten, o, o forbid
verbringen, verbrachte, verbracht spend (time)
die **Vereinigten Staaten** (*pl.*) United States
vergessen, a, e, (i) forget
das **Verhältnis, -(ss)es, -(ss)e** circumstances
  in guten Verhältnissen leben be well-to-do, well-off
verkaufen sell
der **Verkäufer, -s, ___** salesman
die **Verkäuferin, -nen** salesgirl
verlassen, ie, a, (ä) leave behind, abandon
sich verlieben (in + *acc.*) fall in love (with)
verlieren, o, o lose
die **Verlobung, -en** engagement, betrothal
verschütten spill
Versehen:
  aus Versehen by mistake, out of misunderstanding
sich verspäten be late
verstehen, verstand, verstanden understand
versuchen try, attempt
der **Verwandte, -n, -n** relative
verzeihen, ie, ie (*dat.*) excuse
Verzeihung! Excuse me!
viel much
viele many
vielleicht perhaps, maybe
vielmals many times
  Danke vielmals! Thank you very much!
vier four

Viertel:
   Viertel nach a quarter after
   Viertel vor a quarter to
die Vogelstimme, -n voice like a bird
voll full
von (*dat.*) of, about; by
vor (*acc., dat.*) before; in front of
   vor einer Woche (*etc.*) a week ago (*etc.*)
vorbei over, past, finished
   an . . . vorbei past . . .
vorbei-kommen, kam, ist o come by, come past
vorgestern the day before yesterday
vor-haben, hatte vor, vorgehabt have on the agenda, have plans
vorig:
   vorige Woche, vorigen Monat, voriges Jahr, *etc.* last week, last month, last year, *etc.*
vor-lesen, a, e, (ie):
   etwas vorlesen read something aloud
die Vorlesung, -en class (lecture)
der Vormittag, -s, -e forenoon (morning)
vormittags in the forenoon
der Vorname, -ns, -n first name
Vorsicht! Watch out!
vorsichtig careful
vor-stellen introduce, present (to)
sich vor-stellen imagine

W
wach awake
der Waffenstillstand, -s Armistice
der Wagen, -s, __ car
wählen choose; dial (a 'phone number)
wahr:
   nicht wahr? isn't it? aren't you? doesn't it?, *etc.*
während (*gen.*) during
die Wahrheit truth
   die __ sagen tell the truth
der Wald, -(e)s, ⸚er forest
wann when
das Warenhaus, -es, ⸚er department store

warm (⸚er, ⸚st) warm
warten (auf) wait (for)
warum why
was what
was für (*nom.*) what kind of
sich waschen, u, a, (ä) get washed
das Wasser, -s water
wechseln change (get another), exchange
der Wecker, -s, __ alarm clock
der Weg, -(e)s, -e way
   auf dem Wege nach Hause on the way home
wegen (*gen.*) because of
weg-werfen, a, o, (i) throw away
weh:
   weh tun (*dat.*) hurt
weil because
der Wein, -(e)s, -e wine
weinen cry (weep)
weiß white
weit far
weiter:
   ohne weiteres without any further trouble
welcher, welche, welches which, what (*adj.*)
die Welt, -en world
   zur Welt kommen be born, come into the world
der Weltkrieg, -s, -e world war
wenig little (*adv.*), not much
weniger less
wenn if; whenever
wer, wen, wem, wessen whom, whose
werden, wurde, ist geworden, (wird) be going to, will; become
der Westen, -s west
das Wetter, -s weather
wie how
wieder again
wiederholen repeat
wiederhören:
   Auf Wiederhören! Good-bye (over the 'phone)
Wiedersehen! 'Bye! Be seeing you!
wiegen, o, o weigh
der Winter, -s, __ winter

der Wintermantel, -s, ∺ winter coat
wir we
wirklich real
wissen, wußte, gewußt, (weiß) know
der Witz, -es, -e joke
   Witze machen make jokes, be silly, "kid"
wo where
die Woche, -n week
wohin where (to)
wohl fine, well; indeed, surely; probably
wohnen live (in a place), dwell
die Wohnung, -en apartment
wollen, wollte, gewollt, (will) want to
wo-:
   womit? with what?
   worauf? on what?
   worüber? over (about) what?
das Wort, -es, ∺er word
das Wörterbuch, -s, ∺er dictionary
wunderbar wonderful
die Wurst, ∺e sausage

Z
der Zahn, -es, ∺e tooth
die Zehe, -n toe
zeigen show
die Zeit, -en time
   vor langer Zeit a long time ago
   zur Zeit (*gen.*) at the time of

die Zeitschrift, -en magazine
die Zeitung, -en newspaper
das Zentrum, -s, Zentren center
zerbrechen, a, o, (i) break
zerreißen, zerriß, zerrissen tear
ziemlich rather, "pretty," quite
ziehen, zog, ist gezogen:
   ziehen nach move (change residence) to
die Zigarre, -n cigar
die Zigarette, -n cigarette
das Zimmer, -s, __ room
zu (*dat.*) to
   zu Hause at home
   zur Mahlzeit with a meal
zu too (= excessively); (+ *infin.*) to; in, at
der Zug, -s, ∺e train
   mit dem Zug by train
zufrieden satisfied
zu-hören (*dat.*) listen to
zu-lassen, ie, a, (ä) admit
   zugelassen werden be admitted (to a University)
zu-machen close
zunächst at first
zurück-kehren return, go back
zusammen together
zwar to be sure, of course
zwei two
zwischen (*acc., dat.*) between

Index

INDEX

[All numbers refer to *lessons*.]